JONATHAN EDWARDS
among the Theologians

JONATHAN EDWARDS
among the Theologians

Oliver D. Crisp

WILLIAM B. EERDMANS PUBLISHING COMPANY
GRAND RAPIDS, MICHIGAN / CAMBRIDGE, U.K.

© 2015 Oliver D. Crisp
All rights reserved

Published 2015 by
Wm. B. Eerdmans Publishing Co.
2140 Oak Industrial Drive N.E., Grand Rapids, Michigan 49505 /
P.O. Box 163, Cambridge CB3 9PU U.K.

Library of Congress Cataloging-in-Publication Data

Crisp, Oliver.
Jonathan Edwards among the theologians / Oliver D. Crisp.
    pages   cm
Includes bibliographical references and index.
ISBN 978-0-8028-7172-5 (pbk.: alk. paper)
1. Edwards, Jonathan, 1703-1758.
2. Reformed Church — Doctrines.   I. Title.

BX7260.E3C666   2015
230′.58092 — dc23

2015018105

www.eerdmans.com

To Claire:

[T]he uncommon union, which has so long subsisted between us, has been of such a nature as I trust is spiritual and therefore will continue forever.

— Jonathan Edwards's final words about his wife, 1758

Contents

	Acknowledgments	ix
	Abbreviations	xii
	Preface	xiii
1.	Edwards and Reformed Theology	1
2.	Anselm and Edwards on the Doctrine of God	16
3.	Edwards on the Excellence of the Trinity	36
4.	Arminius and Edwards on Creation	60
5.	Girardeau and Edwards on Free Will	80
6.	Edwards on Original Sin: Another Look	107
7.	Bellamy and Edwards on the Atonement	124
8.	Edwards on Preaching	143
9.	On the Orthodoxy of Jonathan Edwards	164
	Bibliography	183
	Index	195

Acknowledgments

I am grateful to Michael Thomson and Jon Pott at Eerdmans for their encouragement to publish the studies contained within the covers of this volume. Over the years I have benefitted from the advice, conversation, and opinions of a host of Edwards scholars. This book reflects that debt in particular ways (the footnotes tell their own story). As in any field of intellectual endeavor, interpreters of Jonathan Edwards disagree on many things, often amounting to questions of substance. Nevertheless, the Edwardsian scholarly community is a collaborative and dialogical one. Work is often done in concert and ideas and drafts of work are often shared and discussed together. Perhaps this is an instance of the harmonious interaction that the Sage of Northampton was so concerned to commend to his readers. The scholars from whom I have learned and profited include Ava Chamberlain, Elizabeth Agnew Cochran, Robert Caldwell III, William Danaher, Paul Helm, Steve Holmes, Sang Hyun Lee, George Marsden, Michael McClymond, Gerald McDermott, Kenneth Minkema, Adriaan Neele, Alvin Plantinga, Amy Plantinga Pauw, Mike Rea, Bill Schweitzer, Harry Stout, Steven Studebaker, Kyle Strobel, Doug Sweeney, William Wainwright, and Avihu Zakai. Mark Hamilton deserves special mention for reading through and commenting on a penultimate draft of the whole, to my considerable benefit. Jordan Wessling has challenged me about a number of important philosophical issues that Edwards's views raise and I hope I have learned from those discussions. Keith Stanglin has encouraged me to read more Arminius alongside Edwards, some of the fruits of which can be found in Chapter 4. My colleagues at Fuller Seminary have provided the happy and constructive

Acknowledgments

theological environment in which much of this work took shape. I am grateful to them.

I would also like to register my thanks to several institutions for their support of my work. Earlier versions of Chapters 3 and 8 were given to audiences at Trinity Evangelical Divinity School in the spring of 2013, under the auspices of the Jonathan Edwards Center and the Carl F. Henry Center, respectively. I am grateful to Douglas Sweeney and Thomas McCall for their invitations to give these talks and for their hospitality. An earlier version of Chapter 5 began as a paper for a panel on sin and evil for the Reformed Theology and History group at the Evangelical Theological Society in the fall of 2013. My thanks to Mark Bowald and Kelly Kapic for the invitation to contribute on that occasion. The index was prepared by David Hunsicker on a research assistantship granted by the Center for Advanced Theological Study at Fuller Seminary. I am grateful to him for his efficient and careful work.

Previous versions of a number of the chapters have been published elsewhere, and are used here with permission of the copyright holders. All have been revised for inclusion in the present volume:

"Jonathan Edwards and Reformed Theology," in *The Cambridge Companion to Reformed Theology*, ed. David Fergusson and Paul Nimmo (Cambridge: Cambridge University Press, 2014). (Chapter 1)

"Anselm of Canterbury and Jonathan Edwards on God," in *The Ecumenical Edwards: Jonathan Edwards and the Theologians*, ed. Kyle Strobel (Farnham: Ashgate, 2014). (Chapter 2)

"Jacob Arminius and Jonathan Edwards on Creation," in *Reconsidering Arminius: Reformed and Wesleyan Theology for the Church Today*, ed. Keith D. Stanglin, Mark G. Bilby, and Mark Mann (Nashville: Abingdon Press/Kingswood Books, 2014). (Chapter 4)

"The Moral Government of God: Jonathan Edwards and Joseph Bellamy on the Atonement," in *After Jonathan Edwards: The Courses of the New England Theology*, ed. Oliver D. Crisp and Douglas A. Sweeney (New York: Oxford University Press, 2012). (Chapter 7)

"Jonathan Edwards on Preaching," in *Text Message: Preaching Scripture in the Multimedia Age*, ed. Ian Stackhouse and Oliver D. Crisp (Eugene, OR: Pickwick Publications, 2014). (Chapter 8)

"The Orthodoxy of Jonathan Edwards," *Scottish Journal of Theology* 67.3 (2014): 304-22. (Chapter 9)

Acknowledgments

* * *

Finally, this volume is dedicated to my wife and best friend, Claire. For over two decades she has welcomed the shade of the periwigged New England parson in our house, even though she is sometimes somewhat baffled by my interest in an eighteenth-century thinker. I am sure, however, that *he* would not be perplexed by my abiding interest in *her*.

Abbreviations

The standard critical edition of Edwards's works published by Yale University Press is now complete. The letterpress edition runs to 26 volumes. The website of the Jonathan Edwards Center at Yale University (http://edwards.yale.edu/) hosts an online version of the Yale Works. It includes many additional volumes of Edwards sermon skeletons and notebooks not published in the letterpress edition of the Works. In the present volume, the printed books in the Yale Edition are cited by series number, followed by colon and page number, e.g., YE1: 50. References to online volumes not included in the letterpress edition are given as WJE Online, followed by volume number and section. A complete list of the Yale letterpress volumes is given in the bibliography.

Preface

There is something about Jonathan Edwards. He is fascinating and intriguing, as well as infuriating and frustrating. A true original, a minister and inceptor of modern evangelicalism, a high Calvinist enamored of the work of key early Enlightenment philosophers, and a writer possessed of an unusually keen intellect and logical bent of mind. Until relatively recently, his work was not accorded the eminence it deserves. Thankfully, that situation has now changed decisively in recognition of Edwards's importance as a Christian thinker of the first rank.

Part of the reason for the earlier neglect is that Edwards died before his life's work was complete, so that much of his creative thought remained buried in university libraries, in manuscripts and notebooks that few could access. That has now changed thanks to the pioneering work of the Jonathan Edwards Center at Yale University, and the painstaking editorial transcription of Edwards's difficult, crabbed handwriting that has been the life work of a previous generation of scholars. The result of this herculean effort has been made available to all by means of the internet, so that anyone may now look up chapter and verse of Edwards's published and unpublished writings in a fully searchable platform hosted at the Center's website.

Difficulty accessing some of his writing is, however, only part of the reason for the historic neglect of Edwards from the end of the nineteenth century to the period following World War II. There is also the matter of the intellectual demands Edwards places upon his readers. He writes clearly enough, but he is uncompromisingly orderly and methodical in the way he traces out his thought on paper. The austerity and precision of his

Preface

prose, coupled with his relentlessly logical bent of mind, mean that serious engagement with Edwards is not for the fainthearted. Additionally, his thought is difficult to fit into neat categories. Over the years he has been labeled by some as too philosophical, and by others as not philosophical enough — depending upon the sort of philosophy in vogue. Some have regarded him as a kind of medieval hangover, dedicated to perpetuating the picture of a ghastly deity casting sinners into the inferno. Still others have thought of him as so ahead of his time that we are only just beginning to catch up with him.

Probably the single most important reason for Edwards's temporary modern eclipse (likewise the principal reason for his literary return in scholarship and popular works of the last half century) can be summed up in a single word: *evangelicalism*. The full-blooded religious zeal Edwards brings to bear on his writings about God, creation, salvation, and consummation, in sermons, notebooks, letters, dissertations, treatises, and essays on matters ranging from semiotics, through theology and metaphysics, to natural science is shot through with evangelical concern. He regards the examination of a "flying" spider and the agonies of those in hell with equal fascination. Intellectuals of the early twentieth century found this repulsive, preferring writers more in keeping with a time beguiled by the hope of endless human progress. Today, with that illusion in tatters, and with a return to the serious study of religion, as well as an industry of historical scholarship devoted to uncovering every detail of early American life and letters, Edwards is once more the subject of high-level academic study. But there is also widespread popular interest in the intricacies of his theology; Edwards is read by both scholars and laypersons with equal fascination. Some recent interpreters of his thought have even suggested that he may be the most widely read Christian theologian today, a "global theologian for twenty-first century Christianity."[1] His appeal encompasses Pentecostal pastors in the majority world as well as Harvard historians. Few theologians of any stripe can claim that.

Edwards is also important for another reason. He was the progenitor of a school of thought that was a force to be reckoned with for a century after his demise. This was the New Divinity and (subsequently) New England Theology, which died out at the end of the nineteenth century and, as a consequence, had no natural heirs to take forward its constructive theo-

---

1. Michael J. McClymond and Gerald R. McDermott, *The Theology of Jonathan Edwards* (New York: Oxford University Press, 2012), p. 727.

Preface

logical program. The Princetonian theologians of the nineteenth century, who held Edwards in high regard but worried about the tendency of his theology towards pantheism and idealism, placed their own imprimatur upon Reformed theology in North America. Their intellectual progeny have perpetuated this Princetonian version of Reformed theology ever since. Thus, those familiar with the writings of Benjamin Warfield or the Hodges may not know the works of Joseph Bellamy, Samuel Hopkins, or Nathaniel Taylor. Yet they were all Edwards's disciples in various ways, part of a theological movement that spanned the century after his death and bore fruit in what is arguably the first, and to date the only, truly *American* Christian theology.

Both for evangelical theologians who laud him as a defender of orthodoxy and for scholars in a range of academic disciplines intrigued by his intellectual precocity and innovative thought, Edwards has "arrived." Yet nagging doubts remain. Did he hold to a traditional, classical doctrine of the Trinity? Did his adherence to philosophical idealism yield strange and unorthodox conclusions for his theology? Is his thinking truly *orthodox*?

Each of these questions is addressed in the studies that follow. There are also chapters that deal with Edwards's work in dialogue with other great Christian theologians of the past. The four figures featured prominently in this regard are the medieval Benedictine theologian, Archbishop Anselm of Canterbury; the seventeenth-century Dutch Reformed divine, Jacob Arminius; the nineteenth-century Southern Presbyterian theologian, John Girardeau; and Edwards's close disciple, friend, and proponent of the New Divinity, Joseph Bellamy. In each case, setting these men in conversation is instructive.

Anselm is one of the greatest of all Christian theologians, although his thought is sometimes stranger than one might think at first glance. Comparing him with Edwards on the doctrine of God throws up some important issues about their common Augustinian heritage as well as the rather different ways in which they understand the Augustinian legacy for Theology Proper. It also appears that Anselm's careful and systematic account of the doctrine of God may offer some "correction" to the sometimes more speculative and (over)confident reasoning of the early Enlightenment Edwards.

Arminius might be thought the nemesis of the Calvinist Edwards. Where Arminius was a theological revisionist who departed in significant respects from the Reformed tradition in which he had been formed, Edwards chose to buttress that tradition with judicious appeals to Enlightenment philosophers like John Locke and Nicholas Malebranche — or so one might think. In fact, as the chapter on their respective accounts of creation shows, Arminius was not the revisionist he is often portrayed as being, and Edwards was no mere defender of the Reformed status quo. If anything, the reverse is the case. It is Edwards's doctrine of creation that is revisionist in important respects, and Arminius who (by and large, and with certain qualifications) reiterates much that can be found within western Catholic tradition.

In the case of Bellamy and Edwards, it turns out that Bellamy's doctrine of the atonement, a sort of transition to the New Divinity governmental model of Christ's work, is different from that of Edwards in important respects. Yet Edwards endorsed it, writing a preface to the published version of Bellamy's volume on the atonement. Perhaps the reason for this strange state of affairs is that Edwards regarded Bellamy's position as within the bounds of certain confessional constraints, and as opposing the latitudinarian tendencies that both theologians rejected. Though Bellamy was an ally and friend, his view of the work of Christ is not slavishly imitative of his master's. Like Edwards himself, Bellamy was his own man. One of the characteristics of the New England Theology is the way in which the leaders of this movement adopted the Edwardsian style of questioning everything in the cause of truth, whilst being unafraid to dissent from the master when it came to particular points of doctrine. We might say that, to some extent, and increasingly as the movement developed and diversified, the Edwardsian method was more influential on the divines of the New England Theology than the substantive doctrines of its founder.

One area of renewed interest in recent years is the theological legacy of Jonathan Edwards. His doctrine of free will has been influential on much subsequent Reformed thought, and remains one of the most intimidating and exhaustive treatments of the topic in theological literature. But is his doctrine that God determines all things, and that this is consistent with human free will (rightly understood), the only theological option open to those of the Reformed faith? Can one be Reformed and also hold to a more expansive account of human free will, one which does not require God's determination of all that comes to pass? Some Reformed theologians have taken issue with Edwards on this score, particularly in the nineteenth-century Anglophone world that was the principal recipient of his account. One of these is John Girardeau, today a little-known

Preface

Southern Presbyterian theologian.[2] At the close of the nineteenth century Girardeau published a study of free will that took aim at Edwards, and offered in place of his doctrine of divine determinism a Reformed version of theological libertarianism, which allows that many human actions are not determined by God or anything else aside from the moral agent making a choice. Girardeau argued that the common Reformed view, from which Edwards departs, is that in matters pertaining to salvation determinism does obtain, but in more mundane choices, fallen humans, like unfallen Adam and Eve, enjoy libertarian free choice. In comparing Girardeau and Edwards we are faced with the ancient problem of how to characterize human freedom and divine sovereignty, as well as the tradition-specific question of whether Reformed theology requires some doctrine of divine determinism. Comparing the views of these two thinkers therefore throws light on much larger theological issues pertaining to the integrity of Reformed theology, as well as to what is deemed theologically permissible within the bounds of historic discussion of this topic.

This brings us to the matter of Edwards and the tradition. We have already noted that the New England theologians were notorious for their willingness to conjecture and adopt unusual theological positions that pressed at the very limits of what was considered acceptable Reformed doctrine. This reflects something of Edwards's own relationship to the tradition that formed him. He was no maverick — to argue that would be to traduce Edwards's legacy. However, he ended up attempting to shore up key tenets of Reformed theology by appeal to sophisticated metaphysical notions that eventually did land him with rather odd views about a range of issues. In this volume, we consider his relationship to the Reformed tradition in several places. Earlier scholarship has emphasized the ways in which Edwards departed from the theology of his forebears; that has often led to an overstatement of the novelty of his positions. Although

---

2. An account of his life can be found in George A. Blackburn, ed., *Life Work of John L. Girardeau, D.D., LL.D.* (Columbia, SC: The State Company, 1916). Girardeau was schooled in the commonsense tradition of nineteenth-century American Presbyterianism, which shaped the way he approached Edwards's more speculative philosophical theology. This can be seen in Girardeau's *Philosophical Questions*, ed. George A. Blackburn (Richmond, VA: The Presbyterian Committee of Publication, 1900), which, his editor writes in the introduction, may be read as having as their "main purpose" the advance of "the Scottish school of philosophy. They are not intended to be a system in themselves." Indeed, "This book is really a supplement to Hamilton's *Metaphysics*, in connection with which it ought to be studied" (p. 7).

Preface

Edwards did embrace doctrines that would have been regarded as suspect by some theologians in his own tradition, he did so in order to preserve what he saw as the theologically non-negotiable absolute sovereignty of God. This is hardly the exclusive property of the Reformed tradition, but Reformed scholars have given that doctrine a particular emphasis and centrality in matters of dogmatic theology. Edwards might be thought of as an intellectual attempting to reconfigure the Reformed Orthodox theology of the early modern period in a new key, drawing on developments in the philosophy of the time in order to show the enemies of revealed religion that it was not inferior to the more fashionable options of Deism, Socinianism, and latitudinarianism.

That said, some of the key aspects of Edwards's metaphysics do appear to press in unorthodox directions. Here we come to one of the themes that run through many of the studies in this volume: how orthodox was Edwards's thought? To what extent could he restate the theology of his own tradition whilst pressing at its borders? Does his thinking ultimately collapse into something that is less-than-orthodox in some respects? That is a difficult question. Edwards's thinking does present his interpreters with some hard choices. Perhaps that is not terribly unusual. The work of many great thinkers, when analyzed in detail, turns out to include tensions and even significant revisions that present hermeneutical challenges for readers and interpreters. (One thinks of St. Augustine, and his late work entitled *The Retractions*.) Edwards is no different in this regard. That does not make him a lesser theologian, or even someone whose work is largely a theological dead-end. However, it may mean his interpreters must engage in theological repair as well as retrieval when assessing his work. There may be aspects of his project that seem to be problematic, even mistaken. But there are deep themes in his work that may provide the basis for further theological reflection today. That is the mark of a great thinker: not that he always had it right, but that he saw the important issues clearly, and returned to them time and again in his own work, refusing easy answers while attempting to elevate the discussion to a new level of clarity and sophistication.

Edwards is claimed by a number of different constituencies. Yet the "popular" Edwards and the "scholarly" Edwards are not two different people; they represent two vocational expressions of the same individual. A pressing concern for Edwards scholarship as it goes forward is finding ways in which the gap between the "popular" and the "scholarly" can be bridged. Both constituencies need to speak to one other so that each can recover aspects of Edwards's legacy that the other has more completely apprehended. For instance, those for whom the evangelical Edwards is the whole of Jonathan Edwards would find some of the things the scholarly Edwards says both startling and potentially troubling, as several of the chapters that follow point out. Yet Edwards himself saw no conflict between pursuing his vocation as a minister serving a settled congregation and engaging in the most complex philosophical and theological speculations. Indeed, he regarded these two tasks as symbiotic. Edwards the pastor was able to make the careful discriminating theological judgments he did because he was at the same time Edwards the scholar. A greater appreciation of this especially amongst those with a more popular or pastoral interest in Edwards would be of great benefit to the future of the sort of heartfelt religion for which he was such an important and influential advocate.

Although the chapters of this book can be read in sequence and share the common threads that I have already touched upon, they could also be read as discrete studies of key aspects of Edwards's thought. Nevertheless, whether read seriatim or individually, what emerges is a consistent theme. Edwards was both a theologian who thought of himself as an heir to the Reformed tradition, and a thinker facing the new task of rethinking the Christian faith in light of the significant intellectual challenges presented to eighteenth-century European Christians. In one respect this is a perennial concern of Christian dogmatics. Constructive theology must always hold on to what has gone before, engaging the theological tradition and Scripture with seriousness and reverence whilst also dealing with the new and pressing challenges facing those of faith in the present. Edwards is a remarkable example of someone doing this in a particular time and context, engaged at the coal face as a minister of Word and Sacrament and leader of the emerging evangelical movement.

Writing about this tension in Edwards's work between received tradition and theological construction, Amy Plantinga Pauw writes, "Following Edwards's example, it would be entirely appropriate for contemporary Reformed theologians to recast doctrines with the aid of a variety of intellectual approaches current in their own day, such as analytic philosophy, feminist thought, or narrative approaches to Scripture. In so doing they may genuinely hope for an 'addition of light.'"[3] As Edwards attempted

---

3. Amy Plantinga Pauw, "The Future of Reformed Theology: Some Lessons from Jonathan Edwards," in *Towards the Future of Reformed Theology: Tasks, Topics, Traditions*, ed. David Willis and Michael Welker (Grand Rapids: Eerdmans, 1999), p. 459.

to use the tools of early Enlightenment philosophy for a theological end, so contemporary Christian thinkers today may borrow ideas, concepts, tools, and methods from modern intellectual disciplines in order to place theology on a firmer footing in today's intellectual climate. This need not mean the rejection of tradition in favor of theological construction. However, those wanting to imitate Edwards's example may find themselves driven to more theological revision than they had anticipated, as new light is shed upon old truths. It may even be that in reading Edwards we will be furnished with ways of tackling longstanding theological conundrums and uncovering fresh aspects of the truth once delivered to the saints. It seems Edwards still has things to teach us today, in matters of theological method as well as doctrinal substance.

CHAPTER 1

Edwards and Reformed Theology

According to Wallace Alston and Michael Welker, "It is characteristic of Reformed theology to be in constant search of the Reformed identity and to define this identity time and again.... The continuous search for Reformed identity is by no means a desperate and hopeless endeavor. It takes place in response to the word of God and in the midst of the challenges of the world."[1] Indeed, the Reformed church itself is said to be *ecclesia reformata semper reformanda secundum verbum dei*.

Although this impulse is at the very heart of Reformed theology, it is not the whole story. At least two important factors are missing. The first is what we might characterize as the "five solas," which became the doctrinal rallying cry of the Reformation churches: *sola scriptura, solus Christus, sola gratia, sola fide,* and *soli deo gloria*. According to historic Reformed theologians, right theology depends upon Scripture as the final norm in matters of theological judgment this side of the grave, through Christ alone as the mediator of salvation, by divine grace alone, expressed and appropriated by faith alone, towards the ultimate goal of glorifying God.

The second missing component is the fact that Reformed Christianity is also confessional in nature. Reformed theology is not merely expressed in the great confessions that have marked this expression of Christianity since the sixteenth century. It is part of the identity of the historic Reformed communions that in each generation there is a confessional impetus born out of the desire to be always reforming, and expressed in confes-

---

1. Wallace M. Alston and Michael Welker, eds., *Reformed Theology: Identity and Ecumenicity* (Grand Rapids: Eerdmans, 2003), p. x.

sions both historic and modern. Of these confessions the Three Forms of Unity (i.e., the Canons of the Synod of Dordt, the Heidelberg Catechism, and the Belgic Confession), and arguably the Thirty-Nine Articles in the sixteenth century, as well as the Westminster Confession and catechisms of the seventeenth century, stand out as foundational Reformed documents that have had a deep, formative influence on subsequent Protestant traditions. Yet these are just the most influential among many such documents, from the Scots Confession to the Barmen Declaration.

There are other things about the Reformed churches that are important, of course. An emphasis on liturgical and sacramental theology, particular dogmatic emphases, and so on. Nevertheless, methodologically speaking, these three things are particularly important to the identity and form of historic Reformed communions. They provide a ready set of criteria that can be found in different churches shaped by Reformed theological commitments and standards. Some theologians in this tradition emphasize one or more of these identifiers, and in so doing press Reformed theology into slightly different shapes. The philosophical predilections of these divines is also an important factor in the particular form their contributions to Reformed theology take. Thus, the confessional theology of the nineteenth-century American Charles Hodge is shaped in important respects by his commitment to the tradition of Westminster Calvinism, as well as the commonsense realism of the Scottish Enlightenment in which he was schooled. By contrast, the theology of the contemporary German Reformed theologian Jürgen Moltmann is characterized in large measure by his desire to find a way of presenting the tradition in the context of late twentieth-century thought, informed by the philosophical influences of Ernst Bloch, among others, and the intellectual aftermath of the holocaust. Hence, his project involves greater emphasis upon the *semper reformanda* aspect of his Reformed heritage than does that of Hodge. Somewhere between these two we might place the work of a theologian like Karl Barth. His *Church Dogmatics* is characterized by a deep engagement with the whole Christian tradition as well as the Reformed confessions. Yet his work is also shaped in profound ways by his commitment to the "solas" of the Reformation churches and an attempt to recover these from the clutches of classical liberal theology at the beginning of the twentieth century.

Edwards and the Reformed Tradition

Jonathan Edwards is most certainly a Reformed theologian of the first rank, and the most influential theologian yet to appear on the American continent. Nevertheless, he was not a confessional theologian in the mold of Hodge, who famously boasted that no new doctrine had been taught at Princeton during his tenure. Edwards was not concerned merely to transmit a tradition, or to reiterate certain confessional standards, though he was willing to abide by the doctrinal norms of the New England Congregationalism that formed him and the Westminster Confession towards the end of his life, leading up to his brief tenure as the President of the College of New Jersey (now Princeton).[2] He was a constructive theologian whose appeal was to Scripture rather than tradition, and who "called no man father" — not even John Calvin. Thus, in the preface to his great work, *Freedom of the Will*, he wrote, "I should not take it at all amiss, to be called a Calvinist, for distinction's sake: though I utterly disclaim a dependence on Calvin, or believing the doctrines which I hold, because he believed and taught them; and cannot justly be charged with believing in everything just as he taught" (YE1: 131).

This is not to deny that Edwards regarded himself as one who stood on the shoulders of those who had gone before him. His theological formation was in the Puritan and continental post-Reformation traditions to which he regarded himself an heir. To the end of his life he delighted in Protestant scholastics like Petrus van Mastricht and Francis Turretin, recommending them to his students. Yet he viewed the writings of these theologians, as he viewed all the intellectual material he came across and devoured, as grist to his own theological mill. He was not an imitator of others, though his work is in some respects a synthesis of ideas gleaned from reading the works of many different writers. His earliest biographer, Samuel Hopkins, reports that he always read with pen in hand, and traced out his thoughts on paper to their logical ends, even if it meant missing a meal to do so. His fingers were permanently stained with ink as a consequence.[3]

---

2. Letter 117 to Rev. John Erskine, Northampton, July 15, 1750, in YE16: 355. Subsequent references to the Yale edition of Edwards's works appear parenthetically in the body of the text.

3. See Samuel Hopkins, *The Life and Character of the Late Reverend, Learned, and Pious Mr. Jonathan Edwards, President of the College of New Jersey, Together with a Number of Sermons on Various Important Subjects* (Boston: S. Kneeland, 1765).

Such observations are of more than passing biographical interest. Edwards's scholarly habits involved carefully working through on paper the implications of a particular problem with which he was fixated, adding corollaries and addenda, cross-referenced in a series of miniature notebooks he kept throughout his career. These he then plundered in his published works, often lifting gobbets verbatim and copying them into the text of his treatises. Thus, his method lent itself to a certain semi-detachment from tradition and confessional encumbrance, and to greater freedom of expression and thought than that enjoyed by some of his theological contemporaries. Although he did not set out to be a revisionist, his intellectual project could be characterized as an attempt to re-envision Reformed theology using aspects of early Enlightenment philosophy. Rather than regarding with suspicion all the literary products of the "new philosophy" exemplified by thinkers like the Cambridge Platonists, Isaac Newton, Nicholas Malebranche, John Locke, Lord Shaftesbury, David Hume, and Thomas Hobbes, Edwards thought of these authors as providing (amongst other things) new tools by means of which he could undergird Christian theology. As Amy Plantinga Pauw puts it, Edwards "lacked, on the one hand, any pretension to metaphysical purity and, on the other, any illusions about a permanent alliance between Christian faith and a particular philosophical tradition."[4] In other words, he was no Thomist. He did not think in terms of a perennial Christian philosophy. Instead, he sought to provide a new synthetic account of Christian theism that reflected the Reformed tradition that had formed him, drawing on early modern philosophy to do so. He was a kind of intellectual magpie, gathering up useful material wherever he found it and copying it into his notebooks, all the while guided by the assumption (reflecting the rational optimism of the age) that "all truth is God's truth" wherever it may be found. Although he regarded some philosophical notions and doctrines espoused by his peers as pernicious (he had a particular aversion to Hobbesian materialism and to Deism), he did not consider rubbish everything written by thinkers with whom he disagreed. Quite the reverse. He was willing to plunder ideas from every quarter, even those that appeared to many to be inimical to Christian doctrine. "I confess," he writes at one point in *Freedom of the Will*, "it happens I never read Mr. Hobbes. Let his opinion be what it

---

4. Amy Plantinga Pauw, "The Future of Reformed Theology: Some Lessons from Jonathan Edwards," in *Towards the Future of Reformed Theology: Tasks, Topics, Traditions*, ed. David Willis and Michael Welker (Grand Rapids: Eerdmans, 1999), p. 458.

will, we need not reject all truth which is demonstrated by clear evidence, merely because it was once held by some bad man" (YE1: 374). Such careful discrimination meant he was not prone to the genetic fallacy, which confuses the provenance of an idea with its truth value.

However, the philosophical eclecticism that characterized his habits of mind did lead him to make more significant adjustments to received Reformed doctrine than some enamored only of his more practical or evangelical writings have presumed. It is to these developments in his major writings that we now turn.

Doctrinal Developments

Edwards made significant contributions to the doctrines of divine and human freedom, original sin, the Trinity, personal eschatology, theological aesthetics, theological ethics, religious psychology, and hagiography. In the course of setting out his views on these topics, he embraced a number of counterintuitive philosophical claims as well. At the time of his death, Edwards had published two major treatises, *Freedom of the Will* (1754) and *Original Sin* (1758), a collection of sermons, several public lectures, the *Life of David Brainerd* (a missionary to the Native Americans), several works of critical reflection on the revivals of the Great Awakening that culminated in the publication of the *Religious Affections* (1746), and some controversial works defending his revised views on the qualifications for communion which precipitated his dismissal from the pastorate at Northampton, Massachusetts, where he was minister for much of his career. The *Two Dissertations*, on *God's End in Creation* and *True Virtue* (often published and read separately, though they are two parts of one whole) remained unpublished at his death, though they were bound and ready to go to the printers. His fragmentary works on idealism and on the Trinity, and his voluminous notebooks were unpublished and not in a state that indicate he would have permitted their publication. Yet they form an important part of modern interpretations of Edwards as a Reformed theologian. Much of this unpublished work should be treated with caution, however, for it is not always clear that Edwards would have endorsed without cavil the views he expressed privately. His theological method allowed for much that was metaphysically and theologically speculative, not all of which he was willing to commit himself to in public discourse. This is not to imply that Edwards was a sort of Reimarus-like figure, preaching in public doctrines he secretly repudiated or revised. Rather, it is to say that Edwards was very careful about what he published and the fact that certain works remained in notebook form with no indication that he was ready to publish them should give any reader of Edwards pause when assigning a place of prominence to such works in his corpus. For this reason, we shall consider his most important published works first, then his *Two Dissertations*, before offering some remarks on important themes from his unpublished works, especially his doctrine of the Trinity, and his idealism.

The work by which Edwards's name was remembered until quite recently was his monumental treatise, *Freedom of the Will*. It stands as one of the most comprehensive accounts of divine and human freedom in theological literature. In it, Edwards delineates an uncompromising vision according to which human and divine freedom have to do with acting according to one's strongest desire. This, of course, is consistent with determinism, the view that all things that obtain have a cause (or causes) which is (are) necessary and sufficient for the bringing about of the effect in question. Edwards believed that God is "determined" to act in the way he does because of the nature he has. Yet, Edwards averred with respect to the deity, "'Tis no disadvantage or dishonor to a being, necessarily to act in the most excellent and happy manner, from the necessary perfection of his own nature" (YE1: 377). Edwards also thought that God could not have failed to create because he is essentially self-diffusive. In later works such as *God's End in Creation* and his unpublished *Book of Controversies* he goes even further than this, concluding in a manner reminiscent of Leibniz that God must create this world because it is the best possible. According to Edwards, God must act as he does because of the sort of being he is, one whose nature is immutable, eternal, perfect, and (as he puts it) "excellent." (We shall return to the Edwardsian notion of excellency in the chapter on the Trinity.) Humans, on the other hand, are constrained by their desires. Utilizing a distinction (that can also be found apparently independent of Edwards's discussion in earlier Amyraldian theology) between moral and natural ability, he reasons that fallen human beings have no natural impediment to turning to God for redemption, and are thus culpable for not doing so. However, all fallen humans have a moral inability to turn to God of their own initiative, which is a certain and complete obstacle to penitence. There is no possibility that this moral inability might be overcome without interposing divine grace. This distinction was to have considerable impact upon the subsequent New England Theology that grew out of his work.

Edwards and Reformed Theology

Edwards was implacably opposed to what he called "Arminianism." Whether this is identical to historic Arminianism, or a broader category covering various freethinking philosophies that were the product of the early Enlightenment, he insisted that theological libertarianism was not merely unacceptable, but incoherent. A libertarian choice is not caused by anything; otherwise (so it is said) it is not truly free. The agent in question makes the choice from a state of moral equilibrium having no predisposition to one option over another. However, reasons Edwards, this is equivalent to choices obtaining on the basis of no cause whatsoever. Far from establishing human freedom and responsibility, such thinking undermines both freedom and responsibility by removing any reason for the human agent choosing one thing over another. Edwards's devastating critique not only influenced the New Divinity that followed him in the early American Republic; it also found admirers in nineteenth-century Scottish Presbyterianism. Thomas Chalmers regarded it as irrefutable, and William Cunningham discussed it at length in the context of whether Christian theological anthropology implied philosophical necessity.

Recent historiographical work has argued that Reformed theology is not aboriginally deterministic and that Edwards's doctrine represented a significant step-change in the way Reformed theologians dealt with the twin concerns of human freedom and moral responsibility.[5] Whether this is right (a matter to which we shall return in Chapter 5), two things about Edwards's position on this nodal theological doctrine stand out as signal contributions to the discussion within and beyond the bounds of the Reformed tradition. The first is that Edwards provided the basis for a systematic Reformed species of theological determinism, grounded not in the scholastic distinctions of his immediate forebears, nor in the faculty psychology that accompanied it (dividing human persons into apparently semi-autonomous faculties of intellect, will, and so on), but in the ideas of John Locke's philosophy of mind. This was a significant and important contribution, articulating a strong doctrine of divine predestination and meticulous providence in the vocabulary of early modern philosophy.

---

5. See Willem van Asselt, J. Martin Bac, and Roelf T. te Velde, eds., *Reformed Thought on Freedom: The Concept of Free Choice in Early Modern Reformed Theology* (Grand Rapids: Baker Academic, 2010); and Richard A. Muller, "Jonathan Edwards and the Absence of Free Choice: A Parting of the Ways in the Reformed Tradition," *Jonathan Edwards Studies* 1.1 (2011): 3-22. Edwards himself resisted calling his position deterministic without careful qualification. See his Letter 227 to John Erskine, dated July 25, 1757, in YE16: 705-18.

Here, Edwards was engaged in the age-old theological project of articulating Christian doctrine in the mode of contemporary thought. Second, his views about divine freedom or the lack thereof represent at best a minority report in the Christian tradition. This is an important example of how his theological method of tracing out the implications of particular views to their utmost end placed him outside the theological mainstream of western Catholicism, and, as a consequence, the Reformed community that had formed him.[6]

Another doctrine to which Reformed theology has made an important contribution is original sin. In his titular work on that subject, Edwards first set out a Reformed view, including a fascinating discussion of the primal sin of our first parents; the doctrine of original sin and guilt; and the double guilt associated with the ascription of original guilt to the sinner, followed by the guilt associated with actual sin. He went on to espouse an interesting doctrine on the transmission of original sin that has been the subject of recent discussion in the philosophical literature (a matter to which we shall return in Chapter 6). To anticipate: Edwards reasons that sin is not transmitted from one individual to another down through the ages, for this would appear to be monumentally unjust. After all, how can I be punished for a sin I did not commit? Instead, he argues that Adam and his progeny all share in original sin because all are parts of one metaphysical whole scattered throughout space and time. He remarks, "there is no identity or oneness in the case" of objects existing across time, "but what depends on the *arbitrary* constitution of the Creator; who by his wise sovereign establishment so unites these successive new effects, that he *treats them as one*, by communicating to them like properties, relations, and circumstances; and so, leads us to regard and treat them as one" (YE3: 403, author's emphasis). In other words, Edwards denies that we are things that endure through time, being wholly present at each moment we exist. He thinks we have temporal parts just as we have physical parts. The part of me that existed yesterday is numerically different from the part that exists today. Yet both are parts of one whole that exist across time according to divine convention, which is what makes it true that the different temporal parts form one whole thing across time.

Applied to the thorny question of the transmission of original sin, this

---

6. For further discussion of this point, see Oliver D. Crisp, *Jonathan Edwards on God and Creation* (New York: Oxford University Press, 2012).

means that Adam and his offspring may be treated by God as temporal parts of one whole thing, that is, humanity, existing across time. In which case, God does not merely ascribe the sin of Adam to you or me, strictly speaking, for we are parts of the entity that includes Adam. Just as an oak tree may share in the disease of the acorn from which it grew, as a later stage in the life of the one organism, so human beings today may share in the sin of the progenitor of the race, as different stages or phases of the life of the one entity that is the fallen human race.

In his *Religious Affections*, Edwards set out to provide, amongst other things, a set of guidelines for distinguishing true from false affections, against the backdrop of increasing antipathy towards the reported emotional and spiritual excesses of the Great Awakening. For him, an affection is not identical to an emotion, since it has a cognitive as well as conative component. For this reason, religious affections that are appropriately formed are quite different from emotional excesses, such as those associated with the Great Awakening in its more exuberant moments. Such excesses do not provide a reliable gauge of a real secret working of the Holy Spirit; they are purely emotional and psychological responses to various phenomena. True spiritual character is formed via the affections, not via the emotions.

Edwards's mature work on this subject came too late to influence the trajectory of the revivals, which had already passed into history. Nevertheless, it affords a profound study of religious psychology in the Reformed tradition, with affinities to the work of both John Calvin and Friedrich Schleiermacher. In many ways Edwards's discussion of the affections complements that of Calvin on the internal instigation of the Holy Spirit and the *sensus divinitatis* (sense of the divine) in the opening book of his *Institutes*, as well as his careful account of faith in the third book. And like Schleiermacher, Edwards was preoccupied with religious experience, affections, and consciousness, as a litmus test of encountering the divine. Having said that, his way of thinking about this in relation to the formation of doctrine was somewhat different from that of his German-speaking successor. *Religious Affections* is testimony to Edwards's intense concern with the internal dynamic of the spiritual life, and with the saving work of the Holy Spirit in the order of salvation that marked his own spiritual journey (as can be seen in his *Resolutions* and his *Personal Narrative*). He combined the fervor of Puritan spiritual writings with the doctrinal casuistry of the continental Reformed tradition. The lasting influence of *Religious Affections* can be seen in William James's discussion of it in his *The Varieties of*

Religious Experience,[7] as well as in the more recent philosophical work of William Wainwright and Alvin Plantinga.[8]

Edwards's *Two Dissertations* have also had enduring significance. The first of the two, *God's End in Creation*, is a profound study of eschatology, in which Edwards advocates a version of the doctrine of theosis. He speculates that those enjoying heavenly bliss are eternal viators, forever engaged on a journey into God. Becoming "partakers of the divine nature" does not mean being "godded with God." Instead, rather like a mathematical asymptote, those saints in the divine presence are on an infinite trajectory towards God that will never yield complete union with the divine essence, though it will involve ever closer communion with the divine nature. "If the happiness of the creature be considered as it will be, in the whole of the creature's eternal duration, with all the infinity of its progress, and infinite increase of nearness and union to God," says Edwards, "in this view, the creature must be looked upon as united to God in an infinite strictness" (YE8: 534). However, "there will never come the moment," Edwards observes, "that now this infinitely valuable good has been actually bestowed" (YE8: 536), since we are forever finite beings in communion with an infinite God.

True Virtue, the second of Edwards's *Two Dissertations*, is famous as a pithy treatise on virtue ethics, which is unusual in the Reformed tradition, and for having no biblical references whatsoever. It is a philosophical work; that much is undeniable. However, it appears more peculiar than it ought to when read apart from the first dissertation, *God's End in Creation*, which in many ways supplies the theological underpinning for the vision of the good life set forth in the sequel. Edwards's language is clear, careful, and nuanced; the fact that his argument occasionally demands rereading before his point is grasped owes not to obscurity but to extraordinary precision. For all that, *True Virtue* is perhaps the most difficult of Edwards's works to understand. This is mainly due to his use of technical terms that have different connotations in modern theology or that belong to eighteenth-century moral discourse, such as "being," "benevolence," and

---

7. William James, *The Varieties of Religious Experience: A Study in Human Nature, Being the Gifford Lectures on Natural Religion Delivered at Edinburgh in 1901-1902* (New York: Longmans, Green, and Co., 1902).

8. See William J. Wainwright, *Reason and the Heart: A Prolegomenon to a Critique of Passional Reason*, Cornell Studies in Philosophy of Religion (Ithaca: Cornell University Press, 2006); and Alvin Plantinga, *Warranted Christian Belief* (New York: Oxford University Press, 2000).

"complacence." It is also due to the close connection Edwards sees between the good life, i.e., that which is truly virtuous, and Beauty, which functions something like a transcendental in his thinking. In the opening paragraphs of the work, Edwards remarks that, "True virtue most essentially consists in benevolence to Being in general. Or perhaps to speak more accurately, it is that consent, propensity and union of heart to Being in general, that is immediately exercised in a general good will" (YE8: 540). Using the double love command of Christ in Matthew 22 as a sort of organizing principle, Edwards goes on to claim that true virtue involves love to being in general, identified with God, and love to others, as instances of created being, reflecting the beauty and harmony of the creator. The truly virtuous life is a life characterized by happiness, and by delight in the good, which is an aspect or dimension of the true and the beautiful. This makes sense if the good life is a life lived in and through the being of God that sustains all creatures and gives them life.

Earlier I remarked that Edwards did not live to complete a publishable treatise on the Trinity. That being said, his doctrine of the Trinity has garnered a great deal of critical attention over the years, beginning in the nineteenth century when it was rumored that he was a closet Arian. More recently, various accounts of Edwards's theology have argued that his Trinitarianism profoundly shaped other aspects of his thought. For this reason, it seems appropriate to say *something* about this vexed issue in Edwardsian studies, not least because his position does represent an innovation in Reformed theology. The main sources for Edwards's doctrine of the Trinity have been gathered together in YE21. They comprise his *Discourse on the Trinity, On the Equality of the Persons of the Trinity*, and *Treatise on Grace*. Like many in the Reformed tradition, he adopted a basically Augustinian account of the divine persons and essence. However, such a statement must be carefully qualified because Edwards offers certain important — indeed, crucial — modifications to the Augustinian account.

Those influenced by an Augustinian approach to the doctrine of the Trinity tend to think of divine persons as individuated by the relations they bear to one another, nothing more. Edwards takes up this model, but adapts it in two important respects.

First, he has a particular notion of "excellency," with both an aesthetic and an ontological aspect. It is a quality a thing possesses provided it exemplifies beauty, proportion, and a certain sort of aesthetic complexity (between parts and their relations to a whole). Edwards thinks God is the supreme example of excellency because "one alone cannot be excellent."

He presumes that a truly perfect being would be an excellent being. Since God is a perfect being, he must be excellent. So he cannot be without internal differentiation. This differentiation is provided by the divine persons of the Godhead.

Alongside this doctrine of excellency, Edwards maintains that the only real distinctions to be found in God are the divine persons. These divine persons he identifies with God (the Father), the understanding of God (the Son), and his will (the Holy Spirit), respectively. They exist perichoretically in such a way that the relation of mutual indwelling is itself person-constituting. That is, the divine persons exist because they are perichoretically related to one another. This is why Edwards can affirm that there is only one understanding and one will in God shared between the divine persons. He does not deny that there is a divine essence; this essence contains those attributes that are not person-constituting, but which are nonetheless part of the divine nature — such as omnipotence and omniscience. This doctrine, which is only now being given the attention it deserves, represents an important variation on an Augustinian model and an original contribution to Reformed theology.[9]

Edwards's theological project was intimately related to his idealism, although he never published a specific work on that subject. The view that matter is a sort of fiction, that all that truly exist are divine and created minds and their ideas, was "in the air" in the eighteenth century. Edwards's position is rather like that of Bishop George Berkeley, although it appears that they came to their own views independently. His early philosophical notebooks, written whilst he was still in college, demonstrate a clear dependence on the Cambridge Platonists, although he moved beyond Henry More's claim that God is space to the view (developed in his later works) that the world is contained "in" God, an immaterial substance. Utilizing Neoplatonic imagery, Edwards argues in *God's End in Creation* and elsewhere that the deity emanates himself in the creation, which is like his shadow. He also holds to a doctrine of continuous creation. Although he does not spell it out in quite this way, it appears that Edwards's doctrine is that God creates the world (emanates it), whereupon it immediately ceases to exist. He then creates a second, facsimile world that is qualitatively iden-

---

9. See Chapter 3 for more on the Trinity. In the recent literature, two of the most important treatments of Edwards's views can be found in Steven M. Studebaker and Robert W. Caldwell III, *The Trinitarian Theology of Jonathan Edwards: Text, Context and Application* (Aldershot: Ashgate, 2012), and Kyle C. Strobel, *Jonathan Edwards's Theology: A Reinterpretation* (London: T&T Clark, 2012).

tical to the previous one, with incremental changes built into it. This action continues with the creation of numerically distinct but qualitatively near-identical world-stages that he segues together so as to produce what appears to be action across time. This four-dimensionalist picture of how God creates denies the doctrine of divine conservation, strictly speaking, since there is no world to uphold across time. When Edwards's idealism is factored into other central doctrines he espouses, the resulting picture is rather exotic, to say the least. It would appear that Edwards held to a species of what we would now call panentheism, and a view of creation that makes the world like a series of momentary photographic stills run together into a motion picture and projected out from God like a movie on the silver screen. Although these themes are deeply indebted to his Augustinian heritage, they can hardly be described as part of the theological mainstream of the Reformed tradition.

The Edwardsian Legacy for Reformed Theology

Edwards's intellectual legacy is a mixed one. His immediate disciples, theologians and ministers in New England such as Samuel Hopkins, Joseph Bellamy, and Edwards's son and namesake, Jonathan Edwards Jr., were instrumental in transmitting his ideas to a new generation of ministers in New England. Through the "New Divinity" that they propounded, the first truly indigenous movement of American theology grew and flourished over the next century, mainly on the eastern seaboard and some of the midwestern cities of the continental United States. It became known as the New England Theology, although there were various perorations as the movement developed and diversified. The most important of these was the New Haven Theology associated with the Divinity School at Yale, the college at which Edwards himself had been educated. Nathaniel Taylor, the main proponent of this brand of New England Theology, was, like his theological master, somewhat theologically eccentric and very much a constructive theologian who called no man master.

In the process of its maturation and differentiation the New England Theology also came to include thinkers whose writings were very much at odds with the stated views of Edwards himself. This has been something of a puzzle to historians interested in the movement. However, it is easier to understand if one recognizes that what Edwards transmitted to his theological heirs was a method of working through a theological problem for oneself with meticulous attention to detail and careful theological distinctions, but without much reliance upon confessions and the tradition. Alongside this method, he bequeathed to his disciples a certain set of theological problems to which successive generations of New England theologians returned, often with very different solutions. He did not leave behind him a carefully worked out system of doctrines to which his disciples adhered, or which represented the movement as a whole. (That task was taken up by his disciple Samuel Hopkins in his *System of Doctrines*, published in 1793.) In this sense, the New England Theology reflected the theologically entrepreneurial attitude of its founder; it was also a good fit for the developing American republic of the nineteenth century. New England theologians concerned themselves with similar sorts of problems to those addressed in Edwards's published writings (e.g., human freedom in relation to divine sovereignty, original sin, religious affections, and so on), but without slavish emulation of Edwards's views. Consequently, some later theologians in the movement, on the basis of a similar method of careful, rigorous argumentation and reflection, ended up espousing views on human freedom completely at odds with Edwards.

As the movement developed and grew, it was kept together largely through personal networks and allegiances, just as had been the case with Edwards and the immediate disciples who had studied under him in preparation for ordination. This was both a strength and a weakness. It meant there was a strong set of loyalties in those schools in which Edwardsian teaching flourished (e.g., Andover, Yale Divinity School, Brown, Union College, Mount Holyoke, and elsewhere). Yet it also meant that the movement suffered from having few doctrines upon which all were agreed, and around which they could unite. Themes such as free will and original sin characterized much of the movement; particular positions on those topics did not. Those who held views contrary to those of Edwards himself felt free to appeal to him as their theological mentor because he had paved the way for constructive reflection on these topics. He was a model of good scholarship and serious divinity even if his particular views were not adopted by all those who claimed allegiance to him.

The New England Theology disintegrated at the end of the nineteenth century, and Edwards's influence as a constructive theological force came to a temporary halt. The reasons for the movement's demise are complex, but in part reflect its increasing theological diversity, with its leaders eventually spinning off in different directions, away from the Edwardsian center. By contrast, the more confessional Princetonian theology of

Hodge, Warfield, and latterly Gresham Machen and others, survived into the twentieth century at least in part because there was a dogmatic core around which its adherents could gather. Nevertheless, both the Princetonian and Edwardsian divinity were in decline at the close of the nineteenth century when the more optimistic outlook of thinkers like Walter Rauschenbusch and the social gospel were much more in vogue.

Despite having been a force to be reckoned with for a century after Edwards's death, New England Theology is today largely unknown outside the limited circle of those with a professional research interest in the movement.[10] This is unfortunate. It means that the theological impact of Edwards's views is often overlooked. It also means that the way in which Edwards's ideas influenced those who adopted his methods has been largely forgotten. After a period in which interest in Edwards languished, the revival of his work since the late 1940s has led to his being an interlocutor for a new generation of theologians and church leaders. He is one of the most widely read major theologians today. Some recent interpreters maintain that this is largely because his theological interests give him an appeal across denominational and intellectual boundaries.[11] There is much to be said for this claim. Edwards was not just a theologian or a Christian intellectual. He was a minister, a missionary, someone professionally interested in the life of the church in New England, and (eventually, and briefly) a president of Princeton. His influence continues as a founding father of modern evangelicalism, and his spiritual and psychological writings (e.g., his sermons, the *Life of David Brainerd* — a major influence on the nineteenth-century missionary movement — and his *Religious Affections*) have never been out of print since their initial publication. In this respect Edwards's reach, and the diversity of those interested in his writings, makes him a theologian with whom many will continue to grapple, within and beyond the Reformed tradition that formed him.

---

10. Having said that, a recent anthology of excerpts from the work of major theologians in the movement and a major symposium reassessing the importance of the New England Theology represent encouraging signs of renewed interest. See Douglas A. Sweeney and Allen C. Guelzo, eds., *The New England Theology: From Jonathan Edwards to Edwards Amasa Park* (Grand Rapids: Baker Academic, 2006); and Oliver D. Crisp and Douglas A. Sweeney, eds., *After Jonathan Edwards: The Courses of the New England Theology* (New York: Oxford University Press, 2012).

11. See Michael J. McClymond and Gerald R. McDermott, *The Theology of Jonathan Edwards* (New York: Oxford University Press, 2012).

CHAPTER 2

Anselm and Edwards on the Doctrine of God

Despite the fact that they are separated by seven centuries and lived on different continents, the accounts of the doctrine of God found in the works of St. Anselm of Canterbury and Jonathan Edwards are similar in many respects. This owes in large measure to the fact that both share a common Augustinian heritage, though each "received" this inheritance in different ways. The legacy of Augustine in both cases involves a large dose of baptized Neoplatonism, and a preoccupation with understanding the divine nature in terms of the dialectic between divine simplicity and triunity — which is arguably the central problematic of classical Christian theism. Yet there are also differences between these two Augustinian theologians. One concerns the way in which they understand the doctrine of the Trinity. Although I shall refer to Anselm's discussion of the generation of the Second Person of the Trinity in what follows, Edwards's Trinitarianism is complicated enough to require a separate discussion. This I have postponed until the following chapter. Here, the focus is more on the classical, orthodox doctrine of God (what is often referred to as classical theism), and the distinction between creatures and the creator. We shall see that although Anselm and Edwards work from the same broad tradition of Augustinian theology, Anselm is in several respects quite guarded about what he is willing to say about the divine life. By contrast, Edwards is willing to countenance a certain amount of speculation about God's nature, as well as the relation between creatures and the creator, all of which leaves him open to objection from theologians of a more Anselmian persuasion.

Anselm and Edwards on the Doctrine of God

Anselm on God

Anselm's doctrine of God has been one of the most influential aspects of his theological legacy. Today there is a whole literature devoted to "perfect being theology" that takes his work as an important point of departure.[1] Although later medieval schoolmen developed the doctrine of God with ever greater sophistication (e.g., St. Thomas Aquinas, John Duns Scotus), and although Anselm is deeply indebted to an earlier Christian tradition (e.g., St. Augustine), his work has become a sort of benchmark against which later accounts of the doctrine of God are measured. We shall see that Edwards's understanding of the divine nature, like that of many other thinkers educated in the technicalities of Reformed orthodox theology, shares important features with the classical account of the doctrine of God indebted to Anselm, amongst others. We shall also see that there are important respects in which Edwards displays a willingness to experiment with or adapt aspects of this doctrinal deposit to suit his own theological predilections. Although Edwards is in one respect a theologian immersed in the classical doctrine of God that owes so much to Anselm, he is not merely a transmitter of classical theism. He is, in many ways, a constructive theologian indebted to a tradition of thought, though not its slavish imitator.

We begin with divine simplicity, which is so central to Anselm's doctrine in *Monologion* and *Proslogion*. Like the vast majority of classical, traditional Christian theists, Anselm believes that God is a simple being. That is, he is an entity very unlike any creature, being essentially non-composite, such that (amongst other things) there is no real distinction to be made between the different attributes he possesses. This is not so much one among many things we can predicate of God, as it is a way of conceiving the whole divine nature, as the following gobbets from Anselm demonstrate:

1. Perfect being theology does not begin with Anselm. He inherits a tradition going back to Platonism via St. Augustine. However, in the contemporary literature "perfect being theology" often goes hand-in-hand with "Anselmianism." Some of the history of perfect being theology is discussed by Brian Leftow in "Why Perfect Being Theology?" *International Journal for Philosophy of Religion* 69 (2011): 103-18. The Augustinian roots of the Anselmian doctrine are discussed in Edward Wierenga, "Augustinian Perfect Being Theology and the God of Abraham, Isaac, and Jacob," *International Journal for Philosophy of Religion* 69 (2011): 139-51. In a recent textbook, Michael J. Murray and Michael Rea say that "Although perfect being theology has a very long history, it emerges as an explicit driving consideration first in the writings of the eleventh-century philosopher Anselm of Canterbury" (*An Introduction to the Philosophy of Religion* [Cambridge: Cambridge University Press, 2008], p. 8). This seems right.

Now the supreme nature cannot properly be said to *have* justice [*habet iustitiam*] but rather to *exist as* justice [or: to *be* justice — *existit iustitia*]. Therefore, when he is said to be just, he is properly understood as existent justice, not as having justice.... Therefore, when someone asks what he is, "Just" is no less fitting an answer than "Justice."... Now it is clear that whatever good thing the supreme nature is, he is that thing supremely [*summe illud est*].[2]

Therefore, since that nature is in no way composite... [i]t must be that all those things are not several but one. So each of them is the same as all the others, whether all at once or individually.... Whatever is truly said of his essence is not understood as expressing what sort of thing or how great he is, but rather as expressing what he is. For whatever is a thing of a certain quality or quantity is something else with respect to what it is, and so it is not simple but composite.[3]

What are you, Lord, what are you? Surely you are life, you are wisdom, you are truth, you are goodness, you are happiness, you are eternity, and you are every true good. These are many things; my narrow understanding cannot see so many things in one glance and delight in all of them at once. How then, Lord, are you all these things? Are they parts of you? Or rather, is not each of them all that you are? For whatever is composed of parts is not completely one. It is in some sense a plurality and not identical with itself, and it can be broken up either in fact or at least in the understanding. But such characteristics are foreign to you, than whom nothing better can be thought.[4]

As these excerpts indicate, Anselm's doctrine of divine simplicity privileges a certain apophaticism about the divine nature. Rather than

---

2. All citations to Anselm's works in English given in the body of the text are from *Anselm: Basic Writings*, ed. and trans. Thomas Williams (Indianapolis: Hackett, 2007). Where relevant, I have also supplied references to *S. Anselmi, Cantuariensis Archepiscopi, Opera Omnia, Tomus Primus et Tomus Secundus*, ed. F. S. Schmitt (Stuttgart: Friedrich Frommann Verlag, 1984 [1968]), henceforth given as *Opera Omnia*, followed by volume number and page reference. References to *Proslogion* will be given parenthetically in the body of the text as "P," followed by chapter number, e.g., P1. Similarly, *Monologion* will be cited as "M," followed by chapter number. In this case the reference is to M16; *Opera Omnia* I. 30-31.
3. M17; *Opera Omnia* I. 31-32.
4. P18; cf. *Opera Omnia* I. 114.

giving a complete description of divine simplicity, he emphasizes the claim that God is without parts and without distinct attributes, all of which are identical to the divine essence as such.[5] There are numerous treatments of Anselm's perfect being theology and his notion, central to the early chapters of *Proslogion*, that God is that than which none greater can be thought. Such accounts often pass over *Proslogion* 15 in silence. Yet what he says in that chapter is crucial to understanding rightly his doctrine of divine simplicity, because there he makes it clear that God is greater than anything that can be thought. He is beyond any human conception of him, a point that is underlined in *Proslogion* 18, where Anselm declares that his own "narrow understanding" cannot grasp all the different attributes of God in a single glance. This is not because God has so many distinct predicates that Anselm cannot see them all at once. Were that the case God would not be a perfect being since he would be a very large composite, having many parts. But that is impossible because he is a perfect being (the implication being that fissiparous entities of whatever size are imperfect because they can be diminished through division). So it cannot be that he has distinct attributes. "You are in fact unity itself," says Anselm. He goes on to say, "you cannot be divided by any understanding. Therefore life and wisdom and the rest are not parts of you; they are all one. Each of them is all of what you are, and each is what the rest are" (P18).

What is more, according to Anselm's way of thinking, although God can be said to be a substance-like thing (M26), he is not like created sub-

---

5. This touches on a wider point about rightly conceiving the doctrine of divine simplicity. The historical theologian Richard Muller says that "If some of the late patristic and scholastic expositions of the doctrine class as philosophical and perhaps speculative, the basic concept is not: from Irenaeus to the era of Protestant orthodoxy, the fundamental assumption was merely that God, as ultimate spirit, is not a compounded or composite being. It is also the case that, from the time of the fathers onwards, divine simplicity was understood as a support of the doctrine of the Trinity and as necessarily defined in such a manner as to argue the 'manifold' as well as the non-composite character of God." Richard A. Muller, *Post-Reformation Reformed Dogmatics: The Rise and Development of Reformed Orthodoxy, ca. 1520 to ca. 1725* (Grand Rapids: Baker Academic, 2003), vol. 3, p. 276. Similar things could be said of other medieval theologians, such as St. Thomas Aquinas. See, e.g., Brian Davies, "Simplicity," in *The Cambridge Companion to Christian Philosophical Theology*, ed. Charles Taliaferro and Chad Meister (Cambridge: Cambridge University Press, 2010), pp. 31-45. For a somewhat different account, see William E. Mann, "Anselm on the Trinity," in *The Cambridge Companion to Anselm*, ed. Brian Davies and Brian Leftow (Cambridge: Cambridge University Press, 2004), chap. 11.

stances. For there is no distinction between substance and accident in God as there is in other substances. Uniquely with God, his substance is identical to his essence, because God has no distinct properties or attributes: all divine attributes are identical with each other and with the divine nature. So, Anselm remarks, "a general analysis of substance does not include that substance whose essence is special and exclusive, having nothing in common with that of other natures" (M27). At the close of *Monologion*, in chapter 79, he even goes as far as to say that the divine essence is not a substance strictly speaking, for substances are property bearers, and God has no properties (i.e., "accidents").[6]

In addition to conceiving God as a simple, unique substance-like thing, Anselm maintains divine aseity according to which God exists "from himself" *(per se)*. He is independent of all other (created) beings, and he generates all other entities, which exist by or through him *(per aliud)*. God's *aseity* is his independence of created things; his *ultimacy* is his being the entity through which all other entities, including abstract objects, exist.[7] These two notions play fundamental roles in the *Monologion*. In chapter 14 Anselm remarks, "where he [God] does not exist, nothing exists. Therefore he exists everywhere, both through all things and in all things. . . . he undergirds and transcends, [as well as] encompasses and penetrates all other things. . . . it is he who exists in all things and through all things, and from whom and through whom and in whom all things exist." Similar ideas are present in M18. There he comments, "he in no way exists from another or from nothing, or through another or through nothing." What is more, "he cannot have a beginning from himself or through himself, although he does exist from himself and through himself. For he exists from himself and through himself in such a way that the essence he is through himself and from himself is in no way different from the essence through which and from which he exists."

Given his endorsement of this package of metaphysical notions concerning the divine nature, it is not surprising that Anselm maintains that God is distinct from the creation. For he exists from and through himself, that is, *a se*, without composition, without potency, and lacking any capac-

---

6. He says "the supreme essence, which does not underlie any accidents, cannot properly be called a substance unless 'substance' is being used instead of 'essence'" (M79). Cf. *Opera Omnia* I. 86: "Unde iam supra manifestum est summam essentiam quae nullis subiacet accidentibus proprie non posse dici substantiam, nisi substantia ponatur pro essentia."

7. Sandra Visser and Thomas Williams make this distinction between divine aseity and ultimacy in *Anselm* (New York: Oxford University Press, 2009), p. 96.

ity for change. He remarks that, "the supreme nature never yields a place in his simplicity for accidents that bring about change" (M25). What is more, "since he alone among all natures has from himself whatever existence he has, without the help of any other nature, is he not uniquely what he is, having nothing in common with his creatures?" To which he adds, "Accordingly, if any word is ever applied to him in common with others, it must undoubtedly be understood to have a very different signification" (M26). By contrast, the creation exists via the agency of some other entity (i.e., *per aliud*), is created *ex nihilo*, is finite, and contains creatures whose being or essence is distinct from their actions and the properties they possess. As Anselm puts it, "the supreme essence alone, through himself, produced so great a mass of things — so numerous a multitude, so beautifully formed, so orderly in its variety, so fitting in its diversity — from nothing" (M7).

In Anselm's hands, the doctrine of divine ultimacy means that nothing exists independent of God's knowledge of it; and that God's knowledge is causal, bringing about the existence of all creatures. As Katherin Rogers puts it, "Not only is there no primal matter out of which He makes things, but there is no independent existing abstracta; that is, there is no world of Platonic forms, or properties, or necessary truths, or propositions of any sort, existing independently of God."[8]

Anselm thinks that the deity knows all things in a single, simple eternal moment that is identical with his essence. Given that Anselm thinks God's knowledge is causal, the eternal moment of divine knowledge is not a passive act like gazing into a crystal ball. Divine knowledge is that means by which God brings the world about and sustains it. We have also seen that Anselm's doctrine of divine simplicity implies that God has absolute qualities like Goodness and Justice. Yet these things are not distinct. They are identical with one another because they are something like aspects of the one, simple divine nature. On this basis, Anselm thinks he has established that "this [divine] substance is not included in any common classification of substances, since every other nature is excluded from having an essence in common with him" (M27).

In one sense, creatures are but shadows in comparison to the divine substance — things that barely exist. God is "in a certain sense the only thing that exists, whereas all other things that appear to exist do not exist

---

8. Katherin A. Rogers, *Anselm on Freedom* (Oxford: Oxford University Press, 2008), p. 16.

at all compared to him" (M28).[9] God alone exists "in an unqualified sense" perfectly and absolutely, whereas all other things "nearly do not exist at all, and barely do exist" (M28). His existence is immutable, eternal. Ours is contingent, changeable, fleeting. What is more, unlike God, creatures begin to exist through the agency of another *(per aliud)*, having been created out of nothing, to which they return unless God sustains them in existence. So everything apart from God is created and sustained by God and is radically dependent upon God, compared to whom they barely exist. What is more, there is no place in Anselm's ontology for objects that exist independent of God's agency. As he puts it in *Monologion* 13, "whatever is not the same as the supreme nature was made through him."

Anselm proceeds in *Monologion* 29-36 (and thereafter) to explain how the created order came to be. The argument of this section is an intriguing and sometimes perplexing combination of an Augustinian *a priori* argument for the eternal generation of the Second Person of the Trinity, coupled with elements of a doctrine of divine exemplars, which he reinterprets in a radical way. Caution should be exercised in interpreting it, for at its close, Anselm frankly admits that he has no idea how the things that were made were made via divine speech (M36).

We can give a *précis* of the argument as follows. Everything apart from God is made through his divine utterance. No created thing is made from itself. God is not made; he is eternal and (therefore) uncreated. God's locution is not made but eternally generated because it is the utterance of an eternal, immutable being. Moreover, God's utterance is identical to God, since God has no parts (i.e., is simple). Hence, God's utterance is not itself a creature. Rather, God utters the exemplar of creatures by uttering himself.

It looks like Anselm thinks there is an exemplar of particular creatures in the mind of God. This exemplar (for it is singular) is eternally generated in the act of eternally generating, or uttering, the Word (i.e., God the Son). It is as if the Word somehow "contains" the exemplar, or blueprint of creation. Plus — a closely related point — it is through the Word that God knows all things (since his uttering the Word is his uttering of himself and, consequent upon this, is equivalent to a perfect and complete act of self-understanding [M29]). Now, we have seen that Anselm thinks

9. Cf. *Opera Omnia* I. 42-43: ". . . quadam ratione solus sit, alia vero quaecumque vindentur esse, huic collate non sint." He goes on to say, "ille [i.e., the deity] solus videbitur simpliciter et perfecte et absolute esse, alia vero omnia fere non esse et vix esse." Creaturely existence is very much an attenuated existence at best when compared to the absolute and unqualified existence of God.

God is identical to transcendentals like Goodness and Justice via divine simplicity. But he is not said to be identical to a rabbit or a rhino. Yet the ideas of rabbits and rhinos are eternally generated in the divine mind and are identical with God. They are, we might say, "aspects" of this one simple divine act, the numerous effects of which are distributed across time. Rabbits and rhinos exist "in" God in one sense, as aspects of the exemplar of these things that exists in the divine mind. But in another sense they are not identical to God in the way that, say, Justice or Goodness are identical to God. As Anselm puts it in *Monologion* 31, every created essence is greater and more excellent the more it is like the supreme essence of which it is an imitation. The nearer a created essence is to God, the closer it approaches his essence, the higher its dignity. But there is no transgression of the boundary between creator and creature here:

> the supreme spirit's verbalization is the supreme spirit. . . . But you cannot possibly count the spirit's verbalization as something created. This is because everything created was made through it, and it cannot have been made through itself. And this is because nothing can be made through itself: whatever something is made into is later than that through which it is made, and nothing is later than itself. Therefore the verbalization of the supreme spirit cannot be a creature. (M29)

Anselm's account of the divine ideas includes three different ontological "layers" or strata.[10] The first is the divine nature itself, which, through an eternal act of self-reflection, perfectly comprehends all things. This includes the exemplar of created things, which exist by means of the utterance of the divine Word. This is like a blueprint of all created things from which, as it were, God creates. "After all, there is no way anyone could make something rationally unless something like a pattern (or, to put it more suitably, a form or likeness or rule) of the thing to be made already existed in the reason of the maker" (M9; cf. M11). The second layer comprises the instances of divine ideas as God creates them — that is, the creatures themselves, created essences existing in created substances. The third layer is creaturely ideas, which he calls "likenesses." When we perceive a person, we do not perceive their essence. Rather, we

---

10. Or, as Katherin Rogers puts it, three ontological levels — although what constitutes these levels is slightly different on her reckoning. Rogers, *The Neoplatonic Metaphysics of Anselm of Canterbury* (Lampeter: Edwin Mellen Press, 1997), p. 230.

perceive some likeness of their essence — an image of it. "After all," says Anselm, "in themselves they exist through their own essence, whereas in our knowledge it is not their essences but their likenesses that exist" (M36; cf. M62).

Each stage is somehow less "real," or has less "being" than the one above it (recall Anselm's comments about creatures "barely existing" in comparison to God). Think of a portrait painting. We creatures are like the painting — a dim copy of the real thing — the Word, which is like the person whose image the painting bears. And like the painting we might be said to "participate" in the life of the real thing, though we are distinct from the thing of which we are an "image" in some fashion. The contemporary Dutch philosophical theologian Gerrit Immink puts it like this: "God's Word is the original exemplar and created reality is made in the likeness of God's Word, whilst human speaking is in turn a likeness of created reality.... as a Christian thinker, [Anselm] cannot accept that God is ultimately subject to any kind of reality. Therefore universals must exist (so to say) in the mind of God."[11]

Coupled with this rather heady account of creation via the divine Word, Anselm maintains that all creatures are immediately and continually dependent upon God for their existence. He also affirms that all things that he creates exist "in" God. In *Monologion* 13 he says that by parity of reasoning the one who exists *per se* must also be the one who sustains *per se*, whereas that which exists *per aliud* must be sustained in the same fashion. Creatures do not become ontologically independent of God once created. They remain dependent upon God at all moments after the first moment of their existence. Or as Anselm sums it up, "nothing remains in existence except through his conserving presence" (M13). So nothing exists "beyond" God, as it were. To this, Anselm adds a rather strong doctrine of the presence of God in all things. God "undergirds and transcends" as well as "encompasses and penetrates all other things," which leads him to the conclusion that "it is he who exists in all things and through all things, and from whom and through whom and in whom all things exist" (M14).

Another relevant consideration comes in *Monologion* 16. In that chapter Anselm argues that God cannot be said to participate in a quality, like

---

11. F. Gerrit Immink, "The One and Only: The Simplicity of God," in *Understanding the Attributes of God: Contributions to Philosophical Theology*, ed. Gijsbert van den Brink and Marcel Sarot (Frankfurt am Main: Peter Lang, 1999), vol. 1, pp. 113-14.

justice. He must be Justice itself. Otherwise he would be just in virtue of something other than himself, which is impossible. But the implication of this passage is that all other things besides God do participate in justice, and they participate in justice as a quality that reflects the Just nature of God. Now, let us compare this with what he says about the nature of truth in the second chapter of his dialogue, *De Veritate*. In reply to a question about the nature of truth in a given statement, the "Teacher" (i.e., Anselm) says this: "nothing is true except by participating in the truth, and so the truth of what is true is in the true thing itself, whereas the thing stated is not in the true statement." A statement is true insofar as it measures up to the Truth, in which all true things participate.[12] And we know from *Monologion* that God is the Truth. I suggest that when we put such statements about participation in God beside the other aspects of his philosophical theology we have discussed thus far, a fairly clear picture emerges.

In summary: according to Anselm, God is a simple substance-like uncreated entity. His nature is unique, for he alone has no distinction between his essence or nature and his accidents. He is essentially non-composite in a very strong sense; this yields a version of the doctrine of divine simplicity. God is also unique in the manner of his existence, which is entirely independent of the creation (i.e., *a se*). Indeed, he is the means by which all created things exist (i.e., he is *ultimate*). Finally, Anselm offers an account of creation that depends on the claim that creatures in some sense exist "in" God, as constituents of his exemplar, the Word of God. Somehow, by means of the eternal generation of the Word, God knows all things. Thus, Anselm's understanding of the divine nature makes a clear distinction between the creator and his creatures in a way reminiscent of Augustine's argument for the eternal generation of the Son.

Edwards on God

Even a cursory look at Edwards in comparison to Anselm shows that their views on Theology Proper share a strong family resemblance. Like Anselm, Edwards was unapologetic in his use of metaphysics in theology. As Michael McClymond and Gerald McDermott put it,

---

12. It is noteworthy that this notion of participation is here joined to Anselm's doctrine of rectitude, which plays such an important role in other areas of his philosophical theology (such as his doctrine of free will).

Edwards's embrace of metaphysics and metaphysical argumentation distinguished him from Reformation thought (Luther, Calvin) as well as twentieth-century Neo-Orthodoxy or Neo-Reformational theology (Karl Barth). It placed him nearer to such patristic and medieval thinkers as Augustine, Anselm, Aquinas, and Bonaventure.[13]

Both Anselm and Edwards regard God as the greatest being. In a manner that recalls this Anselmian notion, Edwards speaks of the deity as "infinitely the greatest and best of beings."[14] What is more, "the Creator is infinite, and has all possible existence, perfection and excellence, so he must have all possible regard. As he is every way the first and supreme, and as his excellency is in all respects the supreme beauty and glory, the original good, and fountain of all good; so he must have in all respects the supreme regard."[15] The terms "all possible existence" and "all possible regard" reflect the language of Edwards's eighteenth-century context. I suppose he does not mean to say that God alone exists or has regard. Rather, he means to express something of the superlative regard due to God because of his peerless state. Edwards also writes of God's "infinite regard or love to himself, he being infinitely the greatest and most excellent Being." Given that he is such a being, "a meet and proper regard to himself" as being "infinitely greater than . . . all other beings" is entirely appropriate. For he "is as it were the sum of all being, and all other positive existence is but a communication from him, hence it will follow that a proper regard to himself is the sum of his regard."[16] What is more, Edwards like Anselm has a healthy regard for the infinite qualitative difference between creature and creator. A superior perceptive nature "may well be supposed, in some respects, to include and comprehend what belongs to an inferior, as the greater comprehends the less and as the whole includes a part."[17] However, "an inferior nature don't include what belongs to a superior."[18] God is beyond our ken precisely because he is infinitely greater than we are, a different order of being, and therefore in many ways puzzling and incomprehensible to us. Edwards writes:

13. Michael J. McClymond and Gerald R. McDermott, *The Theology of Jonathan Edwards* (New York: Oxford University Press, 2012), p. 105.
14. YE8: 421.
15. YE8: 424.
16. YE20: 460, entry 1077, "God's Holiness."
17. YE23: 371, entry 1340, "Reason and Revelation."
18. YE23: 371, entry 1340, "Reason and Revelation."

if a revelation be made [to] us concerning that Being that is uncreated and self-existent, who is infinitely diverse from and above all others in his nature, and so infinitely above all that any improvement or advancement of our nature can give us any consciousness of, in such a revelation it would be very strange indeed if there should not be some great mysteries quite beyond our comprehension and attended with difficulties which it [is] impossible for us fully to solve and explain.[19]

The concepts Edwards employs would not have been foreign to Anselm, even if the language is rather different. In both cases God is conceived of as a being of maximal perfection, as well as beyond our comprehension in important respects.

Some recent scholars have written of Anselm's "theistic idealism." Certainly, his account of the eternal generation of the Son as the very act by means of which the exemplar of the creation is also brought about is suggestive of idealism of a Christian Neoplatonic variety. It is also very much a variation on an Augustinian doctrine of the Trinity. However, Anselm does not deny that the things created are physical objects. His "idealism," if we may call it that, is more like an Augustinian doctrine of divine ideas, with certain important modifications.

By contrast, Edwards embraces the notion that the world is ideal all the way down. This is developed most fully in his early philosophical notebooks *On Being* and *Of Atoms*, as well as *The Mind*. But the same sentiments can be found scattered in his other notebooks. For instance, in his "Miscellanies," he reminds himself at one point: "remember that the world exists only mentally, so that the very being of the world implies its being perceived or discovered."[20] He thinks that there is no such thing as matter. Our bodies are not material objects. They, like human and divine minds, are essentially non-corporeal.[21] However, this does not stop Edwards from speaking with the vulgar whilst he continues to think with the learned. At one point in *The Mind* he makes this explicit:

---

19. YE23: 371, entry 1340, "Reason and Revelation."

20. YE13: 360, entry 247, "Glory of God." Compare "Miscellany" f in YE13: 166, which has: "contrary to the opinion of [Thomas] Hobbes (that nothing is substance but matter), that no matter is substance but only God, who is a spirit, and that other spirits are more substantial than matter."

21. Compare "Seeing the brain exists only mentally, I therefore acknowledge that I speak improperly when I say, the soul is in the brain only as to its operations." Edwards, "The Mind," in YE6: 355, §35.

Though we suppose that the existence of the whole material universe is absolutely dependent on idea, yet we may speak in the old way, and as properly and truly as ever: God in the beginning created such a certain number of atoms, of such a determinate bulk and figure, which they yet maintain and always will; and gave them such a motion, of such a direction, and of such a degree of velocity; from whence arise all the natural changes in the universe forever in a continued series. Yet perhaps all this does not exist anywhere perfectly but in the divine mind. But then, if it be inquired what exists in the divine mind, and how these things exist there, I answer: there is his determination, his care and his design that ideas shall be united forever, just so and in such a manner as is agreeable to such a series.[22]

God has a perfect, stable idea of the creation which he communicates so that things appear to behave in the created world in an orderly fashion according to physical "laws," which God has established and which govern the world.[23] God "supposes the existence"[24] of every atom at every point in space, but this is all an immediate communication of ideas, relations, phenomena, in an ordered series ordained by divine fiat.

In an idealist world such as Edwards supposes the creation to be, it is not surprising to find that he thinks bodies have "less being" than spirits; and that created spirits are but shadows compared with the excellency of God.[25] In this regard, and like Anselm, he thinks that God alone is the fount and origin of being. Creatures exist in an attenuated state. This is because the world is a communication or "emanation" from God, a sort of shadow projected by the deity that is renewed every moment. This picture

---

22. "The Mind," §34 in YE6: 353-54.
23. This is made clear in "Miscellany" 1263 in YE20. I have discussed this at greater length in Crisp, *Jonathan Edwards on God and Creation* (New York: Oxford University Press, 2012), chap. 1. For a rather different interpretation of "Miscellany" 1263, see Sang Lee, *The Philosophical Theology of Jonathan Edwards*, expanded ed. (Princeton: Princeton University Press, 2000 [1988]). See also YE6: 344. Here Edwards says, "that which truly is the substance of all bodies is the infinitely exact and precise and perfectly stable idea in God's mind, together with his stable will that the same shall gradually be communicated to us, and to other minds, according to certain fixed and exact established methods and laws: or in somewhat different language, the infinitely exact and precise divine idea, together with an answerable, perfectly exact, precise and stable will with respect to correspondent communications to created minds, and effects on their minds."
24. The phrase Edwards uses later in the same section of "The Mind" in YE6: 354.
25. Both claims made in "The Mind."

of absolute metaphysical dependence on God is captured rather nicely in one of his early entries in the "Miscellanies" notebook, where he writes:

> 'Tis certain with me that the world exists anew every moment, that the existence of things every moment ceases and is every moment renewed. For instance, in the existence of bodies, for there to be resistance, or tendency to some place; 'tis not numerically the same resistance that exists the next moment.[26]

The world is continuously created or, as he puts it in his later writings, *emanated*, by God.[27] However, God, like created spirits, is not extended in space. He has no location: "That is a gross and an unprofitable idea we have of God, as being something large and great as bodies are, and infinitely extended throughout the immense space. For," writes Edwards, "God is neither little nor great with that sort of greatness, even as the soul of man." He is "not at all extended, no more than an idea, and is not present anywhere as bodies are present." He drives the point home thus, "God is present nowhere any otherwise than the soul is in the body or brain, and he is present everywhere as the soul is in the body."[28]

What characterizes physical bodies is not their extension, as with Cartesianism, but their possessing *resistance*. In *Of Atoms* Edwards states that

> since . . . solidity or body is immediately from the exercise of divine power, causing there to be resistance in such a part of space, it follows that motion also, which is the communication of body, solidity, or this re-

---

26. YE13: 288, entry 125(a) on God's existence. William Wainwright has a helpful article on this point. See his "Jonathan Edwards and 'Particular Minds,'" *International Journal for Philosophy of Religion* 68 (2010): 201-13.

27. "Emanation" is a term that crops up a lot in *God's End in Creation*, chap. 2, §VII, in YE8: 526-36, written at the end of Edwards's life. "Here is both an *emanation* and *remanation*. The refulgence shines upon and into the creature, and is reflected back to the luminary. The beams of glory come from God, and are something of God, and are refunded back again to their original. So that the whole is *of* God, and *in* God, and *to* God; and God is the beginning, middle and end in this affair" (YE8: 531, emphasis in original).

28. YE13: 334-35, entry 194, "God." Some commentators have mistakenly thought that Edwards's early infatuation with Henry More's view that God is space represents his mature view on this matter (an example of this can be found in Richard R. Niebuhr's essay, "Being and Consent," in *The Princeton Companion to Jonathan Edwards*, ed. Sang Hyun Lee [Princeton: Princeton University Press, 2005], chap. 3). Edwards repudiated More's position as he worked through the implications of his idealism.

sistance, from one part of space to another successively (that is, from one part of space to the next immediately adjacent, and so on to the next, etc.) is from the immediate exercise of divine power so communicating that resistance, according to certain conditions which we call the laws of motion. How truly then is it in him that we live, move and have our being.[29]

He goes on to say this:

We by this also clearly see that creation of the corporeal universe is nothing but the first causing resistance in such parts of space as God thought fit, with a power of being communicated successively from one part of space to another, according to such stated conditions as his infinite wisdom directed; and then the first beginning of this communication, so that ever after it might be continued without deviating from those stated conditions.[30]

Physical laws, on this Edwardsian way of thinking, are just "the stated methods of God's acting with respect to bodies, and the stated conditions of the alteration of the manner of his acting."[31] There are no physical laws independent of divine action, as if the creation, once begun, is able to continue under its own steam, according to certain nomological conditions written into the world. The world does not work independently of God, programmed to run in certain ways like some sophisticated organic machine. Rather, God is immediately involved in the sustenance of creation at each moment, as he is the sole cause of its generation.

This indicates a clear distinction between the creator and what he creates — even if the creation turns out to be a series of stable ideas communicated or projected by God outside of himself. Yet, somewhat paradoxically, Edwards also maintains that created spirits are simply finite, limited

---

29. YE6: 215-16. In his editorial introduction to YE6, Wallace Anderson says this of Edwards's notion of resistance: "because a body perseveres or continues to exist only so far as it resists being divided through its continuously extended parts, its being or essence must consist in such a resistance. Indeed, resistance to division and solidity are the same, and they are the same as body itself. All the real properties of bodies are modes of or dependent upon solidity; the extension of a body, as distinct from that of space, results from solidity; shape is a modification of the extension, and mobility is the communicability of solidity from one to another part of space" (YE6: 64).
30. YE6: 216.
31. YE6: 216.

versions of the same sort of fundamental entity as the deity. This seems to undercut his commitment to the absolute difference between God and the created order. He writes:

> Many have wrong conceptions of the difference between the nature of the Deity and created spirits. The difference is no contrariety, but what naturally results from his greatness and nothing else, such as created spirits come nearer to, or more imitate, the greater they are in their powers and faculties. So that if we should suppose the faculties of a created spirit to be enlarged infinitely, there would be the Deity to all intents and purposes, the same simplicity, immutability, etc.[32]

In a later "Miscellanies" notebook entry, he makes much the same point:

> That [the] first supreme and universal principle of things, from whence results the being, the nature, the powers and motions, and sweet order of the world, is properly an intelligent willing agent, *such as our souls only without our imperfections*, and not some inconceivable, unintelligent, necessary agent, seems most rational; because, of all the beings that we see or know anything of, man's soul only seems to be the image of that supreme universal principle.[33]

It is difficult to know what to say about these passages. For it is certainly not obvious that created spirits lack only the perfecting or "enlargement" of their natures "infinitely" in order to have the same attributes as the deity. Even if, like Richard Swinburne in the recent philosophical literature, we think that it is logically possible for a finite spirit to become an omnipresent one,[34] it is not at all clear that a finite spirit may become metaphysically simple as God is. For then, as we have already seen in Anselm's work, the spirit in question would have ceased to have any distinct properties, which seems to be much more than a change in the degree to which one instantiates a particular property (i.e., from having a certain limited power to possessing maximal power). What is more, Edwards himself in other passages makes it clear that the difference between God and

---

32. YE13: 298, entry 135 (150), entitled "Deity."
33. YE13: 451-52, entry 383, "Being of God." Compare "Miscellany" 896, "Being of God, God an Intelligent, Voluntary Being," in YE20: 154-55.
34. See Richard Swinburne, *The Coherence of Theism*, rev. ed. (Oxford: Oxford University Press, 1993 [1977]), pp. 106-7.

rational creatures is not one of mere degree, but kind (recall "Miscellany" 1340 cited earlier; he says similar things in some of his sermons as well[35]). If God is non-composite because simple, then he cannot have properties attributed to him essentially as creatures can. Elsewhere, in his passing endorsements of the divine simplicity tradition of Reformed Orthodoxy, Edwards appears to agree with this.[36]

The language he uses here is, to say the least, unguarded. Perhaps he really did think that an expanding finite spirit would simply reach a point at which it would develop into the sort of infinite spirit that God is. However, he also thought that one cannot generate an actual infinite series by the addition of finite stages, however many one adds.[37] It is difficult to see how the expansion of the powers belonging to a creature, however exalted, would result in its elevation from finitude to infinitude, since, by Edwards's own lights, a finite series can never become an infinite one by mere addition (and so, by extension, a finite power cannot be made infinite by mere addition). What is more, it is hard to understand how enlarging a creature with powers distinct from its essence would in-and-of-itself and without further explanation provide grounds for thinking that an expanded version of the same entity would yield a being which was non-composite. Enlarging and perfecting a being of one sort does not by itself transform it into a being of another sort. Nor does it transform an imperfect being to a maximally great one, in the Anselmian sense of this term. It seems that even Edwards, like Socrates, nodded on occasion.

35. Compare his sermon, "God's Excellencies," where he writes, "God is infinitely exalted above all created beings in excellency and loveliness. It all runs upon infinities in God: so great as is his duration, so great as is his being and essence, so great is his excellency and loveliness" (YE10: 420).

36. I have dealt with this elsewhere at length. See Crisp, *Jonathan Edwards on God and Creation*.

37. At the close of *God's End in Creation*, Edwards says: "'Tis no solid objection against God's aiming at an infinitely perfect union of the creature with himself, that the particular time will never come when it can be said, the union is now infinitely perfect. God aims at satisfying justice in the eternal damnation of sinners; which will be satisfied by their damnation, considered no otherwise than with regard to its eternal duration. But yet there never will come that particular moment, when it can be said, that now justice is satisfied. But if this don't satisfy our modern freethinkers, who don't like the talk about satisfying justice with an infinite punishment; I suppose it will not be denied by any that God, in glorifying the saints in heaven with eternal felicity, aims to satisfy his infinite grace or benevolence, by the bestowment of a good infinitely valuable, because eternal: and yet there never will come the moment, when it can be said, that now this infinitely valuable good has been actually bestowed" (YE8: 536).

Anselm and Edwards on the Doctrine of God

To sum up: Edwards thinks that God is a uniquely simple being; his view is similar to (though not the same as) Anselm's conception of divine non-composition. However, his remarks in support of the doctrine, which can be found scattered through his published writings, are piecemeal. They largely reiterate the sort of classical conception of the divine nature common to those working in the Reformed Orthodox and Puritan communities in post-Reformation Protestant theology. He offers no detailed account of how or in what respect God is said to be non-composite, let alone whether his view is closer to the Thomist account than the Scotist one — the two historic views on divine simplicity postdating Anselm, which were taken up by the Reformed in the post-Reformation period. He does believe God is independent of the creation, which is radically dependent upon him for its existence and conservation. He also makes a clear distinction between God as the infinite uncreated spirit, and creatures as ideas emanated or communicated by God. Like Anselm, Edwards thinks that the creatures are only substances in an attenuated sense, and that creaturely substance is significantly different from that of the deity, given the fact that he possesses aseity, is uncreated, and does not have attributes distinct from his essence as creatures do, because he is metaphysically non-composite. God is infinite. Yet curiously, in at least one place in his corpus Edwards speculates that this infinite existence is something that, conceivably, creatures might enjoy, if their natures were sufficiently "enlarged." This strange claim is difficult to square with other aspects of Edwards's doctrine of God. I suggest it also intimates an important difference between the Anselmian conception of God and the variation on a classical, Augustinian doctrine countenanced by Edwards.

Between Canterbury and Northampton

We have seen that there are a number of ways in which the views of Anselm and Edwards overlap regarding the doctrine of God. This is largely due to their shared Augustinian heritage. Both hold to some sort of theistic idealism. Both think God is a non-composite being, in some ways beyond our comprehension of him. Both think of God as the greatest being, and as in some sense the entity that is the source of all other created entities, though the reason for thinking this is somewhat different in Anselm than in Edwards. However, there are also differences between the two Augustinian theologians just as there are differences between two siblings born of the same parents. This is due in part to the different contexts in which they wrote and the different times that shaped their respective modes of thought: for Anselm, the medieval world of monastic spirituality influenced by the Augustinian heritage he learnt at Bec; for Edwards the frontier of European civilization in early modern New England, at the beginning of the Enlightenment.

Their "reception" of Augustinian modes of thought is in some ways refracted through these different contexts, so that Anselm's understanding of God is more meditative, shaped both by attention to the contemplative life of monasticism (the *Proslogion* is, after all, a prayer), as well as a high view of the reason of faith (what Anselm calls the *ratio fidei*) that guided his optimistic view of sanctified human rationality. Edwards also had a high view of what reason teaches. At one point he even allows that "naked reason" may perceive that there are three distinct persons in the Godhead![38] Elsewhere, in his treatise *Freedom of the Will* he maintains that reason can be deployed to demonstrate that there is a God in the following manner: "We first ascend, and prove *a posteriori*, or from effects, that there must be an eternal cause; and then secondly, prove by argumentation, not intuition, that this being must be necessarily existent; and then thirdly, from the proved necessity of his existence, we may descend, and prove many of his perfections *a priori*."[39] His confidence in human reason is striking not only as an example of early modern intellectual optimism, but also because he stands in a tradition of theology usually marked by a much more pronounced emphasis upon the noetic effects of sin in human reasoning. It is perhaps this strain of intellectual optimism one can detect in his musings on Theology Proper that distinguishes Edwards's doctrine of God most clearly from that of Anselm. Although both have much to say about the divine nature, hedged about with caveats regarding the mystery and (at least partial) incomprehensibility of God's essence, Edwards appears to be more sanguine about what we can know of God, especially given his unguarded remarks about the expansion of creaturely intellects into infinite ones. Neither theologian has all the answers, of course. Both admit at various points their own inadequacies in approaching the topic of the doctrine of God. Yet it may be true to say that in several important respects Anselm provides a more measured, cautious approach in thinking about the divine nature than Edwards does.

---

38. See "Miscellany" 94 in YE13: 257.
39. YE1: 182.

Perhaps it borders on caricature to say that Anselm's prayerful probing of Theology Proper in a state of meditative reflection and humility is in contrast to Edwards's expectation that reason alone can ascertain that there is a Trinity, or that it is conceivable that a creature might be transmogrified into something approaching a being of simplicity and infinity. Nevertheless, there is some truth in this picture. In his more unguarded remarks it does at times appear that Edwards is willing to venture where Anselmians fear to tread.

CHAPTER 3

Edwards on the Excellence of the Trinity

There was a time in the mid-nineteenth century when Jonathan Edwards was rumored to have held an Arian or even incipient Sabellian view of the doctrine of God.[1] Now, he is lauded as a Trinitarian theologian, a divine for whom the three persons of the Godhead are a touchstone for all other doctrines.[2] Yet, although his orthodoxy is endorsed by almost all scholars at work on his corpus, the form of his doctrine of the Trinity is the subject of an ongoing scholarly debate. Much of this depends on whether his views were commensurate with standard models of the Trinity, or whether he developed his own ideas in such a way as to move

---

1. These allegations were begun by Horace Bushnell and caused scandal when repeated and elaborated upon by Justice Oliver Wendell Holmes. In the preface to *Christ in Theology* (Hartford, CT: Brown and Parsons, 1851), p. vi, Bushnell writes that he wanted to present some illustrations from "a manuscript dissertation of President Edwards" on the Trinity, of which he had recently received word. This included an *a priori* argument for the Trinity, the contents of which, he was told, "'would excite a good deal of surprise' if communicated to the public." But he was denied access to it. This was probably the *Discourse on the Trinity*, which can be found in YE21 — hardly a dubious or theologically unorthodox text. A helpful overview of this material is given in the introduction to Steven M. Studebaker and Robert W. Caldwell III, *The Trinitarian Theology of Jonathan Edwards: Text, Context and Application* (Aldershot: Ashgate, 2012).

2. Amy Plantinga Pauw writes, "It is only in the last twenty-five years that the doctrine of the Trinity has received much attention in studies in Jonathan Edwards' theology." "The Trinity," in *The Princeton Companion to Jonathan Edwards*, ed. Sang Hyun Lee (Princeton: Princeton University Press, 2005), p. 44. Edwards did not publish any doctrinal or philosophical work on the Trinity during his lifetime. His reputation as a Trinitarian theologian stems from several works that were only published much later, gathered together (for the most part) in YE21.

beyond variations of the doctrine to which theologians have historically been held accountable.

There are several issues involved in this discussion. These are: whether Edwards held to a doctrine of divine simplicity, and if he did, how this was related to his Trinitarianism; the place of his doctrine of divine excellency, according to which God is irreducibly plural; his understanding of the relationship between the divine essence and the divine persons, including the manner in which the divine persons are individuated; and the place of the doctrine of perichoresis in his account of the Trinity. There is also discussion about which model of the Trinity Edwards endorsed. Rather than focusing on this matter initially, we shall spend time addressing the other questions about his doctrine of the Trinity. Only then will we tackle the question of the model of the Trinity he adopts. The reason for this is twofold. First, if we were to place the question of the model of the Trinity center-stage, it might possibly occlude or at least skew our assessment of the particular shape of Edwards's doctrine. As we shall see, Edwards does have some surprising and original things to say about the Trinity. If we were to begin by assimilating him to one or other traditional model of the doctrine, we would run the risk of obscuring the ways in which his views contribute to, and differ from, the sort of Trinitarian models extant in the tradition. Second, by beginning with the detail of Edwards's doctrine, we may arrive at an understanding of the overall model he was developing before asking whether or to what extent it can be assimilated to existing models of the Trinity with which he would have been familiar. A more synthetic or abductive approach to analysis of Edwardsian Trinitarianism has thus several advantages over a more deductive one.

In the process of attending to key facets of the Edwardsian doctrine of the Trinity we shall engage a number of recent scholars who have been at work in this area. Amy Plantinga Pauw's account of the Trinitarianism of Edwards has been influential in the recent literature and is often taken as a point of departure.[3] Significant contributions to Edwards scholarship have also been made by, amongst others, Stephen Holmes, William Danaher, Sang Lee, and, more recently, Steven Studebaker and Robert Caldwell III.[4]

---

3. Amy Plantinga Pauw, *"The Supreme Harmony of All": The Trinitarian Theology of Jonathan Edwards* (Grand Rapids: Eerdmans, 2002).

4. See Stephen R. Holmes, *God of Grace and God of Glory: An Account of the Theology of Jonathan Edwards* (Edinburgh: T&T Clark, 2000); William J. Danaher Jr., *The Trinitarian Ethics of Jonathan Edwards* (Louisville: Westminster John Knox, 2004); Sang Hyun Lee, ed-

I shall have things to say about each of these interpretations, but will spend more time responding to the recent work of Kyle Strobel.[5] His account takes the discussion forward in important respects by focusing on the key developments to the doctrine that Edwards sets forth. However, as I shall argue, his conclusions are not always on target. In dialogue and, in some cases, collegial disagreement with these various interpretations of Edwards's doctrine I shall propose a reading of the Edwardsian position that pays attention to his debt to the Reformed and western Catholic doctrine of the Trinity, whilst also taking account of the ways in which he presses certain innovative ways of thinking about the nature and persons of the Godhead. I hope to show that my own understanding of Edwards makes better sense of what the Northampton Sage says about this nodal doctrine than other recent attempts to do so, including that of Strobel. However, as will become clear, I owe a great deal to these other authors in the development of my own position.

We proceed in the following manner. In the first section, I set out the key issues in the Edwardsian doctrine of the Trinity. Then, in a second section I give an account of Edwards's doctrine, letting Edwards speak for himself wherever possible. In a third section, I offer a constructive critical interaction with several recent interpretations of Edwards's doctrine, with a particular focus on Lee, Holmes, and Strobel. I close by indicating some of the potential obstacles that need to be removed so that Edwards's contribution to the doctrine of the Trinity might be of use to contemporary Christian theologians.

---

itor's introduction to YE21; Studebaker and Caldwell, *The Trinitarian Theology of Jonathan Edwards*; Steven M. Studebaker, "Jonathan Edwards' Social Augustinian Trinitarianism: An Alternative to a Recent Trend," *Scottish Journal of Theology* 56 (2003): 268-85; also his *Jonathan Edwards' Social Augustinian Trinitarianism in Historical and Contemporary Perspectives* (Piscataway, NJ: Gorgias Press, 2008); and Robert W. Caldwell III, *Communion in the Spirit: The Holy Spirit as the Bond of Union in the Theology of Jonathan Edwards* (Milton Keynes: Paternoster, 2006). I will also have cause to refer to my own contribution to this literature in Crisp, *Jonathan Edwards on God and Creation* (New York: Oxford University Press, 2012), to which this essay is a sequel.

5. Kyle C. Strobel, *Jonathan Edwards's Theology: A Reinterpretation* (London: T&T Clark, 2012).

Key Issues in the Edwardsian Doctrine of the Trinity

Divine Simplicity

A number of recent works on Edwards's doctrine of God deny that he held to a traditional doctrine of divine simplicity as a corollary to his understanding of the Trinity. The opinion of Michael McClymond and Gerald McDermott is typical in this regard. They write, "Edwards's Trinitarianism was original in a number of ways. First, Edwards departed from the Western Trinitarian tradition by rejecting its emphasis on divine simplicity, which was one of the ways in which Augustine and his successors guarded the faith against recurring Arianism." They go on to suggest that Edwards privileged the threeness of the divine persons over the oneness of the divine essence. Following Amy Plantinga Pauw's interpretation of Edwards's Trinitarianism, they declare that he held to "an alternative conception of divine oneness that revolved around the notions of excellency, harmony and consent"[6] rather than the traditional simplicity-Trinity axis.

Others, however, have taken the opposite view. Steven Studebaker and Robert Caldwell are typical of this line of interpretation. Setting Edwards within the context of his Reformed Orthodox schooling, they claim that his "treatment of divine simplicity and God as pure act are quite standard." "In sum," they remark, "Edwards's doctrine of the Trinity and doctrine of God can be broadly categorized as belonging to the Reformed scholastic tradition."[7]

It certainly looks like Edwards advocated divine simplicity. He never disavows or distances himself from the doctrine and in both his published

---

6. Michael J. McClymond and Gerald R. McDermott, *The Theology of Jonathan Edwards* (New York: Oxford University Press, 2012), pp. 197 and 199, respectively. The latter citation draws on Plantinga Pauw's work, "*Supreme Harmony of All*," p. 69. Plantinga Pauw argues that Edwards pays nominal lip service to divine simplicity in his work, though in fact his doctrine of the Trinity implies a departure from simplicity as traditionally understood.

7. Studebaker and Caldwell, *Trinitarian Theology*, pp. 152-53. Others who take this view in recent studies of Edwardsian Theology Proper include John J. Bombaro, *Jonathan Edwards's Vision of Reality: The Relationship of God to the World, Redemption History, and the Reprobate* (Eugene, OR: Pickwick Publications, 2012); Crisp, *Jonathan Edwards on God and Creation*; Paul Helm, "The Human Self and the Divine Trinity," in *Jonathan Edwards as Contemporary: Essays in Honor of Sang Hyun Lee*, ed. Don Schweitzer (New York: Peter Lang, 2010), 93-106; Holmes, *God of Grace and God of Glory*; and Strobel, *Jonathan Edwards's Theology*.

and unpublished works at each stage of his career when the doctrine is raised it is always with a view to endorsing it. Consider his published works. In his *Religious Affections*, published in 1746, Edwards says that the divine moral "attributes can't be without his natural attributes: for infinite holiness supposes infinite wisdom, and an infinite capacity and greatness; and all the attributes of God do as it were imply one another" (YE2: 256-57). Yet this is just a constituent of the doctrine of divine simplicity. Similarly, in the products of his final years in Stockbridge, where one would expect him to at least demonstrate some diffidence towards a doctrine he is supposed to be an opponent of, he endorses the doctrine. For instance, in *Freedom of the Will*, published in 1754, four years before his death, he says in passing that the First Being "is self-existent, independent, of perfect and absolute simplicity and immutability, and the first cause of all things" (YE1: 377). Even in his *Discourse on the Trinity*, the unpublished reflection on the Trinity which has been the source of many of the revisionist claims of McClymond, McDermott, Lee, and Plantinga Pauw, Edwards begins by saying, "there are *no* distinctions to be admitted of faculty, habit and act, between will, inclination and love" in God, "but that it is all *one simple act*" (YE21: 113, emphasis added). What is more, in speaking of the Second Person of the Trinity as the Divine Idea later in the same work, Edwards says that the perfect view God has of his own essence is one "in which there is *no distinction of substance and act, but it is wholly substance and wholly act*" such that the "idea God hath of himself is absolutely himself" (YE21: 116, emphasis added). Such language is just what one would expect from a theologian who wishes to signal his agreement with the pure act account of the divine nature well known to the Reformed Orthodox divines Edwards read, in which the doctrine of divine simplicity is embedded.

This pattern can also been seen in his sermon corpus. Edwards affirms that God is a pure act in no uncertain terms and without picking out the Holy Spirit in particular. In a very traditional-sounding passage, he says, "we must take heed that we han't to[o] Gross a notion of God's Immensity and Omnipresence[;] we must not Conceive of it as part of God." He goes on, "for God is not made . . . up of Parts for he is a simple pure act." What is more, when "we say that God is in this house this must not be understood to mean that Part of God is . . . in this house but God is here. 'Tis not part of God that is in us but God is in us."[8]

---

8. WJE Online Vol. 42, §44, sermon skeleton on Psalm 139:7-10. See also the sermon outline on Ezekiel 8:8 in WJE Online Vol. 53, §477. There Edwards says God "is a pure act,

Finally, in his "Miscellanies" notebooks, which were a source for many of the ideas he later developed in his publications, and which he used as a sort of sourcebook for the training of ministers lodging in his house, Edwards endorses both the pure act view of the divine nature and divine simplicity in early and late entries. In "Miscellany" 94 he speaks of God as a pure act (which he particularly associates with the Holy Spirit, as he does in the later *Discourse on the Trinity*). And in "Miscellany" 1357 he writes that God is "a pure act whose essence is energy; without all extension [or] bulk; indivisible; unmultipliable; one most simple; everywhere present yet not properly in place; perfectly immutable" (YE23: 657).[9]

Whether Edwards held to the doctrine of divine simplicity is important for at least two reasons. First, the doctrine has historically played a vital role in anchoring Trinitarianism firmly within monotheism. Versions of the doctrine have been endorsed by the vast majority of classical, orthodox Christian theologians in a bid to hold together monotheism along with divine aseity and perfection alongside a doctrine of the Trinity. We might say that divine simplicity and the divine Trinity are two sides of a coin, or two aspects of one metaphysical package, to which most Christian theologians have ascribed.[10] Second, if Edwards denies divine simplicity, then his doctrine amounts to a much more significant departure from the tradition than it might appear to be at first glance. For without a doctrine of divine simplicity other resources would need to be found in order to ensure that the sort of robust Trinitarianism that Edwards endorses does not end up being decoupled from its moorings within western monotheism, and drifting towards tritheism.

In some versions of modern social Trinitarianism it has been thought that the doctrine of Trinitarian perichoresis can perform this function, keeping the prospect of tritheism in check. Whatever one makes of such proposals, this is not a theological development that would have made much sense in the early modern period, where deism, unitarianism, and socinianism represented the views of many of Edwards's most prominent opponents. These different views all shared a tendency towards a doctrine

---

i.e. he is nothing but mere act without any passiveness . . . he cannot be passive in any thing whatsoever." (I have corrected the orthography given in WJE Online Vols. 42 and 53, and left ellipses where Edwards has crossed out material in the original — material that is transcribed by the editors.)

9. "Miscellany" 94 can be found in YE13: 256-63.

10. I have argued this in some detail in Crisp, *Jonathan Edwards on God and Creation*, chap. 5.

of God that had little or no place for plurality, let alone triunity. Writing in this context, and having been schooled in the theology of Protestant scholasticism and Puritanism, Edwards was principally concerned to uphold orthodoxy, recast in terms that would have been acceptable to the debates of the early Enlightenment. It would be anachronistic to think his conception of the Trinity, like that of much modern theology, involved casting off the divine simplicity of a previous age, much less throwing over the sort of traditional understanding of the Trinity that informed the heirs of Reformation theology with whom Edwards interacted in his own writings.[11]

Divine Excellency

Hard on the heels of the question of the relationship between divine simplicity and the Trinity in Edwards's thought is the question of his peculiar doctrine of divine excellency. Edwards says that excellency is a concept in need of definition. His treatment of the topic can be somewhat baffling to the uninitiated because of the number of terms of art he deploys in doing so. I shall content myself by offering an abstract of what he says here. For Edwards excellency functions as a semi-technical term that has several constituents: an aesthetic component (having to do with beauty, symmetry, and "similarness"[12]); a relational component (having to do with "agreement," "consent," and the "equality" between parts of things of a whole, and their "communication"[13]); and an ontological component (having to do with being[14]). As Edwards puts it in his early and unpublished work entitled "The Mind," §14, "Excellence, to put it in other words, is that which is beautiful and lovely. . . . That which is beautiful with respect to the university of things has a generally extended excellence and a true

---

11. For discussion of this point, see Sang Hyun Lee's editorial introduction to YE21: 4-5. Edwards addresses himself to his anti-Trinitarian opponents directly in, e.g., "Miscellany" 94, which begins with his comment about there having been "much cry of late" against the doctrine (YE13: 256).

12. YE6: 336.

13. "The Mind," in YE6: 332. See also Edwards's Dissertation, *God's End in Creation*, in YE8, especially pp. 432-35 and 526-36 where he sets forth his account of God's communicative being.

14. "This is an universal definition of excellency: The consent of being to being, or being's consent to entity. The more the consent is, and the more extensive, the greater is the excellency" (YE6: 332).

beauty; and the more extended or limited its system is, the more confined or extended is its beauty" (YE6: 344). But since an excellent entity must be one that includes internal relations between its component "parts," as well as "consenting" to (that is, being in accord with, even generating) other existing beings in the great system of beings, Edwards realizes that a truly excellent being must be one in which there is something irreducibly plural. He sums it up in these famous words:

> One alone, without any reference to any more, cannot be excellent; for in such case there can be no manner of relation no way, and therefore, no such thing as consent. Indeed, what we call "one" may be excellent, because of a consent of parts, or some consent of those in that being that are distinguished into a plurality some way or other. But in a being that is absolutely without any plurality there cannot be excellency, for there can be no such thing as consent or agreement. One of the highest excellencies is love. As nothing else has a proper being but spirits, and as bodies are but the shadow of being, therefore, the consent of bodies to one another, and the harmony that is among them, is but the shadow of excellency. The highest excellency, therefore, must be the consent of spirits one to another. But the consent of spirits consists half in their mutual love one to another, and the sweet harmony between the various parts of the universe is only an image of mutual love. (YE6: 337-38)[15]

Evidently, God is the truly excellent being, for he is the uncreated spirit upon whom all created spirits depend for their existence moment-by-moment. Moreover, reasons Edwards, since God was excellent before he created the world, his excellence must consist in some relation he has *within* himself — what we might call an intrinsic relation. This is a relation something bears to itself independent of any extrinsic relations to other things. It cannot be something that pertains to the creation if he possesses it independent of any creation. Edwards maintains that God

---

15. Elsewhere in his "Miscellanies" notebooks he argues that divine goodness is essentially an intrinsic, communicative attribute. That is, it is an attribute God has in himself, but which implies some internal differentiation within God in order for it to be exercised internally in the divine life. "God must have a perfect exercise of his goodness, and therefore must have the fellowship of a person equal to himself." "Miscellany" 96, in YE13: 264. As Studebaker and Caldwell put it, "plurality in the Godhead is necessary because the communication of the infinite happiness of God — divine love — requires an infinite object of goodness." *Trinitarian Theology,* p. 63.

exerts himself towards himself no other way than in infinitely loving and delighting in himself, in the mutual love of the Father and the Son. This makes the third, the personal Holy Spirit or the holiness of God, which is his infinite beauty, and this is God's infinite consent to being in general. And his love to the creature is his excellence, or the communication of himself, his complacency [i.e., finding satisfaction] in them, according as they partake of more or less of excellence and beauty; that is, of holiness, which consists in love; that is, according as he communicates more or less of his Holy Spirit. (YE6: 364)

So although God's love does have an outward manifestation in the created order, this is the outworking or "communication," as Edwards puts it, of his intrinsic relation of love, which is person-generating. To put it another way, according to Edwards it is because God is the supremely excellent being that he is tri-personal.

The Divine Essence and the Divine Persons

This leads us to the matter of the relationship between the divine essence and divine persons in Edwards's understanding of the Godhead. We can add to this the issue of the way in which Edwards individuates the divine persons, since this is part-and-parcel of his account of the relationship of the divine persons to the divine essence. Since this is the subject of much of the discussion later in this chapter, my introductory comments here can be brief. Suffice it to say that the way Edwards parses the divine persons has been the cause of some discussion and disagreement in the secondary literature. Part of that is bound up with the question of whether he endorses divine simplicity, and if he does, how it is that God can be excellent. However, this also depends on the extent to which his articulation of the Trinity implies rather untraditional ways of divvying up the divine attributes between the divine essence and persons. For instance, Stephen Holmes makes the following startling claim regarding Edwardsian Trinitarianism:

> The residue of a common "essence" which was so pervasive in Western theological discourse is wholly absent, and Edwards claims to be unable to think of "any rational meaning" behind the standard language that describes the essence. [Furthermore,] Edwards is essentially seeking to appropriate different perfections of the divine *phusis* to particular *hy-*

postases.... This is a move unique in the tradition, a radical extension of the doctrine of appropriation (which classically refers to the external acts of the Trinity). I suspect that, provided the doctrine of perichoresis is remembered and asserted, a form of this move could be developed that would not damage Trinitarian theology in any fundamental way, but Edwards did not live to do this.[16]

As I have pointed out elsewhere,[17] were this true, then Edwards's doctrine of the Trinity would be very peculiar indeed. For if the referents for the concept of God were *all and only* the Father, Son, and Spirit, without any common essence, with the divine individuals making up the Godhead sharing these properties merely in virtue of some doctrine of perichoresis (or mutual interpenetration), then Edwards's doctrine would appear to be tritheistic. We shall return to this matter of how Edwards individuates the divine persons and how this relates to his doctrine of Trinitarian perichoresis presently.

Models of the Trinity

Finally by way of introduction, let me say a word about models of the Trinity. Amy Plantinga Pauw has argued that Edwards's doctrine does not fall cleanly within any particular traditional model of the Trinity. "Edwards gave no hint that he was troubled by the dissonances among these models for the Trinity. That he refused to choose a single model is an indication of the diverse polemical and pastoral situations in which he forged his Trinitarian reflections, as well as his high tolerance for theological tension."[18] Similarly, William Danaher argues that there is both a psychological and social analogy to be found in Edwards's works;[19] and Sang Lee speaks of an evolution in Edwards's thinking, from a psychological to a moderate social analogy for the Trinity.[20]

---

16. See *God of Grace and God of Glory*, pp. 69 and 71 respectively. The doctrine of appropriation refers to the way in which, in classical doctrines of the Trinity, the different divine persons are said to appropriate the divine attributes of each other in their perichoretic divine union.

17. See Crisp, *Jonathan Edwards on God and Creation*, chap. 5.

18. Plantinga Pauw, "The Trinity," p. 48.

19. Danaher, *Trinitarian Ethics*, chaps. 1-2.

20. Lee, editorial introduction to YE21: 12-13.

By contrast, Steven Studebaker and Robert Caldwell have recently argued that Edwards does opt for one traditional model, the Augustinian mutual love model that would have been familiar to him through his Reformed teachers. They write, "Edwards operated consistently with one model of the Trinity, the Augustinian mutual love model." Moreover, "language taken to support the social trinitarian interpretation of his writings (excellency, goodness) is generally found in contexts that either presuppose the mutual love model or are extensions of it." Finally, in this regard, Edwards reproduces "standard definitions and categories employed by Reformed scholastics in their work on the Trinity. . . . [His] doctrine of the Trinity and doctrine of God can be categorized as belonging to the Reformed scholastic tradition."[21] If this is right, then Edwards's Trinitarianism is an instance of a tradition of Reformed thinking about the doctrine, which was broadly Augustinian and Thomist in form. The question is, is this right?

Edwards on the Trinity

We have seen that Edwards endorses a version of the doctrine of divine simplicity and that he thinks God is irreducibly internally plural because he is excellent. There is an important question about how he can affirm both these claims. But our focus here is upon his doctrine of the Trinity, not the relationship between that and God's simplicity — something I have tackled at length elsewhere.[22] Nevertheless, this is important because it indicates that Edwards does not feel the need to reject this aspect of his Reformed heritage. He upholds a strong doctrine of divine unity in Thomistic fashion like a number of his Reformed forebears. That is, for Edwards, as for the Reformed scholastics, God is a simple pure act. Recall that in the *Discourse on the Trinity*, he says, "there are *no* distinctions to be admitted of faculty, habit and act, between will, inclination and love" in God, "but that it is all *one simple act*" (YE21: 113, emphasis added). What is more, in speaking of the Second Person of the Trinity as the Divine Idea, Edwards

---

21. Studebaker and Caldwell, *Trinitarian Theology*, pp. 152, 153. Compare William M. Schweitzer, who says quite bluntly, "Edwards was an orthodox Augustinian in his basic conception of the Trinity." *God Is a Communicative Being: Divine Communicativeness and Harmony in the Theology of Jonathan Edwards* (London: T&T Clark, 2012), p. 11. Evidence for this can be found in, e.g., "Miscellanies" 259 and 362 in YE13: 367 and 435, respectively.

22. See Crisp, *Jonathan Edwards on God and Creation*.

says that the perfect view God has of his own essence is one "in which there is *no distinction of substance and act, but it is wholly substance and wholly act*" such that the "idea God hath of himself is absolutely himself" (YE21: 116, emphasis added). This implies no departure from the language of theological essentialism in which Edwards was schooled.

However, the divine substance is significantly different from created substances, and not only in the fact that there is no distinction between substance and act within the divine life. Like many other theologians in the Augustinian tradition, Edwards thinks of the Second Person of the Trinity as an idea eternally generated and hypostasized by the First Person of the Trinity, and the Third Person as the act or bond of love shared between the other two divine persons:

> And this I suppose to be that blessed Trinity that we read of in the holy Scriptures. The Father is the Deity subsisting in the prime, unoriginated and most absolute manner, or the Deity in its direct existence. The Son is the Deity generated by God's understanding, or having an idea of himself, and subsisting in that idea. The Holy Ghost is the Deity subsisting in act or the divine essence flowing out and breathed forth, in God's infinite love to and delight in himself. And I believe the whole divine essence does truly and distinctly subsist both in the divine idea and divine love, and that therefore each of them are properly distinct persons. (YE21: 131)

Also in keeping with the Augustinian tradition of Trinitarian reflection, he believes that the only real distinctions one can predicate of the divine nature pertain to the divine persons. Indeed, he even thinks that this is a deliverance of reason:

> And it confirms me in it, that this is the true Trinity, because reason is sufficient to tell us that there must be these distinctions in the Deity, viz. of God (absolutely considered), and the idea of God, and love and delight; and there are no other real distinctions in God that can be thought [of]. There are but these three distinct real things in God; whatsoever else can be mentioned in God are nothing but mere modes or relations of existence. (YE21: 131)

Created substances have distinct attributes like size, shape, mass, and so on. God as a simple pure act does not have distinct attributes like this. He has certain attributes that seem to be the preserve of the divine essence, that is, are shared between the divine persons on the Edwardsian way of thinking. He also has attributes that are person-constituting in some respect. These he calls "real" attributes as opposed to "modes or relations of existence." These are the attributes God has essentially, such as his infinity, eternity, and immutability.

Normally, Augustinian theologians distinguish the divine persons by means of their relations of origin — nothing more. Thus, the Father is unoriginate being; the Son is eternally generated by the Father; and the Spirit proceeds from the Father (and the Son). Following Boethius, the tradition spoke of persons as individual substances of a rational nature. This included the persons of the Godhead. Edwards changes this in a subtle but important way. He "thickens" the account of the divine persons by redistributing many of the divine attributes usually held in the divine essence to the divine persons. So, although God has "mere modes and relations of existence" like immutability, eternity, and infinity, the divine persons have attributes in addition to their relations of origin. Take the Second Person of the Trinity, for instance. Edwards says, "There is God's understanding, his wisdom and omniscience, that we have shown to be the same with his idea." And his idea is the Son. Similarly, "There is God's will: but that is not really distinguished from his love, but is the same, but only with a different relation." And that is the Spirit, who also possesses divine goodness, mercy, and grace, which are "but the overflowings of God's infinite love." (YE21: 131). Says Edwards, "The sum of all God's love is his love to himself. These three — God, and the idea of God, and the inclination, affection or love of God — must be conceived as really distinct. But as for all those other things — of extent, duration, being with or without change, ability to do — they are not distinct real things, even in created spirits, but only mere modes and relations. So that our natural reason is sufficient to tell us that there are these three in God, and we can think of no more" (YE21: 131-32).

Edwards is clear that the modes and relations that God possesses (e.g., infinity, immutability, eternity, and so forth) are not person-constituting, nor are they to be identified with one or other divine person. However, if we say that "the real attributes of God, viz. his understanding and love, are God, then what we have said may in some measure explain how it is so: for Deity subsists in them distinctly, so they are distinct divine persons." He goes on to say, "We find no other attributes of which it is said that they are God in Scripture, or that God is they, but Λογος and Αγαπε, the reason and the love of God (John 1:1 and 1 John 4:8, 1 John 4:16)" (YE21: 132).

Edwards on the Excellence of the Trinity

To this picture we must add the doctrine of perichoresis, or the mutual indwelling of the divine persons. Edwards reasons in good Augustinian fashion that there cannot be three centers of understanding and will in God; he must have one understanding and will (presumably because he is one God). Yet there are three divine persons, and persons (so Edwards thinks) are entities that have understanding and will.[23] How can he get around this apparently contradictory position? By means of Trinitarian perichoresis. Recall that on the Edwardsian scheme the divine persons have parceled out to them many of the divine attributes usually thought to reside in the divine essence, apart from those that are "mere modes or relations" of God, such as immutability or eternity. The Son is identified with the divine understanding because he is the Logos. The Spirit is identified with divine love as the bond between the Father and the Son. Well, then, says Edwards, it appears that the Son is the divine understanding and the Spirit is the divine love. There is only one divine understanding and one divine love. And since, as we have seen, he specifically identifies the divine love with the divine will, one will too. Yet these are not attributes of the one divine essence. They are divine persons. However, because each of the divine persons indwells the others via perichoresis, the divine understanding that is the person of the Son is also possessed by the other two divine persons — he *is* their understanding. What is more, the divine love and will that is the Holy Spirit is possessed by the other two divine persons — he *is* their love and their will.

In other words, there is one understanding and will in the Godhead that is shared between the divine persons, but these are not attributes of the one divine essence. The understanding and the love of God are divine persons. As Kyle Strobel has recently put it, "instead of Father, Son and Spirit as persons in their own right, Edwards offers a Trinitarian interpretation of personhood through perichoresis. . . . The great 'twist' [to Edwards's doctrine] is that the triune persons are not persons individually. . . . Just as the Father is not a person without understanding and will . . . so also the Father is not a person without the Son or the Spirit."[24] Since this is crucial to rightly understanding the shape of Edwards's doctrine, we quote Edwards at length:

---

23. "One of the principal objections that I can think of against what has been supposed is concerning the personality of the Holy Ghost, that this scheme of things don't seem well to consist with that, [that] *a person is that which hath understanding and will.*" *Discourse on the Trinity*, YE21: 133. Emphasis added.

24. Strobel, *Jonathan Edwards's Theology*, p. 28.

> If the three in the Godhead are persons, they doubtless each of 'em have understanding: but this makes the understanding one distinct person, and love another. How therefore can this love be said to have understanding? Here I would observe that divines have not been wont to suppose that these three had three distinct understandings, but all one and the same understanding. In order to clear up this matter, let it be considered, that the whole divine essence is supposed truly and properly to subsist in each of these three — viz. God, and his understanding, and love — and that there is such a wonderful union between them that they are after an ineffable and inconceivable manner one in another; so that one hath another, and they have communion in one another, and are as it were predicable one of another. (YE21: 133)

He goes on to say,

> All the three are persons, for they all have understanding and will. There is understanding and will in the Father, as the Son and the Holy Ghost are in him and proceed from [him]. There is understanding and will in the Son, as he is understanding and as the Holy Ghost is in him and proceeds from him. There is understanding and will in the Holy Ghost, as he is the divine will and as the Son is in him. Nor is it to be looked upon as a strange and unreasonable figment that the persons should be said to have an understanding or love by another person's being in 'em: for we have Scripture ground to conclude so concerning the Father's having wisdom and understanding or reason, that it is by the Son's being in him; because we are there informed that he is the wisdom and reason and truth of God. And hereby God is wise by his own wisdom being in him. Understanding and wisdom is in the Father, as the Son is in him and proceeds from him. Understanding is in the Holy Ghost because the Son is in him, not as proceeding from him but as flowing out in him. (YE21: 134)

From these passages it is clear that Edwards is doing something rather unusual. He is, in effect, reconceiving the Augustinian heritage of his doctrine of the Trinity by means of the doctrine of perichoresis so as to retain the Augustinian notion of a single divine understanding and will, but reallocating these to the divine persons rather than retaining them within the divine essence. The three divine persons are more than subsistent relations, on the Edwardsian way of thinking. They are the only real distinctions within God. But their ineffable union together perichoretically means that no one divine person is constituted as a person in isolation from the other divine persons. Indeed, each of the divine persons is only constituted as a person by being ineffably united to the other two divine persons. As the Son and Spirit provide the understanding and will requisite for personhood, there is only one understanding and one will in the Godhead — which is the key Augustinian affirmation of monotheism. Yet these are the preserve of distinct persons and shared perichoretically between the three so that Edwards can affirm that all the following statements are true.

i. The Father has understanding and will, and is a person because the Son (as divine understanding) and Spirit (as divine will) indwell him, constituting him as a divine person;
ii. The Son has understanding and will, and is a person because he just *is* the divine understanding eternally begotten of the Father, and the Spirit (as divine will) indwells him, constituting him as a divine person;
iii. The Spirit has understanding and will, and is a person because he proceeds from the Father and the Son, the Son (as divine understanding) indwells him, and he just *is* the divine will, constituting him as a divine person.

There is excellency here, because there are intrinsic relations of something akin to "parts" (the divine persons) to a "whole" (the Godhead). The Father plays the foundational role of being the source or origin of the other two divine persons, and the Second and Third persons of the Trinity constitute two vital aspects of divine personhood in virtue of their being identified with the divine understanding and will, respectively. Yet Edwards achieves this without lapsing into something like a social view of the Trinity by appealing to perichoresis in order to shore up the singularity of divine understanding and will. Although it is not without problems, this is a truly ingenious argument that makes a significant contribution to the doctrine of the Trinity.

Let us take stock. Edwards argues for the following claims:

1. God is an infinite, eternal, simple pure act.
2. God is excellent.
3. God's excellency is expressed in his Triunity.
4. The divine persons are the Father, the Word *(Logos)*, and the Love of God *(Agape)*.

5. These three divine persons exhaust the real distinctions that can be affirmed in God.
6. The divine persons share together in one divine essence.
7. There is only one understanding and will in the Godhead.
8. These do not constitute further real distinctions in God.
9. The understanding of God is identical to the Second Person of the Trinity.
10. The will of God is identical to the Third Person of the Trinity.
11. The divine persons indwell one another perichoretically.
12. This mutual indwelling is a person-constituting relation.

If we add to this (i)-(iii) above, we have a complete account of the Edwardsian way of understanding the doctrine of the Trinity as set out in his *Discourse* in particular.

Critical Reflections on the Edwardsian Model

In his introduction to the Yale Works of Jonathan Edwards volume on Edwards's Trinitarian writings, Sang Hyun Lee says this of Edwards's model of the Trinity:

> In Edwards' perichoretic approach, we have a vision of God's unity that is profoundly different from the Western church's traditional tendency to see God's unity in the singularity of divine substance. For Edwards, God's unity consists in the "wonderful union" between the persons of the Trinity and "a communion in one another." The concept of God's unity here is one of mutuality, communion, and fellowship rather than a monadic and self-contained individuality. And this perspective is more in line with Edwards' conception of God, according to which there is no underlying substance behind the persons, and also according to which there is a clear emphasis upon the threeness of the Trinity as God and God's two self-repetitions.[25]

Earlier, we noted Stephen Holmes's view that Edwards does away with language of the divine essence altogether, relegating the divine attributes to the divine persons. Lee says something similar: perichoresis is doing the work of

25. YE21: 27.

binding the persons together in Edwards's model of the Trinity; the notion of a divine substance has disappeared from his conception of the divine life.

Neither of these claims seems to be quite right. Perichoresis is doing a lot of work for Edwards. But it is not the means by which he cements the three divine persons together in one life, as is the case in some modern versions of social Trinitarianism. Rather, Edwards uses this doctrine as a means by which to make an assertion that would be recognizable to Augustinians, namely, that the Godhead has one understanding, one love, and one will that is shared between the divine persons. The difference is, he thinks that in order to make good on this claim he must hypostasize these attributes as the Second and Third Persons of the Trinity, respectively. Since the divine persons exist in perichoretic relationship to one another, he can claim that the understanding that is the Son is the understanding had by the Father and the Spirit. He can also claim that the love of the Father and the Son just is the Spirit who indwells the other divine persons of the Trinity. This must be the case because he has already affirmed that the divine persons are the only real distinctions in the Godhead.

However, Edwards does not distance himself from the notion of a divine essence in making this move, as both Lee and Holmes think he does. Kyle Strobel provides the most helpful recent treatment of Edwardsian Trinitarianism in this regard. He says this: "Edwards rethinks the relationship between persons and essence, and is adamant that the divinity of the Son and the Spirit are necessary aspects of the Father's own personhood and life. In contrast to seeing the Father as the only person in whom the divine attributes obtain, Edwards posits that the divine attributes *actually are* the Son and the Spirit!"[26] It is Strobel who has called attention to the fact that Edwards's doctrine requires not just perichoresis, but a particular spin on perichoresis, according to which the Son is the understanding and the Spirit the love and will of God that are person-constituting. This is a significant advance upon previous discussions of Edwardsian Trinitarianism. Moreover, like Holmes (and Lee), he thinks this means Edwards redistributes all the divine attributes apart from "mere modes and relations" to the divine persons so that the notion of a divine essence *shared between the divine persons* is lost to Edwards. Instead, according to Strobel, the divine persons *are* the divine essence.[27]

The "mere modes and relations" that God has are not things intrinsic

---

26. YE21: 34.
27. Strobel, *Jonathan Edwards's Theology*, p. 236.

to God, on Strobel's reading of Edwards. They are extrinsic relations God bears to other things, rather like what philosophers call mere Cambridge properties.[28] Cambridge properties are a paradigm of extrinsic relational properties that one thing bears to another, but which imply nothing about the entity in question. For instance, "I was 10 miles from Cambridge, now I am 5 miles from Cambridge." What has changed here is my position relative to the university town, Cambridge. Nothing about me as an entity has changed. Applied to the Edwardsian picture of God, this means that when Edwards speaks of mere modes and relations in God he does not mean to suggest that God has modes and relations intrinsically, but only as he is related to other things. Strobel makes much of Edwards's claim that "as for all those other things — of extent, duration, being with or without change, ability to do — they are not distinct real things, *even in created spirits*, but only mere modes and relations."[29] If Edwards is saying that modes and relations are not distinct real things even in creatures, then the implication is that these are certainly not distinct real things in God either.

The problem with this is that this does not account for the particular attributes Edwards lists as being "mere modes and relations of existence." Strobel thinks that these are "attributes of God qua deity but not God qua persons and therefore relegated to what is true of an infinite, perfect and eternal spirit" such that they do not imply anything intrinsic about the divine nature.[30] Thus, he thinks the following thesis is true:

> Everything that is in God is God, and this must be understood of *and exhausted by* "real" attributes ("real" in the Edwardsian sense, meaning attributes that pertain to one of the persons of the Trinity), not of modes and relations (meaning relational attributes shared between the divine persons, such as immutability, eternity, and infinity).

This is what I have elsewhere called the *Strong Edwardsian Trinitarian Thesis* (or SETT).[31] Both Strobel and Holmes affirm it, though for slightly different reasons.[32] Whereas the notion of a divine essence has dropped

---

28. Strobel, *Jonathan Edwards's Theology*, pp. 55, 60, and Appendix: Divine Attributes and Essence, especially p. 240.

29. *Discourse on the Trinity*, YE21: 132, emphasis added.

30. Strobel, *Jonathan Edwards's Theology*, p. 239.

31. Crisp, *Jonathan Edwards on God and Creation*, p. 131.

32. Strobel explicitly aligns himself with Holmes on this matter in *Jonathan Edwards's Theology*, p. 239.

out of the discussion as far as Holmes is concerned, the divine persons instantiate the divine essence as far as Strobel is concerned.

However, in assessing Strobel's claim, several things should be noted. First, in setting forth this claim about certain attributes being "mere modes or relations of existence," Edwards is clear that these are predicable of God, not of God's relation to his creation. That is, they are not extrinsic but intrinsic to God. He says, "whatsoever else can be mentioned *in* God are nothing but mere modes or relations of existence."[33] These are not external but internal to God in some sense. Granted, he does go on to say that "But as for all those other things — of extent, duration, being with or without change, ability to do — they are not distinct real things, even *in* created spirits, but only mere modes and relations. . . . [and later in the same passage] It is a maxim amongst divines that everything that is in God is God, which must be understood of real attributes and not of mere modalities."[34] Note, however, that he does not deny that modes and relations are *in* created spirits. And with regard to the "maxim amongst divines" he is indicating that the real distinctions in God are the divine persons alone, not the modes or relations in God. He is not denying that modes and relations of existence, or power, or knowledge are in God in some manner.

This is only reinforced when one turns to one of his last works, the dissertation entitled *God's End in Creation*. There he reduces all the divine attributes to God's infinite knowledge, virtue or holiness, and joy and happiness, without assigning them to specific divine persons as he does in the *Discourse*.[35] But the modes and relations of existence mentioned in the *Discourse* appear again, this time as a way of qualifying the divine internal glory. "God's infinity is not so properly a distinct kind of good in God, but only expresses the *degree* of the good there is in him." Similarly, "God's eternity is not a distinct good; but is the duration of good. His immutability is still the same good, with a negation of change." He goes on, "the fullness of the Godhead is the fullness of his understanding, consisting in his knowledge, and the fullness of his will, consisting in his virtue and happiness. And therefore the external glory of God consists in the com-

---

33. *Discourse on the Trinity*, YE21: 131, emphasis added.
34. *Discourse on the Trinity*, YE21: 132, emphasis added.
35. He says: "his infinite knowledge; his infinite virtue or holiness, and his infinite joy and happiness. Indeed there are a great many attributes in God, according to our way of conceiving or talking of them: but all may be reduced to these; or to the degree, circumstances and relations of these." *God's End in Creation*, in YE8: 528.

munication of these."[36] Even if we make allowances for the different issues Edwards is addressing here, it should be clear that what in the *Discourse* he refers to as the "mere modes and relations of existence" (namely, immutability, eternity, and infinity) are here clearly identified with God's *internal* glory, not with the communication of his glory to the creation. They are simply assumed to be modes and relations of the divine life.

A second and related point is that the modes and relations Edwards lists in the *Discourse*, especially immutability, infinity, and eternity,[37] cannot be extrinsic or even Cambridge properties because they bespeak something about the divine nature independent of anything created. Indeed these are often referred to in classical Reformed theology as incommunicable divine attributes precisely because they are things about the divine nature that cannot be communicated to, or instantiated in, the created order.[38] Since the only extrinsic attributes God could have would be attributes that relate him to the creation on the sort of classical pure act doctrine Edwards espouses (as is the case with Cambridge properties God possesses), these attributes are excluded from being counted as extrinsic.

What is more, in the pure act account of the divine nature that we have seen Edwards affirms (as Strobel himself admits) there can be no divine attributes that are intrinsic but accidental. That is, God cannot have attributes as part of his nature that he might not have had. Extrinsic attributes are precisely attributes that are not part of an entity's nature, but (usually) pertain to some relation that entity has with some other thing; hence Strobel's identification of Edwards's "mere modes and relations of existence" with Cambridge properties. However, immutability, eternity, and infinity cannot be relations of this sort. They must be part-and-parcel of the divine nature because without them God would not be a perfect be-

---

36. YE8: 528.

37. YE21: 132. In the same passage he also lists "God's being without change," "God's being everywhere," and "God's having a right of government over creatures."

38. Edwards does not adopt this distinction, however. He prefers to speak of moral and natural divine attributes: "there are two kinds of attributes in God, according to our way of conceiving of him, his moral attributes, which are summed up in his holiness, and his natural attributes, of strength, knowledge, etc. that constitute the greatness of God" (*Religious Affections*, YE2: 256). This does not mean he thinks modes and relations of God are communicable attributes, however. A number of Reformed theologians who rejected this distinction did so because they thought *all* the divine attributes incommunicable; they regarded it as a distinction without a difference, given the fact that God is a pure act in whom none of these attributes exist "eminently" or as distinct divine properties. See Heinrich Heppe, *Reformed Dogmatics*, trans. G. T. Thomson (London: Collins, 1950), pp. 58-64.

ing (on an Edwardsian way of thinking). Hence, they cannot be attributes God might not have had because all divine attributes are intrinsic and essential. For these reasons, the Edwardsian account of the divine nature, when set alongside what he says in the *Discourse* about the individuation of the divine persons cannot imply SETT. It must imply something weaker, something that allows for the simple pure act that is God to include modes or relations of existence shared within the divine life, so that all the divine persons are immutable, infinite, and eternal. We could put it like this:

> Everything that is in God is God, and this must be understood of real attributes (which pertain to one of the persons of the Trinity), not of modes and relations (such as immutability, and so forth).

This weaker thesis I call the *Edwardsian Trinitarian Thesis* (or ETT). Both Holmes and Strobel have zeroed in on something of fundamental importance to Edwards's doctrine of the Trinity. Of the two, Strobel is closer to the truth, because he maintains that Edwards retains the traditional language of the pure act account of the divine nature and divine essence, though he thinks the divine attributes are all assigned to the divine persons who instantiate the essence in a way that seems to pull against the pure act view.

In my view this goes too far and is not warranted by the cumulative case for the model of the Trinity that Strobel so carefully marshals. Strobel has placed all Edwardsian scholars in his debt by drawing attention to the highly innovative way in which Edwards redeploys the doctrine of perichoresis in his account of the Trinity in order to uphold a basically Augustinian model whilst assigning all the "real" divine attributes to the divine persons. However, he is mistaken if he thinks that Edwards denies that there is an essence of God over and above the individual persons of the Godhead. The divine essence includes some of God's incommunicable attributes — attributes shared by the divine persons, but which (according to Edwards at least) none "own" as their personal property. If anything, this makes Edwards's doctrine of the Trinity more startling and original than even Strobel thinks it is. For if this is right, Edwards manages to pull off something very rare indeed: a variation on the doctrine of the Trinity that takes as its point of departure a basically Augustinian framework, whilst re-describing key aspects of the Augustinian position in a way that makes sense of the irreducible plurality of the Trinity within the bounds of the anti-Trinitarian controversies characteristic of his own early modern context.

Problems with the Edwardsian Doctrine of the Trinity

Edwards's doctrine of the Trinity is both complex and subtle. He wants to hold onto the doctrine of his Reformed heritage, but he refines and reshapes it in important respects. This is just what one should expect of a divine as creative and original as the Sage of Northampton. It also goes a long way towards explaining why it is so difficult to fit Edwards's doctrine into either the "Augustinian" or the "social" model preferred by some earlier studies of Edwardsian Trinitarianism. His proposal is not without its difficulties, however.

We have spent most of our energies in getting clear the shape of Edwards's doctrine. Nevertheless, it is appropriate in closing to at least indicate where some of the main problems with his doctrine lie. If his achievement is to continue to inform contemporary constructive theology (as I hope it will), those sympathetic to an Edwardsian doctrine of the Trinity will have to address these questions in order to move forward.

The first problem has to do with how Edwards can retain both a doctrine of divine simplicity and his doctrine of the Trinity. As I have argued at length elsewhere, this is a problem he shares with much western Catholic theology. It is a particular problem for Edwards because of his doctrine of divine excellency, and because of the idiosyncratic way in which he individuates the divine persons.[39]

The second problem concerns the residue of the divine essence. Suppose Edwards does think that God has modes and relations of existence held in common between the divine persons as part-and-parcel of his being a simple pure act that exists *a se*.[40] Is the divine essence just these modes and relations? Is it related to the divine persons? If it is, how is it? This Edwards does not appear to have made as clear as he might have done.

Third, there is a problem concerning Edwards's particular use of Trinitarian perichoresis. How can the personhood of one divine person be *constituted* by the other two? Trinitarian perichoresis is doing a lot of the metaphysical heavy lifting for Edwards, but it is not at all clear what he means when he says, "there is such a wonderful union between them that they are after an ineffable and inconceivable manner one in another;

---

39. See Crisp, *Jonathan Edwards on God and Creation*.

40. Don Schweitzer in his recent article on Edwards's concept of infinity, says that his "understanding of God as metaphysically infinite meant that his thought assumes a strong sense of divine aseity and transcendence to creation." "Edwards' Understanding of Divine Infinity," in Lee, ed., *Jonathan Edwards as Contemporary*, p. 64.

so that one hath another, and they have communion in one another, and are as it were predicable one of another."[41] It would appear to be the case that if one thing is constituted as a person by another thing, then the first thing is identical to the second, or is at least a component of that second thing. For how can one thing provide one of the necessary conditions for the very personhood of another without being a part of that thing? Let us not mistake the problem here. The issue has to do with the identity of a person, that is, one of the necessary components of a thing's conscious life, psychology, and so forth, not a necessary prerequisite to such-and-such a thing *becoming* a person (at some point), or having the *potentiality* to be a person, or something like that. In other words, this has to do with an intrinsic attribute of divine personhood being provided to one divine person by another divine person. That is very odd indeed. For it implies that one divine person is something very like a part or constituent of another, or (at least) that one divine person partially composes another. But none of these things can be true of divine persons because they are not parts of one another and are not parts of God — on pain of denying the doctrine of the Trinity as well as the doctrine of divine simplicity.

Yet, as Edwards makes plain, these three, though one God, are distinct persons in more ways than via their perichoretically shared understanding and will. The different divine persons have many other attributes shared out between them so that the Son is quite different from the Spirit in (say) his wisdom and knowledge, in virtue of being uniquely the Word of God and the Idea of the Father. But then, how can this second divine person constitute one necessary aspect of another divine person if that divine person has many distinct attributes not shared between the two, even if they do share modes and relations of existence?

Taken together, I suggest that these problems present serious objections to the Edwardsian view. They may not be insurmountable. However, they are pressing and do require his advocates (or those enamored of something like the Edwardsian view) to take up the constructive theological task with seriousness and application.

---

41. YE21: 133.

CHAPTER 4

Arminius and Edwards on Creation

"He suffered much at the hands of his interpreters." This literary proverb could very easily be applied to Jacob Arminius. As Keith Stanglin has put it, the trouble is no one "owns" Arminius; he has no "tribe," as do Luther or Calvin or Cranmer. Lutherans love Luther; the Reformed (by and large) look to Calvin; Anglicans regard Cranmer as their English Reformer. But Arminius is the common property of many who claim his name as their rallying cry, and some who are not even clear about what Arminianism entails. Wesleyans are Arminians of a sort. But then so are Dutch Remonstrants, and many general Baptists and Anabaptists, as are many evangelicals of no particular confession.

What is more, the Harmenszoon of history is not the same as the Arminius of faith. The Arminius of faith undermined Reformed orthodoxy, creating schism in the church by teaching a synergistic doctrine of salvation and denying God's absolute sovereignty in creation and redemption. He tended towards a semi-Pelagian account of human beings post-Fall, made election conditional upon foreseen faith, entertained the notion that the atonement is universal in scope, thought grace was resistible, and doubted that one's election was sure and certain. The Harmenszoon of history was a rather more complex character. He was a biblical theologian, one for whom Scripture is the principal norm for all matters of Christian doctrine. Yet he was also a scholastic theologian, who used the elenctic and disputatious methods of school theology, harnessing them to Ramist logic and a penchant for the doctrine of God's middle knowledge, which he may have introduced to Protestant thought. He was also a Reformed minister and latterly a professor, even if the substance of his doctrine did not comport in every respect with the mainstream of that tradition, and might even be thought antithetical to it in some important respects.[1] Add to the question of the reception of Arminius's thought and his place in the history of Christian theology the problems associated with his writings, not all of which are in the public domain, and most of which are not in a modern critical edition. It seems amazing that the nearest thing to an English translation of the works of a theologian of such influence and importance was last attempted in the nineteenth century as a labor of love.[2]

The focus of this chapter is the doctrine of creation proper. This doctrine overlaps with several others in much traditional theology, including the doctrines of election and providence. But in this chapter, we shall concern ourselves with the doctrine of creation, not with election and providence as they bear upon creation, though these are important and controversial matters in Arminius's thought. The occasion of this piece was the publication of the first introductory work to Arminius's theology for some time in the volume *Jacob Arminius: Theologian of Grace* co-authored by Keith Stanglin and Thomas McCall.[3] There the authors draw attention to the shape and orthodoxy of Arminius's understanding of creation and to the fact that Arminius has often been misinterpreted and misunderstood on this topic as on several others. In order to test Stanglin and McCall's thesis that the Arminius of faith is a rather different theologian from the Harmenszoon of history, I will compare Arminius's doctrine with that

1. One aspect of Arminius's legacy was the Synod of Dordt and its canons. Arminius himself lived and died a Reformed pastor and professor. His immediate disciples, including the formidable Episcopius, formed the Remonstrant party that was the object of the Synod's ire. Arminius was dead and buried by that time. His importance for the Remonstrant movement was arguably less the specifics of the doctrine he espoused than the broad theological trajectory in which his views were thought to tend.

2. I refer to the James Nichols, William Nichols, and W. R. Bagnall edition of his works, first published in the mid-nineteenth century in three volumes, and frequently reprinted as *The Works of James Arminius*, vols. 1 and 2 (London: Longman, Hurst, Rees, Orme, Browne, & Green, 1825-1828); vol. 3 (London: Thomas Baker, 1875); reprinted entire (Grand Rapids: Baker, 1986). Hereafter, these writings are referred to as *Works*, followed by volume number and pagination. A good overview of recent scholarship on Arminius can be found in Keith D. Stanglin, "Arminius and Arminianism: An Overview of Current Research," in *Arminius, Arminianism, and Europe: Jacobus Arminius (1559/60-1609)*, ed. Th. Marius van Leeuwen, Keith D. Stanglin, and Marijke Tolsma (Leiden: Brill, 2009), pp. 3-24.

3. Oxford: Oxford University Press, 2012. A first draft of this paper was read at a panel discussion of this volume at the Evangelical Theological Society Annual Conference in Milwaukee, November 2012.

of a paradigmatic English-speaking Reformed thinker of the eighteenth century, namely, Jonathan Edwards.

Despite the distance in time and geography that separates Arminius from Edwards, the comparison is instructive. Evangelicals usually regard Edwards as an exemplar of Reformed theology. For the "young, restless, and Reformed" constituency, Edwards is a poster boy, whose theology epitomizes what Reformed theology ought to look like, over and against the perceived anthropocentric theology of Arminianism.[4] In the influential popularizing works of ministers like John Piper, Edwards is lionized for his emphasis upon absolute divine sovereignty and divine self-glorification in the creation of the world.[5] However, we shall see that of the two divines it is Edwards whose doctrine presses at the bounds of what is theologically permissible whilst Arminius's doctrine is well within the parameters of orthodoxy, even if it is untypical of Reformed theology in several respects.

Arminius on God and Creation

In his important study of Arminius's doctrines of God, creation, and providence, Richard Muller remarks, "It is apparent not only that Arminius' doctrine of creation, like his doctrine of God, is profoundly indebted to the scholastic tradition, particularly to the tradition of Thomism, but also that his doctrine of creation is one of the fundamental pivots of his theological system."[6] The doctrine of creation was not peripheral or unimportant to Arminius's system: it occupies a central place and is connected to several other *loci* of considerable importance for rightly understanding the shape of his work, particularly (as already indicated) his understanding of election and providence. For this reason, it behooves us to pay careful attention to the form his doctrine takes, beginning with his doctrine of God.

---

4. See Collin Hansen, *Young, Restless, Reformed: A Journalist's Journey with the New Calvinists* (Wheaton, IL: Crossway, 2008). Edwards's portrait even adorns the cover of the book.

5. See, e.g., John Piper, *God's Passion for His Glory: Living the Vision of Jonathan Edwards* (Wheaton, IL: Crossway, 1998), which includes the complete text of Edwards's dissertation, *The End for which God Created the World* (also known by the shorter title, *God's End in Creation*, which I will use throughout this volume).

6. Richard A. Muller, *God, Creation, and Providence in the Thought of Jacob Arminius* (Grand Rapids: Baker, 1991), p. 211.

As in most traditional dogmatic accounts of creation, the work of God *ad extra* is understood to be intimately related to the nature of God as God relates to creation. Arminius endorsed a traditional, classical account of the divine nature according to which God is a simple pure act. He says this of God's simplicity:

> Simplicity is a pre-eminent mode of the Essence of God, by which he is void of all composition, and of component parts, whether they belong to the senses or the understanding. He is without composition, because without external cause; and he is without component parts because without internal cause. . . . The essence of God therefore neither consists of material, integral, and quantitive parts, of matter and form, of kind and difference, of subject and accident, nor of form and the thing formed . . . neither hypothetically and through nature, through capability and actuality, nor through essence and being. Hence God is his own Essence and his own Being.[7]

In keeping with much late medieval and Protestant orthodox theology, Arminius is clear that the essence of God "is that by which God exists."[8] The life of God is, he says, "an Act flowing from the Essence of God, by which his Essence is signified to be [*actuosa*] in action itself."[9] Moreover, the life of God "is the Essence itself, and his very Being; because the divine Essence is in every respect simple, as well as infinite, and therefore eternal and immutable."[10] His views in this regard remain consistent across his public and private disputations. Even on a cursory reading of the relevant sections of his works it is clear that he does not substantially deviate from the norms of western Catholicism regarding the divine nature or the divine life. Thus, in his *Private Disputations* he writes, "this Essence is free from all composition, so it cannot enter into the composition of any thing."[11] Further, "The life of God . . . is most simple, so that it is not, in reality, distinguished from his essence" and therefore "according to the confined capacity of our conception, by which it is distinguished from his essence, it may, in some degree, be described as being 'an act that flows from the

---

7. Arminius, *Public Disputations* (hereafter *Disp. Pub.*), IV. XI, *Works*, vol. 1, p. 438. Cf. *Jacob Arminius: Theologian of Grace*, pp. 57-59, for useful discussion of this issue.
8. *Disp. Pub.*, IV. VII, *Works*, vol. 1, p. 436.
9. *Disp. Pub.*, IV. XXV, *Works*, vol. 1, p. 442.
10. *Disp. Pub.*, IV. XXVIII, *Works*, vol. 1, p. 443.
11. Arminius, *Private Disputations* (hereafter, *Disp. Priv.*), XV. IX, *Works*, vol. 2, p. 339.

essence of God,' by which is intimated that it is active in itself."[12] We cannot know the divine essence, he avers. But we can apprehend some things dimly, and by analogy, about God and about God's life. In this manner, we are able to see that being essentially non-composite and being essentially in act are both predicates that apply to the divine essence.

Stanglin and McCall point out that this endorsement of divine simplicity in Arminius may be more Scotist than Thomist.[13] Thomas Aquinas allowed that there are "rational" or purely conceptual distinctions that can be predicated of God, so that we can speak of the distinct divine persons of the Godhead. But he denied that there are "real" distinctions in God as there are between, say, the parts of creaturely bodies, because God's nature is simple. However, Scotus added to this the idea that there are "formal" distinctions in God, where a formal distinction picks out some differentiation *within* the essence of a thing. Thus, the color and texture of an apple are formally distinct, but belong numerically to the same entity. Arminius echoes this Scotist language at one point in his *Public Disputation*, where, during a discussion of divine simplicity, he remarks that

> whatever is absolutely predicated about God, it is to be understood essentially and not accidentally; and those things (whether many or diverse) which are predicated concerning God, are, in God, not many but one.... It is only in our mode of considering them, which is a compound mode, that they are distinguished as being many and diverse.

He continues, "though this may not inappropriately be said — *because they are likewise distinguished by a formal reason.*"[14]

From simplicity conjoined with divine infinity, Arminius derives divine eternity (i.e., atemporality), immensity, immutability, impassibility, and incorruptibility. These are all incommunicable attributes — that is, divine perfections that God does not share in common with creatures.[15] Out of this perfect, singular life God creates the world *ex nihilo*.[16] Creation

---

12. *Disp. Priv.*, XVI. III, *Works*, vol. 2, p. 340.

13. In this matter they follow Muller's reading of Arminius. See *Arminius: Theologian of Grace*, p. 55.

14. Arminius, *Disp. Pub.*, IV. XI, *Works*, vol. 1, p. 438, emphasis added.

15. See *Disp. Pub.*, IV. XIII, *Works*, vol. 1, p. 439.

16. See, e.g., the terse statement of this doctrine in *Disp. Priv.*, XXIV. III, *Works*, vol. 2, p. 355; and *Certain Examples to Be Diligently Examined and Weighed*, VI. I, *Works*, vol. 2, p. 711. Muller has an interesting discussion of some untypical features of Arminius's

is the product of his communicable attributes, including divine goodness, wisdom, will, and power.[17] More specifically, it is the contingent output of the intrinsic self-diffusiveness of divine goodness, in which all creatures participate. As Muller points out, this aspect of Arminius's doctrine is thoroughly Thomist in nature, and underlines the connection between the classical understanding of the divine nature and what it is that leads to the creation.[18] God wills to create a world in which creatures may participate in God's goodness. However, this is a free act of God; nothing impels God to act in this fashion, not even something intrinsic to the divine nature. For, says Arminius, "the Lord Omnipotent did not create the world by a natural necessity, but by the freedom of his will."[19] (We shall see that by modifying this essentially Thomist component of a classical doctrine of God, Edwards ends up with a very different understanding of God's freedom in creation.)

Yet as Arminius understands divine aseity and freedom, God is free to refrain from creating and has no need of the created order. God's blessedness *(beatitas)* is perfect delight in God's own perfection.[20] This is an incommunicable attribute peculiar to God that is an act both of understanding and will, and the fount of blessing to the creature. But God does not need to create; there is nothing in the divine nature that requires an act of creation to manifest this blessedness, or bring about the instantiation of the divine glory *ad extra*. As Stanglin and McCall put it, "Arminius insists that the simplicity and aseity of God imply that God lacks nothing good — thus the external display of the divine glory is not necessary for God."[21] Moreover, "God can lack nothing and can have no need — not even the need for glorification through the display of justice or wrath."[22] In Arminius's own words,

> God . . . does not need to illustrate his glory extrinsically, by mercy and justice or wrath, nor by grace, as it is here understood. But God

---

conception of creation out of nothing. It appears that Arminius thought of the *nihil* from which God creates as Aristotelian primary matter. See *God, Creation, and Providence*, pp. 215-16.

17. *Disp. Priv.*, XXIV. IV, *Works*, vol. 2, p. 355.
18. Muller, *God, Creation, and Providence*, pp. 213-14.
19. *Disp. Priv.*, XXIV. X, *Works*, vol. 2, p. 357.
20. *Arminius: Theologian of Grace*, p. 79.
21. *Arminius: Theologian of Grace*, p. 80.
22. *Arminius: Theologian of Grace*, p. 81.

can make use of the sinner for the glory of his grace, mercy, wrath, or severity, if he sees fit to do so *(visum fuerit)*.[23]

Other aspects to his doctrine of creation are also relevant to our present concern. For instance, Arminius denies that God could create creatures purely for the purposes of destroying them in hell. Instead, God creates according to God's essentially benevolent nature, so that all God brings into existence is good.[24] What God wills to create, God creates *per se*, or in itself, as good. Evil is not willed *per se*, but *per accidens* — that is, accidentally, or contingently, not as an expression of the essential goodness of God.[25] This reflects the fact that Arminius is an intellectualist, not a voluntarist. That is, he thinks God creates for good reasons that are logically and explanatorily prior to that which he wills. (The voluntarist, by contrast, says that there are no such antecedent reasons that guide God's actions *ad extra*.) Thus in his *Declaration of Sentiments*, Arminius writes,

> Rather than being alien to God, creation is an act quite proper to him. It is eminently an action most appropriate to him. It is an act to which he could be moved by no other external cause. Indeed, it is the primordial act of God, and until it was completed, nothing could have any actual existence except God himself. For everything else that has being came into existence through this act.[26]

Although the topic here is not providence proper, some remarks about Arminius's understanding of the act of creation as it bears upon the divine governance of the world are appropriate at this juncture. For one thing, Arminius does not appear to endorse the scholastic doctrine of continuous creation. On this view, both the act of creation and the sustenance of

---

23. Arminius, *Works*, vol. 3, p. 707.
24. In the *Declaration of Sentiments*, Part II, chap. IX, 2-3, Arminius writes "Reprobation is a hateful act that springs from hate. But the act of creation did not grow out of hatred, and it should not be construed as a way or means to accomplish the decree of reprobation. Creation is a perfect act of God that declares his wisdom, goodness, and omnipotence." See W. Stephen Gunter, trans., *Arminius and His* Declaration of Sentiments: *An Annotated Translation with Introduction and Theological Commentary* (Waco, TX: Baylor University Press, 2012), p. 116. All references to the *Declaration* are to this edition.
25. *Disp. Pub.*, IV. LXIII, *Works*, vol. 1, p. 455; *Arminius: Theologian of Grace*, p. 71.
26. Arminius, *Declaration*, Part II, chap. IX, 4, p. 117. Cf. *Arminius: Theologian of Grace*, pp. 69-70.

that which is created thereafter are two aspects of one eternal timeless divine act, apprehended as distinct events in time by finite human creatures. By contrast, Arminius appears to think these two things are distinct divine actions and (somewhat strangely) that God brings them about *in time:* "it is an act of the practical understanding, or of the will employing the understanding, not completed in a single moment, but continued in the moments of the duration of things."[27] It is difficult to see what can be meant by the claim that a timeless, simple pure act (somehow) brings about different actions in time, because such a being can have no temporal relations. It is easier, I think, to see what might be meant by the claim that the one, eternal, simple, pure act that is God brings about distinct temporal effects: creation with time *and* the conservation of creation thereafter. However, this does not appear to be what Arminius actually says. At least one recent interpreter of Arminius thinks we should take this at face value as a claim about temporal divine actions, which raises a concern about the integrity of Arminius's theology.[28]

Arminius is also a proponent of Molinism — that is, the doctrine of divine middle knowledge. Although he does not mention Luis de Molina by name, it is clear that he endorsed Molina's doctrine.[29] All parties in this period of early Reformed Orthodoxy agreed that God has natural knowledge (i.e., knowledge of all that is necessary and possible) and free knowledge (i.e., knowledge of how things are in the actual world he brings about). The Molinist notion of a pre-volitional middle knowledge was novel within Reformed circles. Stanglin and McCall sum it up well:

> Natural knowledge includes knowledge of all that *must be* (in the sense of logical necessity) as well as all that *could be* (in the sense of logical possibility), while free knowledge is God's knowledge of what *will be.*

---

27. Arminius, *Disp. Priv.*, XXVIII. III, *Works*, vol. 2, p. 367.

28. Compare Muller, who writes, "Arminius appears, consciously, to have narrowed the scope of providence specifically to temporal divine activity in and with the things of the created order and to have maintained this narrow definition by modifying the concept of *continua creatio.*" Muller, *God, Creation, and Providence*, p. 248.

29. Eef Dekker drew attention to this in his paper, "Was Arminius a Molinist?" *Sixteenth Century Journal* 27.2 (1996): 337-52. He writes, "Arminius not only mentions the theory of middle knowledge, but he also has incorporated it into his theology. It appears in all crucial formulations of his doctrine of divine knowledge. . . . Middle knowledge is vital for Arminius since it is a cornerstone in his attempt to build a theory with the help of which he can show that both God and human beings are free" (p. 351).

Between these, however, is middle knowledge: it is God's knowledge of all that *would be*.³⁰

While Arminius's position with respect to middle knowledge has been the subject of some debate in recent studies,³¹ his support for the doctrine seems clear. He says things like this: "it is necessary for that middle [knowledge] to intervene in things which depend on the liberty of created choice."³² That being said, Eef Dekker has argued that the internal logic of Arminius's position with respect to divine ordination and human freedom is actually disordered and collapses into a species of metaphysical determinism. Though Arminius would have denied this, Dekker concludes that the internal tensions in Arminius's theology drive him in this direction. While he "suggests a kind of epistemological indeterminism on the human side," this does not "loosen the ties of metaphysical determinism" all things considered, and may "lead to further incoherences" in his thought.³³

Be that as it may, we can summarize some of the central claims about the doctrine of creation in Arminius's theology in the following numbered statements:

1. God is a simple pure act.
2. God is free and exists *a se*.
3. God perfectly delights in God's own perfection.
4. God's perfect self-delight does not require the creation of a world in which to display this self-delight.
5. Hence, creation is a free act:
   a. God could refrain from creating a world; and
   b. God could refrain from creating this world.
6. God creates according to God's good pleasure and will, reflecting God's own character (this is God's intellectualism).
7. God creates the world *per se* good; evil is generated *per accidens*.
8. Creation and conservation are two distinct, temporal divine actions.

---

30. *Arminius: Theologian of Grace*, p. 67.

31. See William Gene Witt's doctoral dissertation, "Creation, Redemption, and Grace in the Theology of Jacob Arminius" (University of Notre Dame, 1993). Dekker's paper, "Was Arminius a Molinist?" is in part a response to Witt's claims.

32. Arminius, *Disp. Pub.*, IV. XLV, *Works*, vol. 1, p. 449, cited in *Arminius: Theologian of Grace*, p. 68.

33. Eef Dekker, "Jacob Arminius and His Logic: Analysis of a Letter," *Journal of Theological Studies*, NS 44 (1993): 118-42, especially 138.

9. God eternally and pre-volitionally knows all that is necessary and possible.
10. God eternally and pre-volitionally knows all that would obtain in all logically possible states of affairs were God to bring them about.
11. God eternally and post-volitionally knows what will obtain in the world God creates.
12. God creates the world *ex nihilo*.

Apart from the innovative use of middle knowledge (expressed in 9-11 above) and his departure from the scholastic account of continuous creation (in 8), the main contours of Arminius's doctrine of creation appear to be well within the bounds of classical orthodoxy.

Edwards on God and Creation

We come now to Jonathan Edwards. He also defended a classical account of the divine nature and attributes, including in both his unpublished and published works the claim that God is an atemporal, simple pure act.[34] Thus, in his "Miscellanies" notebook, entry 94, Edwards says that the "Holy Spirit is the act of God between the Father and the Son infinitely loving and delighting in each other." What is more, the Holy Spirit is "distinct from each of the other two [divine persons], and yet it [sic] is God; for the pure and perfect act of God is God, because God is a pure act. It appears that this is God, because that which acts perfectly is all act, and nothing but act."[35]

What is more, like Arminius, he thought of divine simplicity as primarily a piece of apophatic theology, emphasizing that the divine nature

---

34. This has been disputed in several recent studies of Edwards's work, especially that of Amy Plantinga Pauw, *"The Supreme Harmony of All": The Trinitarian Theology of Jonathan Edwards* (Grand Rapids: Eerdmans, 2002); and Michael J. McClymond, "Hearing the Symphony: A Critique of Some Critics of Sang Lee's and Amy Plantinga Pauw's Accounts of Jonathan Edwards' View of God," in *Jonathan Edwards as Contemporary: Essays in Honor of Sang Hyun Lee*, ed. Don Schweitzer (New York: Peter Lang, 2010), pp. 67-92. However, there is good evidence that Edwards did endorse this claim. For arguments supporting this conclusion see Crisp, "Jonathan Edwards on Divine Simplicity," *Religious Studies* 39.1 (2003): 23-41; Crisp, *Jonathan Edwards on God and Creation* (New York: Oxford University Press, 2012); and Kyle Strobel, *Jonathan Edwards's Theology: A Reinterpretation* (London: T&T Clark, 2012).

35. YE13: 260.

is non-composite.[36] Edwards endorses divine aseity, but he understands this unambiguously in terms of his doctrine of theological determinism, so that divine freedom amounts to God necessarily acting according to the perfection of his nature.[37] As is well known, Edwards argues in his dissertation, *God's End in Creation*, that God's ultimate end in creation is God's own self-glorification.[38] What is less well known is that Edwards is also committed to the following controversial theological claims in his doctrine of creation: that (a) God is essentially creative so that God must create some world;[39] and (b) that any theater of divine creation must be one in which the full panoply of divine attributes are displayed, including God's justice and wrath as well as God's grace and mercy.

Let us consider these claims. Edwards thinks that God is essentially creative. By this he means that God's nature is such that God must "self-communicate" in some act of creation. It is not merely that a creative God might generate some world or other, though God could refrain from doing so. Rather, God must create a world. In this way, Edwards's God is like an artist for whom creative action is not merely appropriate or expected, but inevitable given the sort of talents and character God has. Some artists speak of their work as being something compulsive. It is as if they cannot help themselves; in some sense they feel compelled to make works of art. Edwards seems to have something similar in mind regarding the deity. God must create; it is God's character to create; God cannot but create, though not through compulsion. God creates because God is essentially self-diffusive. However, this would appear to infringe on two fundamental concerns of much classical Christian theology, namely, divine freedom and the claim that God exists *a se*. If God is free, then (so it is often thought) God must be able to create and refrain from creating. If the act of creation is pictured as something akin to a compulsive act, then something has gone awry with our reasoning. For, so this story goes, a God who is perfect must be perfectly free to create or not as God sees fit. It is often thought

---

36. For discussion of this point, see Crisp, *Jonathan Edwards on God and Creation*, chap. 5.

37. Jonathan Edwards, *Freedom of the Will*, YE1: 377.

38. *God's End in the Creation* can be found in YE8.

39. In fact, Edwards goes beyond this to claim God must create this world because it is the best possible world. Interested readers should consult William J. Wainwright, "Jonathan Edwards, William Rowe, and the Necessity of Creation," in *Faith, Freedom, and Responsibility*, ed. Jeff Jordan and Daniel Howard-Snyder (Lanham, MD: Rowman and Littlefield, 1996), chap. 9. Cf. Crisp, *Jonathan Edwards on God and Creation*, chaps. 3-4.

that a corollary to divine freedom is divine aseity. God is free because God is independent of anything that is created. God does not depend upon creation for happiness and fulfillment, and to deny this is to deny something basic to the divine nature.

Does Edward's theology end up denying one or both of these constituents of the tradition? On the face of it, it looks like it does. Nevertheless, in this case, first appearances may be deceptive. To begin with, Edwards maintains that divine freedom is consistent with determinism. That is, God acts in a way commensurate with necessity, but without this infringing divine freedom. He says, "'Tis no disadvantage or dishonor to a being, necessarily to act in the most excellent and happy manner, from the necessary perfection of his own nature."[40] He also makes use of a distinction between natural and moral ability and inability to do a thing. God may be naturally able to do certain things, like lie or act wickedly. However, God is morally incapable of such acts given God's necessarily benevolent nature. Far from making divine actions inevitable and therefore without moral significance, Edwards thinks that the closer the morality of an action is to necessity, the more praiseworthy it is. "Men don't think a good act to be the less praiseworthy, for the agent's being much determined in it by a good inclination or a good motive," he says, "but the more."[41]

For Edwards, what matters in considering questions of freedom and moral responsibility, whether human or divine, is that the agent in question would have been able to perform the action in question *if she or he had willed to do so*. This is true, Edwards thinks, irrespective of whether the agent in question *could* have performed that action. That is, God would have created a world of unrelieved wickedness if God had willed to do so. However, God's nature is such that God is incapable of bringing this about. It is morally impossible for God to act in this way, though there is no natural impediment to God's doing so.[42]

What, then, of divine aseity? Edwards is clear that God has no need of creation in the sense that without the creation God would be unhappy or unfulfilled. "God stands in no need of his creatures, and is not profited by

40. YE1: 377.
41. YE1: 361.
42. See William Rowe's helpful discussion of Edwards on this point in *Can God Be Free?* (Oxford: Oxford University Press, 2004), p. 50; and Richard Muller's paper, "Jonathan Edwards and the Absence of Free Choice: A Parting of Ways in the Reformed Tradition," *Jonathan Edwards Studies* 1.1 (2011): 3-22.

them; neither can his happiness be said to be added to by the creature."⁴³ Yet, God must create a world, given the sort of nature God has, which is essentially creative. Nevertheless, God does not depend upon the creation *in and of itself* for happiness or glory. It is the means by which God communicates that glory and unites with that which God has created. God does not need this world any more than artists needs paintings in order to continue to exist, though they may be said to be an expression of their character. Thus, in *God's End in Creation*, Edwards remarks:

> There is something in that disposition in God to communicate goodness which shows him to be independent and self-moved in it, in a manner that is peculiar, and above what is in the beneficence of creatures.... God being all and alone is absolutely self-moved. The exercises of his communicative disposition are absolutely from within himself, not finding anything, or any object to excite them or draw them forth.⁴⁴

Rather, "all that is good and worthy in the object, and the very being of the object" proceeds "from the overflowing of his goodness."⁴⁵

It seems that, for Edwards, creation is the communication of God's goodness outside of the divine self. What is more, any such creative act must include some space for the display of the divine attributes since, as Edwards makes plain in the closing sections of the second chapter of *God's End in Creation*, God does all things for God's own glory, and this is the ultimate end of all God's works:

> for it appears that all that is ever spoken of in the Scripture as an ultimate end of God's works is included in that one phrase, "the glory of God"; which is the name by which the last end of God's works is most commonly called in Scripture: and seems to be the name which most aptly signifies the thing.⁴⁶

Even the very many apparently different ways in which God acts in creation, displaying one attribute here, another there, realizing this particular goal here, and another there, are all in fact merely parts of or subordi-

---

43. "Miscellany" 679 in YE18: 237-38.
44. YE8: 462.
45. YE8: 462.
46. YE8: 526.

nate ends towards this larger overarching ultimate end that God envisaged in creating the world, namely, the display *ad extra* of God's internal glory via its communication to the creatures.[47]

One of the startling implications of this deliverance of Edwardsian theology is that he thinks God creates the world that he may be united with elected creatures in *theosis*. Although Edwards does not use the term "theosis" or "divinization," this is clearly the upshot of his position. At the close of *God's End in Creation*, he says this:

> We may judge of the end that the Creator aimed at, in the being, nature and tendency he gives the creature, by the mark or term which they constantly aim at in their tendency and eternal progress; though the time will never come when it can be said it is attained to, in the most absolutely perfect manner.[48]

He goes on to say,

> But if strictness of union to God be viewed as thus infinitely exalted; then the creature must be regarded as infinitely, nearly and closely united to God. And viewed thus, their interest must be viewed as one with God's interest; and so is not regarded properly with a disjunct and separate, but an undivided respect.[49]

This is a significant theological claim for someone formed in the tradition of Reformed scholasticism.

An account of Edwards's doctrine of creation would be incomplete without some mention of his twin doctrines of continuous creation and occasionalism.[50] Unlike Arminius, Edwards thinks continuous creation is one, eternal divine act. In contrast with the scholastic doctrine, Edwards construes this in terms of a continuous creation *out of nothing*, denying

---

[47]. See YE8: 527-28. For a recent discussion of this theme see William M. Schweitzer, *God Is a Communicative Being: Divine Communicativeness and Harmony in the Theology of Jonathan Edwards* (London: T&T Clark, 2012).

[48]. YE8: 535. For discussion of the Edwardsian doctrine of theosis, see Crisp, *Jonathan Edwards on God and Creation*, chap. 8; and Kyle Strobel, "Jonathan Edwards and the Polemics of Theosis," *Harvard Theological Review* 105.3 (2012): 259-79.

[49]. YE8: 535.

[50]. I have attempted a more comprehensive account in Crisp, *Jonathan Edwards on God and Creation*.

conservation. He adds to this the claim that God is the only real cause of what comes to pass (i.e., occasionalism), pressing his doctrine of creation in the direction of a four-dimensionalist account of the persistence of created things across time. That is, unlike Arminius, Edwards thinks the world does not exist whole and complete at each moment of time that it does exist. This is brought out particularly clearly in his treatise on *Original Sin*:

> If the existence of created *substance*, in each successive moment, be wholly the effect of God's immediate power, in *that* moment, without any dependence on prior existence, as much as the first creation out of *nothing*, then what exists at this moment, by his power, is a *new effect*; and simply and absolutely considered, not the same with any past existence, though it be like it, and follows it according to a certain established method. And there is no identity or oneness in the case, but what depends on the *arbitrary* constitution of the Creator; who by his wise sovereign establishment so unites these successive new effects, that he *treats them as one*, by communicating to them like properties, relations and circumstances; and so leads us to regard and treat them as *one*.[51]

Later in the same passage, he underlines the point:

> Thus it appears, if we consider matters strictly, that there is no such thing as any identity or oneness in created objects, existing at different times, but what depends on *God's sovereign constitution* . . . for it appears, that a *divine constitution* is what *makes truth*, in affairs of this nature.[52]

Nothing persists through time — not the constituents of the world; not even the world itself. It would appear that, according to Edwards's way of thinking, "the world" is strictly speaking a sort of approximation. Rather than describing an entity that persists through time, from creation to conflagration, "the world" is actually shorthand for a series of momentary, but complete, worlds that God segues together making it appear that there is action across time, though, strictly speaking "divine constitution is what makes truth" in this matter.

---

51. YE3: 492-503, author's emphasis.
52. *Original Sin*, in YE3: 404, author's emphasis. I have discussed these passages in *Original Sin* at greater length in Crisp, *Jonathan Edwards and the Metaphysics of Sin* (Aldershot: Ashgate, 2005).

Arminius and Edwards on Creation

An analogy will help to make this point clearer. Imagine a nineteenth-century kinetoscope. This was an early motion picture device mounted in a wooden box with a hole through which a viewer could see a "moving picture." It was, in fact, a primitive version of the sorts of images seen on a regular basis on the silver screen of movie theaters. The pictures were photographic stills of action across time that, when run together, produced the illusion of movement and action. Edwards's understanding of continuous creation implies something like this about the world in which we live. It is a series of such "stills" that are numerically distinct, woven together, as it were, by divine convention.

There are at least two ways one could understand this. On the one hand, one might argue that this view of divine continuous creation makes of the world a sort of divine plaything that undermines real creaturely action across time. Any person at one moment is strictly speaking numerically distinct from what we would perceive to be the same person at the next moment, according to the Edwardsian way of thinking. This might be thought detrimental to the Edwardsian if it implies that nothing persists through time, making everything radically dependent on the will of God. By contrast, one might simply accept the sort of metaphysical picture of the world that Edwards presupposes, allowing that some sort of four-dimensionalism is true. Perhaps, we might consider, things persist through time not by being numerically the same at each moment at which they exist, but by having "temporal parts" just as they have physical parts. Just as I have a right arm and a left arm, both of which are different physical parts of me, I also have a part of me that existed yesterday and a part that exists today. These are what are often called *temporal parts* of me. Then, to speak of "me" is to speak of some four-dimensional object that extends across time as well as across space. It is a thing that has physical parts at a given time, and temporal parts across a particular stretch of time. This, or something very like it, is the sort of view Edwards appears to endorse.[53] It is somewhat counterintuitive. But its appeal or lack thereof depends in large measure on whether one is willing to accept the sort of four-dimensionalist view of the world to which Edwards subscribes.

Edwards also embraces a doctrine of panentheism. This is the claim that the world is somehow an emanation from God. In his dissertation, *God's End in Creation* (and elsewhere[54]), Edwards makes it clear that he

---

53. I return to these matters in the following chapter.
54. Some of what he says might suggest pantheism rather than panentheism, but

thinks the world is something like an emanation from God, a shadow-like entity that is the necessary product of divine creativity:

> The emanation or communication of the divine fullness, consisting in the knowledge of God, love to God, and joy in God, has relation indeed both to God and the creature: but it has relation to God as its fountain, as it is an emanation from God; and as the communication itself, or thing communicated, is something divine, something of God, something of his internal fullness; as the water in the stream is something of the fountain; and as the beams are of the sun. . . . Here is both an *emanation* and *remanation*. The refulgence shines upon and into the creature, and is reflected back to the luminary. The beams of glory come from God, and are something of God, and are refunded back again to their original. So that the whole is *of* God, and *in* God, and *to* God; and God is the beginning, middle and end in this affair.[55]

Even if Edwards's panentheism does not push him beyond orthodoxy, it should be clear from this sketch of his doctrine of creation that it looks very different from the sort of view one would expect from a representative of Reformed orthodoxy. In many ways it is closer to the sort of position one finds elaborated by Baruch Spinoza in his *Ethics* than that of Edwards's compatriots in Puritan and continental Reformed theology. As John Cooper says in summing up Edwards's position, "all things considered, his affirmation that 'the whole is *of* God, and *in* God, and *to* God' is best construed philosophically as a panentheism that borders on Spinozan pantheism."[56]

We can sum up what we have seen of Edwards's views as follows:

1. God is a timeless, simple pure act.
2. God is free and exists *a se* (where divine freedom is understood to be consistent with determinism).
3. God is essentially creative so that God must create some world in order to "communicate" the divine self *ad extra*.

---

the preponderance of what he says on this matter is towards the latter, not the former. See, e.g., YE8: 421 and 439; "Miscellany" 27a in YE13: 213; YE18: 281; and "Miscellany" 880, in YE20: 123.

55. YE8: 531.

56. John W. Cooper, *Panentheism: The Other God of the Philosophers — From Plato to the Present* (Grand Rapids: Baker Academic, 2006), p. 77.

4. Any theater of divine creation must be one in which the full panoply of divine attributes are displayed, including God's justice and wrath as well as God's grace and mercy.
5. God creates for the ultimate end of displaying God's glory.
6. God communicates the divine self to elect creatures that he may be united to them via *theosis*.
7. Nothing persists through time.
8. The present world is a momentary stage in a series of such stages created seriatim *ex nihilo* by God and segued together according to divine convention.
9. God is the only causal agent in the world.
10. The world is the emanation of God's essential creativity. It is a shadowy projection from God *ad extra*.

Although there is significant conceptual overlap with Arminius (because both theologians share a common heritage and commitment to the broad contours of a classical doctrine of God), it is clear that Edwards's understanding of God and creation is innovative in several important respects — indeed, much more innovative than the doctrine espoused by Arminius.

Conclusion

This comparison is limited in scope and for that reason alone drawing conclusions from it is a somewhat hazardous endeavor. A complete account of Arminius's doctrine of creation, or that of Edwards, would require much more attention to detail, to aspects of their respective positions that we have only sketched, and to the important ways in which other fundamental motifs in their theologies play a part in what they say about the doctrine of creation, e.g., the Trinity. However, what even this brief survey shows is that the claim that Arminius was a theological maverick or a thinker who played fast-and-loose with the tradition he inherited cannot be sustained when it comes to this doctrine, which is of fundamental importance for his theological system. The most important innovation he makes in his account of creation is the inclusion of a doctrine of middle knowledge. This does take him beyond the Reformed mainstream, and those contemporary evangelical theologians who claim to be both Molinist *and* Reformed would do well to pay more attention to the historical dimension to this debate.[57] However, the more startling conclusion of our comparison is that the supposed paragon of Reformed, evangelical theology, Jonathan Edwards, has a doctrine of creation far more exotic than that of Arminius. We might put it like this: Edwards's hypertrophied account of absolute divine sovereignty expressed in his doctrines of divine determinism, the necessity of creation, and the attenuated, ephemeral nature of the creation, which is emanated by God, lead him to embrace panentheism — a doctrine often thought to be at odds with orthodox Christian theology.[58] Some critics of Edwards, like Charles Hodge, have even claimed that his work collapses into pantheism, given his idealism and robust doctrine of continuous creation.[59] Even if his view is panentheist rather than pantheist, I submit that it requires a much more significant shift in theology than the addition of a doctrine of middle knowledge and temporal account of divine conservation to a basically classical account of the divine nature.

The comparison is instructive. Both thinkers are theologians steeped in the Reformed and western Catholic theological traditions. Both are schooled in scholastic debate and utilize the technical vocabulary of Reformed Orthodox discussion. Both are also biblical theologians in the sense that they are deeply engaged with the biblical tradition, seeking to form their theological judgments in ways that reflect the shape and coherence of what they find in Scripture. Moreover, both were willing to innovate within the traditions that shaped them, where they thought that appropriate. In the doctrine of creation, it transpires that the innovations presented by Arminius were actually less radical than those allowed by Edwards.

I have argued that Arminius's doctrine of creation is an expression of a broadly orthodox account, in the post-Reformation Reformed tradition of what is sometimes referred to as Thomist Calvinism. He is able

---

57. See, e.g., Terrance L. Tiessen, *Providence and Prayer: How Does God Work in the World?* (Downers Grove, IL: IVP, 2000).

58. One standard definition of panentheism states that the "being of God includes and penetrates the whole universe, so that every part exists in Him, but His Being is more than, and not exhausted by, the universe." F. L. Cross and E. A. Livingstone, eds., *The Oxford Dictionary of the Christian Church*, 3rd ed. (New York: Oxford University Press, 1997), p. 1213. This is the position Edwards advocates in *God's End in Creation*.

59. See Charles Hodge, *Systematic Theology* (Grand Rapids: Eerdmans, 1940 [1871]), vol. 2, p. 220. We will return to Hodge's criticism in the final chapter. For a recent discussion of other objections to Edwardsian metaphysics as pantheistic, see Steven Studebaker and Robert W. Caldwell III, *The Trinitarian Theology of Jonathan Edwards: Text, Context, and Application* (Aldershot: Ashgate, 2012), chap. 9.

to hold together divine aseity and freedom in creation, as well as the dependence of creatures upon God. His understanding of the motivation or end of God in creation is also suitably nuanced and careful. By contrast, Edwards retains divine freedom and aseity at the cost of making creation the necessary product of divine creativity. Indeed, as a number of recent studies have argued, Edwardsianism entails panentheism.[60] This is not *necessarily* unorthodox, but it does put Edwards's understanding of God and creation much further from the center of classical, orthodox accounts of the divine nature (including classical, orthodox Reformed accounts) than that of Arminius. This does not show that Arminius is closer to the Reformed mainstream than Edwards, all things considered. But it does give some credence to Stanglin and McCall's view that Arminius is not the bogeyman of much Calvinist apologetic on a central doctrinal locus, namely, the doctrine of creation. Rightly or wrongly, Edwards is often regarded as a paradigm of Reformed theology, while Arminius is thought to be its antithesis. It is ironic that Edwards spent much of his intellectual capital combatting "Arminianism" — not the actual theology of Arminius but a sort of freethinking theological sensibility that implied an anthropological turn that Edwards (rightly) regarded as a threat. This is especially ironic given that the doctrine of creation espoused by the historical Harmenszoon is actually closer to Catholic orthodoxy, including the orthodoxy of Reformed theology, than that of Jonathan Edwards.

---

60. In addition to Crisp, *Jonathan Edwards on God and Creation*, see, e.g., John J. Bombaro, *Jonathan Edwards's Vision of Reality: The Relationship of God to the World, Redemption History, and the Reprobate* (Eugene, OR: Pickwick Publications, 2012); Cooper, *Panentheism*, pp. 74-77; and Douglas Elwood, *The Philosophical Theology of Jonathan Edwards* (New York: Columbia University Press, 1960).

CHAPTER 5

Girardeau and Edwards on Free Will

In a recent volume, Dutch scholars Willem J. van Asselt, Martin Bac, and Roelf T. te Velde have argued that our understanding of the Reformed perspective on freedom of the will needs to be rethought.[1] Negatively, they argue that it is a mistake to characterize Reformed thinking as monolithic, or even preponderating towards one single view on the matter. Positively, they claim that a number of key early Reformed theologians can be shown to have held to something like libertarian accounts of human free will, giving case studies to establish this. If they are right, then the way we think about the character and development of Reformed thought needs some revision. In addition to the descriptive challenges this presents to historians, it has potentially far-reaching normative consequences for those interested in the practice of Reformed theology today. It is the normative issue that I want to address in this chapter, though we shall have to deal with some of the historical claims being made in order to get there.

---

1. Willem J. van Asselt et al., *Reformed Thought on Freedom: The Concept of Free Choice in Early Modern Reformed Theology* (Grand Rapids: Baker Academic, 2010). However, this is not the first time such views have been raised in the contemporary literature. Twenty years ago Richard Muller wrote, "It was never the Reformed view that the moral acts of human beings are predetermined, any more than it was ever the Reformed view that the fall of Adam was willed by God to the exclusion of Adam's free choice of sin. The divine ordination of all things is not only consistent with human freedom; it makes human freedom possible." Richard A. Muller, "Grace, Election, and Contingent Choice: Arminius's Gambit and the Reformed Response," in *The Grace of God, The Bondage of the Will*, ed. Thomas R. Schreiner and Bruce A. Ware (Grand Rapids: Baker, 1995), vol. 2, p. 270.

Preamble

This discussion raises the question of how broad a spectrum of views on human freedom are permissible within the bounds of confessional Reformed theology. Popular accounts of Calvinism describe it as almost synonymous with unrelenting determinism; libertarianism is *ex hypothesi* excluded. On this way of thinking, God determines all that comes to pass, including all the actions of human creatures. In which case, one of two scenarios obtains. The first is that my actions are not free at all because God determines all that comes to pass. In which case, some species of hard determinism obtains and human freedom is a mirage; the world is deterministic all the way down. Alternatively, at least some of my actions are free in some sense consistent with moral responsibility, despite the fact that God determines all that comes to pass — in which case, a species of soft determinism or compatibilism obtains, according to which human freedom (and moral responsibility) is consistent with divine determinism.[2]

Whether one subscribes to compatibilism (as, arguably, a number of Reformed thinkers have done[3]) or hard determinism (a doctrine almost entirely absent from historic Reformed theology[4]), determinism ob-

---

2. Matters are slightly more complicated than this, in point of fact. For one thing, some Reformed theologians that were compatibilists about human freedom nevertheless believed that God has libertarian free will. Francis Turretin held this view. Others, such as Jonathan Edwards, believed that God himself is "determined" to act as he does by the sort of nature he has, such that though God could have willed to do other than he does, he would not have willed other than he does because he necessarily acts in accordance with his nature, and it is in his nature to act precisely in the way that he does. For discussion of this, see Crisp, *Jonathan Edwards on God and Creation* (New York: Oxford University Press, 2012), chaps. 3-4; and William Rowe, *Can God Be Free?* (Oxford: Oxford University Press, 2004), especially chap. 4.

3. However, Muller for one denies that Reformed theology has ever been deterministic in outlook. He writes, "Far from being a rigid metaphysical determinism of all human actions, a form of necessitarianism (which was never Reformed doctrine in any case), predestination applies only to the issue of salvation." In "Grace, Election, and Contingent Choice," p. 271.

4. I say "almost entirely absent from historic Reformed theology" because there may be one or two exceptions. Perhaps the best known is the Swiss Magisterial Reformer, Huldrych Zwingli. In his work *On the Providence of God*, he comes perilously close to what today would be called hard determinism: "Since, therefore, nothing is or exists by its own power, nor lives, nor acts, nor understands, nor deliberates, but the present power of the Deity does all these things, how could human will be free? . . . Since, then, even the poets of the heathen recognize that they depend upon the Deity alone, why, alas, do not the

tains. And on this popular view, it is usually thought that central tenets of Reformed theology imply or entail some species of determinism. It is precisely this adherence to determinism that usually leads to misgivings about the viability of Reformed thought concerning human freedom. The conventional objection is that because Reformed theologians believe God decrees all that comes to pass, no robust doctrine of human freedom and responsibility is possible. For if God brings about all things — including, for the sake of completeness, divine permissive willing — then it looks like human freedom and responsibility are attenuated in important respects, if not altogether vitiated.

But it would be theologically significant if it turned out that Reformed theology does not require adherence to a doctrine of divine determinism of either a soft or hard variety. It would be even more significant if it transpired that Reformed theologians could hold to a doctrine of libertarianism whilst remaining firmly within confessional boundaries. One way of adjudicating this discussion is to turn to the Reformed confessions, to see whether they are conceptually porous enough to admit of more than one interpretation on the matter of human freedom. However, we have already seen in the first chapter that Edwards was not really a confessional theologian. Although he subscribed to the confessional standards of New England Congregationalism, and latterly, in his move to Princeton, to the Westminster Confession, his work is not marked by a deep commitment to confessional theology. Rather, he holds in tension a pronounced biblicism on the one hand and a penchant for metaphysical speculation on the other. This is not to deny his deep engagement with the Puritan and Reformed orthodox theology of his forebears. It is merely to point out that what motivated his theology was his engagement with Scripture and his desire to re-describe Reformed theology using the tools of early Enlightenment thought.

Edwards's place in Reformed discussion of human free will has been the subject of recent discussion in light of the van Asselt volume, especially its claims that Reformed theology was aboriginally libertarian, or at least shared important features with libertarian thinking on the nature of human freedom. Richard Muller has argued that Edwards's thought on the issue of free will represented a watershed, significantly reorienting

---

cultivators of true piety rise to the height of seeing that all the activity of all their faculties and powers is from the same source whence the whole universe flows?" *On Providence and Other Essays*, trans. Samuel Macauley Jackson (Durham, NC: The Labyrinth Press, 1983 [1922]), p. 189.

nineteenth-century Reformed theology in the English-speaking world.[5] While the impact on the New England Theology itself was actually more methodological than doctrinal, Edwards's influence on nineteenth-century Presbyterian thinkers was profound — whether Scots such as Thomas Chalmers and William Cunningham or Americans such as Charles Hodge, whose much more confessional Reformed theology was a kind of alternative to the speculative cast of Edwardsian thought.

Another American for whom Edwards was an important sparring partner was the southern Presbyterian, John Girardeau. He is not widely known outside the narrow confines of scholarly discourse on the history of American Reformed theology. Yet he offered an important theological treatment of free will which is a counterpoint to that of Edwards, and which presents a rather different account of the shape of Reformed thinking on this matter.[6] In a way, Girardeau's view is much more obviously informed by theological precedent, both confessional and personal. This is not surprising since Edwards's treatise *Freedom of the Will* is not so much a theological account of free will as a philosophical one, with some theological application. By contrast, Girardeau's treatment approaches the matter from the other direction, from the theological side of the debate, utilizing certain philosophical notions in the service of his theological agenda.

Rather than spending time outlining the different contexts and influences that formed the respective doctrines of free will espoused by these two thinkers, I want to focus on the ways in which their arguments highlight a fault line running through Reformed theology on this topic. Whereas Edwards is the paradigm of unrelenting theological determinism, Girardeau is a representative of what I have elsewhere called *libertarian Calvinism*.[7] This is the view, similar in some respects to that espoused

---

5. See Richard A. Muller, "Jonathan Edwards and the Absence of Free Choice: A Parting of Ways in the Reformed Tradition," *Jonathan Edwards Studies* 1.1 (2011): 3-22.

6. This can be found in John L. Girardeau, *The Will in Its Theological Relations* (Columbia, SC: W. J. Duffie, 1891). All subsequent references to this work are from this edition. For a brief account of Girardeau's views on the will as part of a larger Southern Presbyterian anti-Edwardsianism in nineteenth-century America, see Sean Michael Lucas, "'He Cuts Up Edwardsism by the Roots': Robert Lewis Dabney and the Edwardsian Legacy in the Nineteenth-Century South," in *The Legacy of Jonathan Edwards: American Religion and the Evangelical Tradition*, ed. D. G. Hart, Sean Michael Lucas, and Stephen J. Nichols (Grand Rapids: Baker Academic, 2003), pp. 200-214.

7. See Oliver D. Crisp, *Deviant Calvinism: Broadening Reformed Theology* (Minneapolis: Fortress, 2014). Note that the term "libertarian Calvinism" is my own invention. Girardeau does not use it, though I shall argue that his position implies it, or something very like it.

by van Asselt et al., that Reformed theology is consistent with a version of libertarianism. In this context libertarianism is a thesis about the metaphysics of human free will. It comprises two claims. The first is that determinism (roughly the thesis that everything, every event, every action, every choice, and so forth is determined) is inconsistent with free will. This is often called incompatibilism. The second is that determinism is false. There are varieties of libertarianism just as there are varieties of determinism. But all of them share these two claims in common. Call the conjunction of these two claims *libertarianism simpliciter*. The libertarian is not committed to the view that all human choices must be libertarian ones. But usually, libertarians take the view that only choices that are libertarian in nature are ones for which we can be held morally responsible, because they are the only truly free choices. Hence, in addition to the foregoing, typical libertarian accounts of the metaphysics of human free will will also include a particular understanding of the relationship between human freedom and moral responsibility.

Libertarian Calvinism is not exactly the same as libertarianism *simpliciter* for several reasons. The principal difference is philosophical in nature: libertarian Calvinists must deny that determinism is false and that it is necessarily inconsistent with moral responsibility. They allow what we might call a *hybrid account of moral responsibility*. We can sketch this as follows. There are two sorts of actions for which humans are morally responsible. The first sort of action is consistent with divine determinism. The second is not.

As to the first, all confessionally Reformed theologians are agreed on the basis of biblical texts such as Ephesians 2:8 that salvation is entirely a work of divine grace. No human being can save herself or himself because no human being is in a position to do so. All are in bondage to sin as a consequence of the Fall. So all choices that yield salvation are not choices fallen human beings are capable of making. They require divine grace. Only the action of the Holy Spirit can ensure such choices are made and are effectual. In which case, all human choices that pertain to salvation are not free in the sense set forth in libertarianism *simpliciter*. The libertarian Calvinist, in keeping with other Reformed theologians, must affirm that God brings about human salvation. No mere human can bring about her own salvation. Choices that yield salvation are not choices that are within the purview or the metaphysical reach of fallen human beings. Hence the need for divine grace. (Compare the case of an alcoholic for whom certain choices, such as the choice to relinquish his addiction immediately and without further ado, is one that is not within his purview or reach. If he is so weak-willed that he cannot choose to stop drinking, or even choose to choose to stop drinking, it may require the intervention of external agencies to bring about his rehabilitation. Suppose that is right. Then the case of the weak-willed alcoholic is an analogue, though not a perfect analogue, to the case of salvation and human choice as understood by the Reformed.)

However, this does not necessarily mean fallen human beings that are without salvation have no moral responsibility for being in that condition. Reformed theologians have also traditionally claimed that all human beings after the Fall are morally responsible for failing to avail themselves of the salvation offered by the work of Christ. It might be thought unjust or grossly unfair for God to hold fallen human beings morally responsible for failing to avail themselves of salvation where they are incapable of doing so. For surely "ought" implies "can." If I *ought* to do a thing, then I am morally responsible if I fail in my duty precisely because I *can* do that thing if I so desire. Yet it appears that the Reformed theologian must deny this. (This is a case where moral questions supervene on metaphysical ones.) Historically, a number of different strategies have been brought to bear on this problem. One common response is to argue that a person may be morally responsible for making a particular choice even if there was no alternative open to the person at the moment of choice. If Jones chooses to blaspheme, and Jones's desires are ordered so that he chooses to choose to act in this way (such that his first order and second order desires are working in harmony), then, to borrow a phrase from the contemporary Princeton philosopher Harry Frankfurt, he chooses *wholeheartedly*.[8] He chooses to blaspheme, and he chooses to choose to blaspheme. Even if his choice is determined (by God, say), it is he that makes the choice; God doesn't. He is the agent choosing, and he is responsible for the choice made.

There are other strategies that could be deployed by the Reformed theologian at this point. Given that our concern is to compare and contrast Edwards and Girardeau on this topic, rather than to articulate a compelling case for a Reformed version of theological determinism, we can leave matters there. The libertarian Calvinist can claim that choices that yield salvation are not free in the libertarian *simpliciter* sense of "free." They

---

8. See Harry Frankfurt, *The Importance of What We Care About* (Cambridge: Cambridge University Press, 1988).

do not originate with the human agent in question, but are acts of divine grace. What is more, they are not choices where the human agent could have chosen in favor of salvation because all human beings after the Fall are in bondage to sin. Consequently, all fallen humans are incapable of choosing salvation. Nevertheless, the failure to choose salvation is something for which God can hold us morally responsible.

This brings us to the second sort of action for which humans are morally responsible. Recall that this class of action is not consistent with divine determinism. According to the libertarian Calvinist, the paradigm of libertarian free choice is the primal sin committed by our aboriginal parents. In the case of Adam and Eve's choice for primal sin, and in the case of many mundane choices we now make every day, libertarianism-plus-moral responsibility obtains. So the libertarian Calvinist is committed to something like a hybrid account of moral responsibility. Like the defender of libertarianism *simpliciter* she agrees that determinism is inconsistent with free will. However, unlike many libertarians, she does not think that all choices that are determined are ones for which we cannot be held morally responsible. What is more, the libertarian Calvinist disagrees with the theological determinist in that she allows that many human choices are ones that are free in the libertarian sense of freedom (e.g., the fall of Adam and Eve).

On the face of it, this position looks internally disordered. How can it be that some actions are determined by God, yet we are morally responsible for them, and that other actions are libertarian in nature and we are morally responsible for them as well? Note, the claim is not that those actions that are determined by God and for which we are morally responsible are actions that are free in the libertarian sense. That is, the claim is not that there are libertarian actions for which we are morally responsible and determined actions that are free. The claim is merely that there are some actions that are determined, and for which we are morally responsible, and also that there are some actions that are free in the libertarian sense, for which we are also morally responsible. The key point has to do with moral responsibility. The libertarian Calvinist is willing to allow that some actions that are determined may also be actions for which we are morally responsible, though there are also many actions that are free (and therefore not determined), for which we are also morally responsible. In other words, moral responsibility is consistent with determinism *and* libertarianism. More specifically, moral responsibility is consistent with certain sorts of actions that are determined by God, and also with certain sorts of actions that are not determined by God (or by anything else). Obviously this does not entail the further claim that *all* actions that are determined are ones for which we are morally responsible, or that *all* actions that are not determined are ones for which we are morally responsible. The class of actions for which we are morally responsible is restricted to some actions that are determined as well as some that are not determined. In other words, moral responsibility is a property of certain determinist as well as certain non-determinist (in fact, libertarian) actions.

Naturally, the libertarian Calvinist must be willing in principle to allow that there is some version of libertarianism that is coherent. But there are many versions of libertarianism that are extremely sophisticated and that offer plausible ways of making sense of choices that are both uncaused and yet for which the agent in question is morally responsible. Some Calvinists, like Edwards, who are committed to the strong claim that there are no such coherent accounts of libertarianism, will baulk at this requirement. However, it is important to see in principle that this is not a theological difference but a philosophical one. The sort of libertarianism we have just outlined is in principle entirely consistent with historic confessional Reformed theology, though I shall not argue for that in detail here.[9] Instead, let us turn to the comparison of Edwards's unrelenting theological determinism with the more libertarian-Calvinist views of Girardeau.

The remainder of this chapter falls into three parts. In the first, some of the main issues in Edwards's position on free will are set forth. This is followed by a second section, which considers the views of Girardeau. A final section draws the threads of the argument together, offering some comparison and reflection on lessons to be learned for contemporary Reformed accounts of human freedom.

Jonathan Edwards on Free Will

Edwards's main concern in his treatise *Freedom of the Will* was to show that only a version of compatibilism (the doctrine according to which human free will is compatible with determinism, in this case divine determinism) was theologically viable. As John E. Smith puts it, "Despite the great length and the intricacies of Edwards's argument, his position rests, like a huge

---

9. I have argued this case in *Deviant Calvinism*, chap. 3.

tower, on one foundation: God alone is *the* cause of all and to allow 'secondary causes' is tantamount to denying the reality of God altogether."[10]

The massive and unrelenting argument of *Freedom of the Will* can be boiled down to two broad strategies: to discredit the opposition, and to establish the credentials of Edwards's own position. In the opening section of the treatise Edwards spends a great deal of time parsing what free will is, what a cause is, and whether necessity is consistent with freedom and moral praiseworthiness and blameworthiness. He then sets out a number of related arguments for the conclusion that libertarianism does not have a clear account of what free will is, how a given free action is caused or brought about, or moral responsibility.

Edwards's principal interlocutor in setting forth his account of free will is the English philosopher John Locke. The chapter titled "Of Power" in Locke's *Essay Concerning Human Understanding* was influential, and Edwards interacts with it in his own presentation of the nature of free will.[11] Thus, at the beginning of *Freedom of the Will*, he writes in good Lockean style, "I observe, that the will (without any metaphysical refining) is plainly, that by which the mind chooses anything. The faculty of the will is that faculty or power or principle of mind by which it is capable of choosing: an act of the will is the same as an act of choosing or choice" (YE1: 137).

The fundamental matter for Edwards is choice. The will, on his way of thinking, might properly be said to be "that by which the soul chooses." For "the mind's making its choice . . . is properly the act of the will: the will's determining between the two [alternative courses of action] is a voluntary determining; but that is the same thing as making a choice" (YE1: 137). There is no faculty of the will somehow *distinct* from the agent that wills. Rather, on the Lockean as on the Edwardsian way of thinking, the agent is the one who wills, and the will is just a way of speaking about certain sorts of actions the agent performs. It is a "power or principle of mind by which it is capable of choosing," nothing more. Edwards was not an uncritical Lockean, however. Whereas the English philosopher had reneged on his earlier claim that will and desire are united, Edwards remained convinced that the two cannot be "so entirely distinct, that they can never be properly said to run counter" to one another (YE1: 139). For

---

10. John E. Smith, *Jonathan Edwards: Puritan, Preacher, Philosopher* (London: Geoffrey Chapman, 1992), p. 60.

11. Useful discussion of this can be found in the editorial introduction to YE1; and in James A. Harris, *Of Liberty and Necessity: The Free Will Debate in Eighteenth-Century British Philosophy* (Oxford: Oxford University Press, 2005).

Edwards it is impossible to will something that one does not desire; on the contrary, one wills according to one's strongest desire in any given act of choice. For if the will is a euphemism for a power possessed by a moral agent, then it is not clear (on Edwards's estimation) how one can will what one does not desire; that would be tantamount to the agent choosing what he does not want to choose, which is hardly a free act.

As to what determines the will, Edwards is clear: "it is that motive, which, as it stands in the view of the mind, is the strongest, that determines the will" (YE1: 141). In extrapolating what he means by this he goes on to say "that the will always is as the greatest apparent good, or as what appears most agreeable" (YE1: 144). This is a more appropriate manner of speaking "than to say that the will is determined by the greatest apparent good, or by what seems most agreeable; because an appearing most agreeable or pleasing to the mind, and the mind's preferring and choosing, seem hardly to be properly and perfectly distinct." Nevertheless,

> If strict propriety of speech be insisted on, it may more properly be said, that the voluntary action which is the immediate consequence and fruit of the mind's volition or choice, is determined by that which appears most agreeable, than the preference or choice itself; but that the act of volition itself is always determined by that in or about the mind's view of the object, which causes it to appear most agreeable. (YE1: 144)

The language is that of theological compatibilism: the will is free to the extent that the agent chooses according to the strongest motive or desire, but this is perfectly consistent with determinism. As he says a little later in the treatise, "Let the person come by his volition or choice how he will, yet if he is able, and there is nothing in the way to hinder his pursuing and executing his will, the man is fully and perfectly free, according to the primary and common notion of freedom" (YE1: 164).

We come to the Edwardsian critique of theological libertarianism, i.e., what he calls "Arminianism." There are several components to the "Arminian" account of free will at which he takes aim. These are: (1) the self-determining power of the will in choosing; (2) indifference or equilibrium in the mind immediately prior to any particular volition; and (3) contingence with respect to particular choices, where "contingence" is opposed to "necessity" (YE1: 164-65).

The basic problem with this libertarian account of free will, as far as he is concerned, is that it is "plainly absurd" and requires a "manifest inconsistence" because it presumes that "the will itself determines all the free acts of the will" (YE1: 171). That is, it presumes that the will brings about action independent of any cause, which is just the first constituent of the libertarian account, that is, (1) above. This he quickly turns into a *reductio ad absurdum*. Suppose that the agent chooses her own actions so that "the will determines the will" (YE1: 172). In that case, "if the will determines all its own free acts, then every free act of choice is determined by a preceding act of choice" (YE1: 172), and so on in a causal chain. But this yields a contradiction, says Edwards. For "it supposes an act of will preceding the first act in the whole train, directing and determining the rest; or a free act of the will, before the first free act of the will" (YE1: 172), which is absurd. If it is objected that this is to beg the question, because the libertarian denies that free choices are caused by previous free choices, Edwards has a ready response. He writes, "if that first volition is not determined by any preceding act of the will, then that act is not determined by the will, and so it is not free, in the Arminian notion of freedom, which consists in the will's self-determination" (YE1: 173). This makes no sense, according to Edwards, for "nothing ever comes to pass without a cause" (YE1: 181), unless the thing in question is eternal and self-existent. All that begins to exist has a cause.[12]

What about the indifference of the will? He says this:

> For how ridiculous would it be for anybody to insist, that the soul chooses one thing before another, when at the very same instant it is perfectly indifferent with respect to each! This is the same thing as to say, the soul prefers one thing to another, at the very same time as it has no preference. Choice and preference can no more be in a state of indifference, than motion can be in a state of rest, or than the preponderation of the scale of a balance can be in a state of equilibrium. (YE1: 207)

The very idea that an agent might choose a particular thing from a state of volitional equilibrium, without a preponderating motive, in fact, without any motivation that might constitute a cause of choice whatsoever, made

---

12. Edwards thinks of causes as "any antecedent with which a consequent is so connected, that it truly belongs to the reason why the proposition which affirms that event, is true. . . . And in agreeableness to this, I sometimes use the word 'effect' for the consequence of another thing, which is perhaps rather an occasion than a cause, most properly speaking" (YE1: 181).

no sense to Edwards. He even parodied the whole idea of such choices in his famous example of the beast of Tierra del Fuego (a cypher for libertarian free choice):

> If some learned philosopher, who had been abroad, in giving an account of the curious observations he had made in his travels, should say, he "had been in Tierra del Fuego, and there had seen an animal, which he calls by a certain name, that begat and brought forth itself, and yet had a sire and a dam distinct from itself; that it had an appetite, and was hungry before it had being; that his master, who led him, and governed him at his pleasure, was always governed by him, and driven by him as he pleased; that when he moved, he always took a step before the first step; that he went with his head first, and yet always went tail foremost; and this, though he had neither head nor tail": it would be no impudence at all, to tell such a traveler, though a learned man, that he himself had no notion or idea of such an animal as he gave an account of, and never had, nor ever would have. (YE1: 345-46)

This brings us to the matter of the contingence of the will. Edwards distinguishes between moral and natural necessity, a matter that was to be of considerable importance in the development of the New Divinity and New England Theology that took up his mantle after his death.[13] It was also a distinction that can be found in earlier French Reformed theology, associated with the Saumur Academy that gave rise to Amyraldism (although Edwards betrays no knowledge of this). In his hands the distinction is a way of preserving the fact that human freedom is consistent with divine determinism, whilst rebutting the claim that a choice is contingent in the libertarian sense of being an action that, up until the moment of choice, may or may not obtain, depending on the course of action the agent decides upon.[14]

---

13. For a discussion of the influence of Edwards's doctrine of free will in subsequent American theology, see Allen C. Guelzo, *Edwards on the Will: A Century of American Theological Debate*, Jonathan Edwards Classic Studies Series (Eugene, OR: Wipf and Stock, 2008 [1989]).

14. It is worth pointing out that this distinction can also be found in the work of the Reformed orthodox divine, Francis Turretin, who may be the source for Edwards's use of it. See Turretin, *Institutes of Elenctic Theology*, vol. 1, ed. James T. Dennison Jr., trans. George Musgrave Giger (Phillipsburg: Presbyterian and Reformed, 1992), 10.2.7, p. 663. I am grateful to Paul Helm for directing me to this reference.

There are different sorts of necessity, on the Edwardsian way of thinking. But a moral necessity may be just as inviolable as a physical or nomological necessity. What is more, such necessity is entirely in accordance with moral praise and blame. Taking up this anticipated objection to his distinction, Edwards outlines two cases of individuals whose circumstances illustrate the two sorts of necessity he has in mind. In the first case he conceives of a man "who has offended his prince, and is cast into prison":

> after he has lain there a while, the king comes to him, calls him to come forth to him; and tells him that if he will do so, and will fall down before him, and humbly beg his pardon, he shall be forgiven, and set at liberty, and also be greatly enriched, and advanced to honor: the prisoner heartily repents of the folly and wickedness of his offense against his prince, is thoroughly disposed to abase himself, and accept of the king's offer; but is confined by strong walls, with gates of brass, and bars of iron. (YE1: 362)

This illustrates what he means by a natural inability that depends on a physical or natural necessity. There is a natural impediment that prevents the prisoner from agreeing to the king's will: he is shut up in prison. For this reason it is physically impossible for him to accede to the monarch's wishes. However, this is to be distinguished from a moral necessity. Returning to the prison thought experiment, Edwards this time conceives of a haughty, rebellious subject who is cast into jail for his treachery. He writes:

> At length the compassionate prince comes to the prison, orders his chains to be knocked off, and his prison doors to be set wide open; calls to him, and tells him, if he will come forth to him, and fall down before him, acknowledge that he has treated him unworthily, and ask his forgiveness; he shall be forgiven, set at liberty, and set in a place of great dignity and profit in his court. But he is so stout and stomachful, and full of haughty malignity, that he can't be willing to accept the offer: his rooted strong pride and malice have perfect power over him, and as it were bind him, by binding his heart: the opposition of his heart has the mastery over him, having an influence on his mind far superior to the king's grace and condescension, and to all his kind offers and promises. (YE1: 362-63)

This illustrates a moral inability to bring about an action that is rooted in a kind of moral necessity. Although there is no physical impediment preventing the prisoner from granting the prince's wish, yet, because of his traitorous and corrupt disposition, he is quite incapable of acting accordingly — indeed, and for the purposes of judging liberty and necessity in this matter, as incapable of acceding to the prince's wishes as if he were physically impeded from doing so. It is important to see that on Edwards's way of thinking, such an individual is blameworthy for acting in this manner, just as the person who is disposed to do the good is praiseworthy for doing so. We don't suppose that a person whose character is so formed that she cannot fail to act graciously towards others is *less* praiseworthy for her actions just because her character prevents her from choosing to do something else that is morally inferior. Rather, we think such persons praiseworthy because they have formed such a character over time. So, according to Edwards, where a moral inability to do a thing exists, so that a person is incapable of performing some action (as with the haughty, traitorous prisoner), the fact that the agent in question is incapable of acting otherwise does not necessarily exculpate the agent. Someone that is morally unable to do an action may nevertheless be blameworthy for failing to do the action — provided that there is no natural inability impeding it.

These arguments are not without problems, and I have attempted some criticism of them elsewhere.[15] For present purposes, what we need to see is that Edwards has a particular strategy for undermining the libertarian understanding of free will and establishing that determinism of the compatibilist variety is entirely consistent with human freedom (understood in terms of choosing what one desires), and moral attitudes of praise and blame. Even if we do not think he demonstrates beyond a shadow of doubt that all forms of theological libertarianism are incoherent, his arguments were extremely influential on subsequent Reformed thinking, and on the shape of theological discussion about human free will in the century after his death.[16] We might say that Edwards's argument established the edifice of theological determinism that quickly became identified with Reformed theology, even though it actually represented an

---

15. See Crisp, *Jonathan Edwards and the Metaphysics of Sin* (Aldershot: Ashgate, 2005).
16. As Guelzo's study amply demonstrates. See *Edwards on the Will*. Muller's article reinforces this picture with other evidence. See Muller, "Jonathan Edwards and the Absence of Free Choice."

important departure from some earlier Reformed thinking on the matter, as we shall see when examining Girardeau's account.

John Girardeau on Free Will

At the very beginning of his study, *The Will in Its Theological Relations*, Girardeau stakes out his own position against that of Edwards. He writes that the publication of Edwards's treatise on free will in the eighteenth century "was attended by singular and apparently contradictory results."[17] On the one hand, there were those who were skeptical about the theological determinism for which it argued, and who used it to fortify their own opposition. On the other hand, there were Reformed theologians in both the United States and Great Britain that "absorbed from it a powerful influence," leading to the incorporation of "its principle of Determinism as a component element of its structure" in order to "vindicate the sovereignty of God and the dependence of man."[18] Warming to his theme, Girardeau goes on, "it is still a matter of serious inquiry whether there were not tendencies in his system legitimately leading to an unhappy result, and whether the Calvinistic theology has not injured itself and crippled its rightful influence, to the extent of their appropriation." In short, he is persuaded that the Edwardsian doctrine of theological determinism is "radically defective," such that he "cannot but regret its continued prevalence, even in a modified form."[19]

According to Girardeau, the will is "precisely the power through which the freedom of the man expresses itself. To affirm or deny the freedom of the will is the same thing as to affirm or deny the freedom of the man."[20] He thinks of the will as one of several intellectual faculties that the person possesses.[21] This means that willing a particular thing is really a matter of the

---

17. Girardeau, *The Will in Its Theological Relations*, p. 18. Hereinafter, cited as TWTR, followed by page reference.

18. TWTR, pp. 18-19. This claim is also argued for by Richard Muller in "Jonathan Edwards and the Absence of Free Choice."

19. TWTR, p. 19.

20. John L. Girardeau, *Calvinism and Evangelical Arminianism* (Harrisburg, PA: Sprinkle Publications, 1984 [1890]), p. 397. Hereinafter, cited as CEA, followed by page reference.

21. He distributes human mental powers into (1) intellect or understanding, (2) the feelings, including desire; (3) the will; and (4) conscience or the moral faculty (TWTR, p. 39).

person engaging the relevant faculty. Hence the rather semi-detached language about the will as the power *through which* the freedom of the person is expressed. The "elements of the Will," as he puts it, include (1) the power to choose in virtue of possessing causal efficiency; (2) choice, which obtains in a given act of will in keeping with the other human mental powers; (3) conation, or a "chosen nisus to action"; and (4) the determinate choice of action, whether for one thing or another. He has no separate account of volition, which is assimilated to willing.[22] It should be clear from this that, in common with many other nineteenth-century southern Presbyterian theologians, he owes a debt to the Scottish commonsense tradition.[23]

Girardeau distinguishes between what he calls *freedom of deliberate election* and *freedom of spontaneity*. "The freedom of deliberate election," he says, "is the freedom of the will to determine itself to either of two opposing alternatives — the power of otherwise determining, and is inconsistent with causal necessity."[24] Such freedom has built into it a principle of alternate possibilities. By contrast, freedom of spontaneity is "the freedom of the will to do as the man pleases, to pursue his inclinations in any one, definite direction, and is consistent with necessity."[25] This view does not include a principle of alternate possibilities. Consequently, it is commensurate with determinism. Girardeau resists the assimilation of freedom of deliberate election to the notion of the liberty of indifference (a common way of conceiving a compatibilist-friendly notion of free will in early modern philosophy), because he denies that choices are made in a state of moral equilibrium, or without motive. The freedom of deliberate election has to do with the freedom of the soul to choose between alternatives, nothing more. It is freedom from causal necessity in making a free and morally responsible choice.[26]

---

22. TWTR, pp. 43-44.

23. This is evident in Girardeau's *Philosophical Questions*.

24. TWTR, p. 401. Compare what he says elsewhere in CEA: the freedom of deliberate action is "between opposing alternatives, of going in either of two directions, the freedom, as it is sometimes denominated, of otherwise determining" (pp. 397-98).

25. TWTR, p. 401. In CEA he speaks of freedom of spontaneity as "the freedom of a fixed and determined spontaneity" (p. 398), and complains (in the same passage) that freedom should really only be applied to the freedom of deliberate action, whereas freedom of spontaneity should be denominated merely "spontaneity." The implication is that only the former properly applies to freedom of the will. This is not an insignificant concession coming from a Reformed theologian.

26. TWTR, pp. 45-46; 132-33. No doubt the Edwardsian would want to know what sort of choice is in view if the agent chooses between alternatives without being in a state of

Girardeau avers that the first human pair had the freedom of deliberate election in their original state of innocence. This, he maintains, the Church has universally believed.[27] Unsurprisingly, therefore, it is a view reflected in the confessions of the Reformed churches. He remarks somewhat dryly, "The Calvinistic Confessions, which surely ought to be accepted as exponents of Calvinism, affirm that man before the Fall was possessed of the freedom of deliberate election between the alternatives of sin and holiness; and they also teach that God decreed to permit — they do not assert that he efficiently decreed — the first sin."[28] We shall return to the matter of the theological authority for his position presently.

After the Fall, a distinction can be made between what he calls natural and spiritual ability. (Here he offers a "correction" to the Edwardsian distinction between natural and moral ability, which we have already encountered.) According to postlapsarian natural ability, fallen humans continue to enjoy freedom of spontaneity. "It is obvious that the liberty of spontaneity was not lost" at the Fall. However, the liberty of contrary choice involved in the freedom of deliberate election was lost as a consequence of the Fall.[29] "In man's fallen and unregenerate state, the will has no self-determining power in relation to the contrasts between holiness and sin. The free decision for sin destroyed man's holy spontaneity, and originated, in its place, a sinful spontaneity."[30] That is, the "freedom of deliberate election between the alternatives of sinfulness and holiness no longer exists." The will "in the spiritual sphere, is under *bondage to sin*."[31]

---

moral equilibrium and without there being a necessary and sufficient cause of the action in question. Although Girardeau does not spell out what he means here, his position seems very similar to some contemporary agent-causal accounts of human free will. See, e.g., Timothy O'Connor, *Persons and Causes: The Metaphysics of Free Will* (New York: Oxford University Press, 2000), who makes an explicit connection between his own view and that of the Scottish commonsense tradition to which Girardeau was indebted.

27. CEA, p. 398.
28. CEA, p. 400. Compare TWTR, where he makes this case at greater length. See also *Deviant Calvinism*, chap. 3, where I set out the case from the Reformed confessions.
29. TWTR, pp. 134-35.
30. TWTR, p. 403.
31. TWTR, p. 403, emphasis in original. He goes on to say, "But while, in the spiritual sphere, the will of man in his unregenerate condition has by its own fatal act lost all self-determining power, it still possesses that power in the merely natural sphere" (p. 404). Interestingly, this is substantially the view of Martin Luther in his *The Bondage of the Will*, trans. J. I. Packer and O. R. Johnston (London: James Clarke, 1957; reissued by Baker Academic in 2012), although Girardeau does not discuss Luther's position in any detail.

It is unfortunate that Girardeau muddies the waters by speaking of a holy spontaneity and a sinful spontaneity, given his initial distinction between freedom of deliberate election and freedom of spontaneity. What he seems to mean is this. Prior to the Fall the moral orientation of human beings was such that if they acted in accordance with their natural moral orientation, they would remain sinless. Nevertheless, it was possible for such prelapsarian humans to act against this moral orientation, in sinning. As he puts it earlier in his study, unfallen Adam was "able to stand, liable to fall."[32] This is because the original human pair enjoyed both a sinless moral orientation and the ability act contrary to that moral orientation — Girardeau's freedom of deliberate election. "The specific difference of such a case is the possession of the power of contrary choice — of the will's power to determine itself *in utramque partem*."[33]

However, after the Fall, this was no longer the case. The moral orientation of humanity had been altered by the primal sin of the first human pair so that fallen human beings act on the basis of a vitiated moral condition, "under bondage to sin," as Girardeau puts it. Fallen human beings still have a natural ability to make all sorts of choices consistent with the freedom of deliberate election. What they lack is such freedom with respect to choices pertaining to their salvation; it is the ability to make appropriate *spiritual choices* that has been impaired in fallen human beings. This is a consequence of corrupting the moral orientation with which the first human pair were endowed. He writes, "But while, in the spiritual sphere, the will of man in his unregenerate condition has by its own fatal act lost all self-determining power, it still possesses that power in the merely natural sphere."[34] The following are indicative examples Girardeau offers by way of illustrating this important point. Fallen human beings may exercise freedom of deliberate election in choosing between choices tainted by sin: in external and civil matters (that is, matters that are mundane, having no personal soteriological significance); with respect to "moral culture" (e.g., refraining from blaspheming); and with respect to certain sorts of actions that "tend towards religion," without making a permanent soteriological change in the sinner, e.g., the arguments of natural theology, acknowledging the divine origin of Scripture, attending to the ordinances of the Church, and so forth.[35] It is

---

32. TWTR, p. 83.
33. TWTR, p. 83.
34. TWTR, p. 404.
35. TWTR, pp. 404-5.

even in the power of a fallen human being to "call on God to show him the truth, to reveal to him his real spiritual condition, to extend to him mercy, and to deliver him from bondage to sin."[36]

At times Girardeau's views are not as pellucid as one might like. For instance, in *Calvinism and Evangelical Arminianism* he says that the fallen human "sins freely, in the sense of spontaneity; in sinning he is urged by no compulsory force exerted by a divine influence either upon him or through him, but follows the bent of his own inclination — in a word, does as he pleases. He is not, however, free to be holy or to do holy acts."[37] So when speaking of free will with respect to fallen human beings in an unregenerate condition, Girardeau thinks that what is in view is merely "the freedom which is implied by a fixed spontaneity in accordance with which he pleases to sin. Only in that sense is he a free agent, as to spiritual things."[38]

On a cursory reading, this suggests that he thinks of human freedom in two distinct phases. The first, unfallen phase, in which human beings have libertarian freedom including a principle of alternate possibilities; and the second, fallen phase, in which human beings are enslaved to sin and incapable of acting in a holy manner. The unwary reader might be led by such reasoning into thinking that Girardeau is affirming something like compatibilism with respect to the free and morally responsible decisions of *fallen* humanity. I am free to continue to make sinful choices, but given that I am bound to sin (being in bondage to sin through original sin), this is consistent with my being determined to act as I do because of my sinful disposition.

However, a more careful analysis of what he writes in this passage of *Calvinism and Evangelical Arminianism* shows that what he says here, though less carefully articulated than in *The Will in Its Theological Relations*, is nevertheless consistent with it. For what he means by the "fixed spontaneity" in accordance with which fallen human beings are pleased to sin is precisely a moral orientation that places beyond the reach of fallen human beings a life of uninterrupted holiness. However, a fallen human being may still make all sorts of mundane choices that include alternate possibilities whilst possessing a sinful disposition. Girardeau's account stipulates that fallen human beings do act from a certain moral

36. TWTR, p. 405.
37. CEA, p. 401.
38. CEA, p. 401.

constraint (what he calls, somewhat unhelpfully, a "moral necessity") as a consequence of the change of moral orientation consequent upon the primal sin of the first human pair. If we are now in bondage to sin, then there is a factor that restricts the choices available to me, because I am no longer free to act sinlessly, from an untainted moral orientation.

To illustrate, consider the case of the fictional high-functioning consulting detective and cocaine addict, Sherlock Holmes. He makes all sorts of mundane choices on a daily basis for many of which he is morally responsible, including the solving of many crimes that baffle conventional law enforcement agencies. Of course, his moral purview is tainted, as it were, by the fact that he is a cocaine user. This puts certain sorts of moral choices beyond his reach. For instance, he is unable to decide forthwith and without any deleterious effects to give up his addiction to the drug. Even if he decides he must rid himself of his physical and psychological dependence on it, he cannot do so immediately. Or at least, he cannot rid himself of his addiction immediately, even if he resolves to begin the long process of rehabilitation forthwith. Nevertheless, we would not think that the mundane choices he makes that are within the ambit of what he is capable of doing immediately are less free because he has an addiction to cocaine. His decision to have tea rather than coffee or to solve a crime rather than sitting sawing at his violin in his rooms in Baker Street are evidence of this.

From this I conclude that Holmes's cocaine addiction is not immaterial to the question of the scope of his free choices. Yet, in any given circumstance, if he has significant moral freedom (i.e., freedom of deliberate election) to choose one thing or another, he has free will in the relevant sense. Girardeau's contribution, then, is to show that libertarian free choices are consistent with a sinful moral orientation (i.e., bondage to sin), although being in bondage to sin means that a certain class of actions, those pertaining to the salvation of the individual concerned, are no longer within metaphysical reach. His is what we might call a chastened libertarianism, or a libertarianism within certain constraints — in this case, the constraints of a hybrid account of moral responsibility. This is not all that strange, given that all careful accounts of libertarianism allow for certain constraints, including things like addiction and moral failure.

As was mentioned earlier, Girardeau also maintains that his view, which admits of a species of libertarianism, is consistent with the Reformed faith, unlike Edwardsianism. This strand of his reasoning has several parts. Negatively, it includes his attack upon the moral consequences of Edwardsian determinism. Positively, it involves an appeal to various authorities as theological precedent for (something very like) his own view. This latter includes detailed exposition of the view of John Calvin as well as reference to the Reformed confessions. Let us take each aspect in turn, beginning with the negative.

According to Girardeau, the question between himself and Edwards is this: "Did [God], in the instance of the first sin, causally determine the will of Adam?" To which he responds:

> There are but two alternatives: either God efficiently determined Adam's will in the first sin, or he did not. There is no middle ground. If he did, the sin was unavoidable, and could not have been attended with just liability to punishment. If he did not, as no other being could have efficiently determined Adam's agency, the sin was avoidable. If avoidable, there was no causal necessity which operated to its production. For, if a thing is causally necessary, it is not avoidable. To suppose that it is, is self-contradictory.[39]

Matters are made worse when we turn to the covenant of works, that covenant between God and human beings that many historic Reformed theologians thought provided the moral framework for the original human pair in the primordial garden. Suppose that there was such a covenant, the condition of which was continued obedience to the divine moral law (symbolized in the command not to eat of the tree of the knowledge of good and evil). Failure to meet this condition would lead to punishment. Some Reformed theologians (including Girardeau) also speculated that had Adam (and Eve) remained upright, resisting the temptation of the serpent, they would have been "confirmed" in their moral orientation, so that they were incapable of sinning thereafter, like the saints in heaven and the elect angels. This is usually referred to as Adam's *probation*. However, if the Edwardsians are right then the covenant of works becomes a "mockery." For "it stipulated conditions which could not be fulfilled, and tendered rewards that could not be secured."[40] That is, if Adam's sin was somehow divinely determined, then holding out the prospect of moral "confirmation" upon fulfillment of the period of probation that is part-and-parcel of a putative covenant of works, is

---

39. TWTR, p. 84.
40. TWTR, p. 85.

insincere. Adam (and Eve) could not fulfill the condition of the covenant because they were determined to act as they did by God "efficiently" bringing about that end.

We turn to Girardeau's positive appeal to theological authority in his effort to trump Edwardsianism on the will. Two in particular draw our attention. These are his appeal to Calvin and his appeal to the Reformed confessions. Calvin's views do not have the status of the confessions as subordinate standards within particular Reformed communions. Nevertheless, his standing as arguably the preeminent Reformed theologian of the sixteenth century meant that appealing to his views, and showing that his position deviated substantially from that of Edwards, was a way of calling into question the bona fides of Edwardsianism as a species of Reformed theology. As Sean Lucas writes, "By claiming Calvin's authority for his position, Girardeau was doing more than simply balancing one cultural authority with another. He was signalling Edwards' deviation from the Reformed tradition through doctrinal novelty."[41]

He cites from a range of Calvin's works, including commentaries, the *Bondage and Liberation of the Will*, and the *Institutes of the Christian Religion*. For instance, in *Institutes* 2.3.10, Calvin seems to endorse the idea that in his unfallen state Adam had freedom, including a principle of alternate possibilities: "We admit that man's condition while he still remained upright was such that he could incline to either side."[42] Earlier in *Institutes* 1.15.8, Calvin says something similar:

> In this integrity man by free will had the power, if he so willed, to attain eternal life. . . . Therefore Adam could have stood if he wished, seeing that he fell solely by his own will. But it was because his will was capable of being bent to one side or the other, and was not given to the constancy to persevere, that he fell so easily. Yet his choice of good and evil was free, and not that alone, but the highest rectitude was in his mind and will, and all the organic parts were rightly composed to obedience, until in destroying himself he corrupted his own blessings.[43]

---

41. Lucas, "'He Cuts Up Edwardsism by the Roots,'" p. 206.

42. From John Calvin, *Institutes of the Christian Religion*, vol. 1, ed. John T. McNeill, trans. Ford Lewis Battles (Philadelphia: Westminster Press, 1960 [1559]), p. 303. All references are to this edition. Compare TWTR, p. 151, where Girardeau cites the same passage.

43. *Institutes*, p. 195. Compare TWTR, pp. 150-51. Space prevents greater appeal to the writings of Calvin. Interested readers may consult TWTR for Girardeau's argument, which includes gobbets from the whole range of Calvin's writings.

According to Girardeau, these passages (and others like them, for he cites Calvin copiously and at length) "clearly prove that Calvin affirmed for man in innocence the power of contrary choice — the liberty of inclining to either of opposing alternatives. He plainly . . . declares that, although Adam freely elected to sin, he might have done otherwise — he might have elected to stand."[44] Support for Girardeau's interpretation of Calvin's views can be found in recent philosophical-theological literature on the subject. Paul Helm, who regards Calvin as, in a qualified sense, a theological compatibilist, *not* a theological libertarian, nevertheless addresses himself to the question of whether Calvin thinks humans have free will in the following way. "Yes, he [Calvin] believes that we have on appropriate occasions the power to choose between alternatives in a way which is uncoerced. No, he does not believe that we naturally possess free will in the sense of the power to choose what is good, at present; but yes, unfallen man had free will in that sense."[45] But this, if it is right, provides some measured support for Girardeau's claim to be defending a Calvinian doctrine of the will — at least in terms of how Girardeau understands the exercise of free will in the primal sin of Adam and Eve. Moreover, if this is right, then Edwards's position is different from that of Calvin in an important respect, for Calvin allows for what looks very like libertarian free will in at least the paradigm case of primal sin. Edwards emphatically denies this.

What of the Reformed confessions? These Girardeau treats more quickly. But he provides gobbets from the Gallic and Scots Confessions, the Canons of the Synod of Dort, the Second Helvetic Confession, the For-

---

44. TWTR, p. 152, cf. p. 158.
45. Paul Helm, *John Calvin's Ideas* (Oxford: Oxford University Press, 2005), p. 161. In the sequel to that volume, Helm writes, "Calvin's doctrine of the bondage of the will . . . has no necessary connection with the issue of the metaphysics of agency." He goes on to say, "When Calvin and Luther deny free will, therefore, they chiefly have in mind not the metaphysical issues being discussed in this chapter, but a spiritual disposition stemming from sin which is, logically speaking, neutral on the question of determinism and libertarianism." Paul Helm, *Calvin at the Centre* (Oxford: Oxford University Press, 2010), pp. 228-29. If that is right, then Girardeau has gone beyond what Calvin avers, making the connection between the theology and a particular metaphysical account of free will that Calvin does not. However, this claim would need to be argued for, and there is not the space to do that here. The literature on the topic of Calvin's views on free will is (understandably) considerable. A useful recent resource on the wider debate about Calvin and the Reformation understanding of the bondage of the will can be found in Kivin S. K. Choy, "Calvin's Defense and Reformulation of Luther's Early Reformation Doctrine of the Bondage of the Will" (PhD dissertation, Calvin Theological Seminary, 2010).

mula Consensus Helvetica, and the Westminster Confession. In each case there appears to be good *prima facie* evidence for the view that these confessions, like Calvin, allow for libertarianism with respect to the primal sin of our first human parents. Representative citations from the Westminster Confession may serve to indicate the sort of evidence he has in mind. The fourth chapter, on creation, says the following:

> II. After God had made all other creatures, He created man, male and female, with reasonable and immortal souls, endued with knowledge, righteousness, and true holiness, after His own image; having the law of God written in their hearts, and power to fulfil it; and yet under a possibility of transgressing, being left to the liberty of their own will, which was subject unto change.

In the ninth chapter, on free will, we read this:

> II. Man, in his state of innocency, had freedom, and power to will and to do that which was good and well pleasing to God; but yet, mutably, so that he might fall from it.
> III. Man, by his fall into a state of sin, has wholly lost all ability of will to any spiritual good accompanying salvation: so as, a natural man, being altogether averse from that good, and dead in sin, is not able, by his own strength, to convert himself, or to prepare himself thereunto.

Finally, in the nineteenth chapter, on the Law of God we are told:

> I. God gave to Adam a law, as a covenant of works, by which He bound him and all his posterity, to personal, entire, exact, and perpetual obedience, promised life upon the fulfilling, and threatened death upon the breach of it, and endued him with power and ability to keep it.

Manifestly, these statements are consistent with Girardeau's claims about prelapsarian human free will. What is more, and importantly for our purposes, it appears that these statements are *not* consistent with the Edwardsian position — which is more than a little odd, given the fact that Edwards is on record as saying that he had no qualms about signing the Westminster Confession.[46] "To sum up the matter," says Girardeau, "the

---

46. In a letter to his Scottish correspondent, John Erskine, in 1750, Edwards writes:

standards say that Adam in innocence had the power of otherwise determining than he did; the Determinist says that he had not that power. The two doctrines are contradictory and mutually exclusive."[47]

Let us take stock: Girardeau's account of human freedom is able to accommodate the constituents of libertarian free will outlined in the first section of this chapter. His account of freedom of deliberate election allows that choices falling under this description originate with the agent; are actions for which the human agent is morally responsible; are actions that are not determined by any agents or factors other than the human agent in question; are actions that are not determined by any factors "internal" to the psychology or character of the agent himself or herself at the moment of choice; are actions that the agent could refrain from; and, are actions which include some alternative state of affairs that the agent could have chosen to bring about at the moment of choice, but did not.

Edwards versus Girardeau

Edwards is clear that libertarian free will is no free will at all. On his reckoning, the very idea of libertarian choice as something that is self-determined, indifferent, and contingent is downright incoherent. As far as Edwards is concerned, an uncaused choice is not a free choice at all but a random, inexplicable event. Clearly such events are not ones for which a person can be morally responsible. So libertarianism actually eviscerates moral responsibility by removing causation from the notion of a truly *free* choice. By contrast, compatibilism makes sense of moral responsibility because it conjoins cause and desire. "The will is as the greatest apparent good," says Edwards. Where action is caused by the strongest motive and desire, a person acts freely. This does not preclude some sort of conditional analysis of free action because, on Edwards's account, an agent would have brought about a different state of affairs if he desired it and chosen accordingly. Whether he could have brought about the alternative is not to the point, for Edwards.

By contrast, Giraradeau provides an account of human moral re-

---

"You are pleased, dear Sir, very kindly to ask me whether I could sign the Westminster Confession of Faith, and submit to the Presbyterian form of church government. . . . As to my subscribing to the substance of the Westminster Confession, there would be no difficulty" (YE16: 355).

47. TWTR, p. 177.

sponsibility that requires a chastened, circumscribed libertarianism — although he offers nothing like the careful account of notions like cause, choice, volition, and so forth that inform Edwards's treatise. Nevertheless, on his way of thinking, it is Edwards that is driving moral responsibility out of the world, and hanging it around the neck of the deity. By insisting on theological determinism all the way down, so to speak, Girardeau thinks Edwards has saddled himself with an insurmountable problem of evil. For if God ordains all things, including wickedness, then there is no hope of exculpating God. It is not clear, however, why theological determinism in and of itself makes God the author of evil. There is a large historic as well as contemporary literature on this, and it is not at all obvious that Girardeau's argument defeats all attempts to show that God may determine all things without being morally responsible for evil. (Much turns on whether God can be responsible for bringing about evil without moral responsibility for bringing about evil, as well as on whether decreeing evil is itself an evil.) Nonetheless, there are peculiarities in Edwards's brand of theological compatibilism that do raise serious concerns with his doctrine as it stands. These I have written about in detail elsewhere.[48] Although Girardeau does not set out these particular problems for Edwards, they are serious and (I believe) fatal for his position.

This episode in the larger, age-old debate about human freedom and divine ordination actually raises an issue that has only recently begun to be reassessed in light of the historical scholarship of people like Willem van Asselt, Antonie Vos, and Richard Muller. This has to do with whether confessional Reformed theology is somehow committed to a particular view (or family of views) on the metaphysics of free will. Often Edwards is held up as an important figure in the development of Reformed views in this area. He is, as Paul Helm has recently pointed out, the first Reformed thinker to give us a systematic philosophical account of free will.[49]

---

48. See Crisp, *Jonathan Edwards and the Metaphysics of Sin*, and the following chapter in this volume. Two excellent treatments of Edwards's doctrine in the recent philosophical literature can also be found in William J. Wainwright, "Original Sin," in *Philosophy and the Christian Faith*, ed. Thomas V. Morris (Notre Dame: University of Notre Dame Press, 1988), pp. 31-60; and Michael C. Rea, "The Metaphysics of Original Sin," in *Persons, Divine and Human*, ed. Dean Zimmerman and Peter van Inwagen (Oxford: Oxford University Press, 2007), pp. 319-56.

49. Paul Helm, "Jonathan Edwards and the Parting of the Ways?" in *Jonathan Edwards Studies* 4.1 (2014): 21-41, located at: http://jestudies.yale.edu/index.php/journal/article/view/141/98.

However, if Girardeau is right, then Edwards's argument is not so much a philosophical restatement of what the Reformed had always believed but never clearly articulated, as it is a departure from the theological views countenanced by an older generation of Reformed thinkers. The notion of the bondage of the will, which is the hallmark of both Calvin and Luther in their excoriations of "free will," may turn out to be consistent with a chastened, circumscribed notion of theological libertarianism such as is found in what I have called libertarian Calvinism. For, on Girardeau's reckoning, the Reformed (*pace* Edwards) have always believed the following tenets about human freedom:

1. Adam and Eve were created with libertarian free will, which they misused in the act of primal sin.
2. After the Fall, human beings are in bondage to sin as a consequence of inheriting original sin from Adam and Eve.
3. This bondage to sin places certain choices beyond the reach of fallen human beings. In particular, it places beyond reach any choices that might yield salvation from sin.
4. This means that fallen human beings no longer have libertarian freedom to serve and love God without the logically prior interposition of divine grace.
5. Nevertheless, fallen human beings still have libertarian freedom with regard to all sorts of mundane choices.

If Girardeau is right, then it is not the libertarian Calvinist whose views are out of step with the tradition, but the Edwardsian. The upshot of this is that Edwards, who believed himself to be defending the Reformed tradition, turns out to be the advocate of a rather different understanding of human freedom than that of his theological forebears, one that is, if Girardeau and his modern epigones are correct, theologically novel.

CHAPTER 6

Edwards on Original Sin: Another Look

In several previous studies, I have attempted to give an exposition and critique of the central components of Jonathan Edwards's doctrine of original sin.[1] His treatise on the subject, *The Great Christian Doctrine of Original Sin Defended*, was published in the year of his death, 1758. It was the last major work he saw to the press before his demise in Princeton. His work on this topic is, to my mind, one of the few significant theological restatements of this doctrine in the early modern period, and perhaps one of a handful of post-Augustinian accounts that can claim to have made a real contribution to our understanding of the doctrine. This is due in large measure to what we might call its *philosophical dimension*, an aspect of the doctrine that has been the subject of some contemporary philosophical and theological interest.[2] Other aspects of his treatise are also worthy of study, e.g., on

---

1. See Oliver D. Crisp, *Jonathan Edwards and the Metaphysics of Sin* (Aldershot: Ashgate, 2005); and "Jonathan Edwards and the Imputation of Sin," in *Retrieving Doctrine: Essays in Reformed Theology* (Downers Grove, IL: IVP Academic, 2011). The latter was originally published in the *Scottish Journal of Theology*.

2. Examples of recent philosophical interest in Edwards's doctrine of sin (in order of publication) include Roderick Chisholm, *Person and Object* (London: George Allen and Unwin, 1976), appendix B; Sang Hyun Lee, *The Philosophical Theology of Jonathan Edwards* (Princeton: Princeton University Press, 1988); William J. Wainwright, "Original Sin," in *Philosophy and the Christian Faith*, ed. Thomas V. Morris (Notre Dame: Notre Dame University Press, 1988), pp. 31-60; Mark Heller, *The Ontology of Physical Objects: Four-Dimensional Hunks of Matter* (Cambridge: Cambridge University Press, 1990), pp. 20-22; Stephen H. Daniel, *The Philosophy of Jonathan Edwards: A Study in Divine Semiotics* (Bloomington: University of Indiana Press, 1994); Paul Helm, "Jonathan Edwards on Original Sin," in *Faith and Understanding* (Edinburgh: Edinburgh University Press, 1997),

the question of the authorship of sin, or on the matter of how it is that a morally upright individual like the traditional Adam can sin. However, the pre-critical assumptions made about the biblical material he uses, especially the primeval prologue of Genesis 1–3, make some parts of his work seem rather antique — very much the product of his time.

In this chapter, I want to revisit one particular aspect of this philosophical dimension of Edwards's doctrine of original sin, re-examining what he has to say about the transmission of original sin to ascertain whether he really is committed to the sort of strange and metaphysically exotic view that previous work (including my own) has attributed to him. To do this, we will need to have an idea of what his doctrine entails. Once this is clear, we will be able to probe the logic of his view, seeing whether it makes sense and what some of its major costs and shortcomings may be. In closing, I will offer some remarks about the enduring significance of Edwards's work in this area.

Edwards on Original Sin

One of the most important theological innovations Jonathan Edwards introduced into Reformed theology stems from his defense of the doctrine of original sin. He supported what we might call a full-orbed doctrine, of the sort common in much classical Protestant thought and that has its roots deep in the theology of St. Augustine of Hippo. He believed that there was an original pair from whom all subsequent human beings are descended. He thought that this human pair, created in a state of original righteousness, nevertheless fell into sin, committing the first or primal sin, which somehow introduced a tendency or disposition to sin into the human race thereafter. This disposition stems from a morally disordered nature, which fallen Adam transmitted to his progeny. Many Christian theologians would have little difficulty in allowing that original sin includes such a moral disordering of human nature, though its transmission is a cause of some disagreement (a matter to which we shall return presently). However, Ed-

---

pp. 152-76; Helm, "A Forensic Dilemma: John Locke and Jonathan Edwards on Personal Identity," in *Jonathan Edwards: Philosophical Theologian*, ed. Paul Helm and Oliver D. Crisp (Aldershot: Ashgate, 2003), pp. 45-60; Jasper Reid, "The Metaphysics of Jonathan Edwards and David Hume," *Hume Studies* 32.1 (2006): 52-82; and Michael C. Rea, "The Metaphysics of Original Sin," in *Persons: Divine and Human*, ed. Peter van Inwagen and Dean Zimmerman (Oxford: Oxford University Press, 2007), pp. 319-56.

wards also held to the Augustinian notion that not only the disposition to sin but the guilt associated with the commission of the primal sin of the first human pair is transmitted to all subsequent human beings, barring Christ. Thus, original sin includes original guilt as well as the moral vitiation consequent upon the primal sin, and both are passed on from Adam to us. Indeed, Edwards thinks that human beings are guilty of what he calls a *double guilt* (YE3: 390). We are born with the original guilt of Adam as part of the deposit of original sin, so that in virtue of possessing original sin we are culpable along with Adam in the eyes of God. Then, upon committing acts of actual sin ourselves, we incur a second guilt, pertaining to the wickedness of those actions for which we ourselves are morally responsible. For this reason, he supposes, we are blameworthy both for possessing original sin (our culpability depending upon the original guilt component of original sin), and for committing actual sins of our own in virtue of having a morally disordered nature as a consequence of Adam's primal sin (which is the additional guilt of which he speaks).

Without the interposition of divine grace no fallen human being can be reconciled to God. In a manner characteristic of the majority report in Reformed theology, Edwards was implacably opposed to the notion that human beings could do anything to prepare themselves to receive divine grace or to contribute to its reception. To use a little theological shorthand, we might say that he was a monergist, not a synergist, in this regard. Following the Apostle in Ephesians 2, he averred that faith itself is a divine gift, bestowed on the elect. On the question of the culpability for sin, as we noted in the previous chapter, Edwards was of the view that fallen humans are morally incapable of refraining from sin, but naturally capable of doing so. This distinction depends on a controversial relationship between the supposed moral necessity of a given action, and a person's moral responsibility for that action. Edwards held that in certain circumstances moral necessity might be a relation as inviolable as logical necessity. When applied to the question of being able to do a thing, in his treatise *Freedom of the Will*, Edwards's thinking takes an interesting turn:

> We are said to be *naturally* unable to do a thing, when we can't do it if we will, because what is most commonly called nature don't allow of it, or because of some impeding defect or obstacle that is extrinsic to the will; either in the faculty of understanding, constitution of body, or external objects. *Moral* inability consists not in any of these things; but either in the want of inclination; or the strength of a contrary inclination; or the

want of sufficient motives in view, to induce and excite the act of the will, or the strength of apparent motives to the contrary. Or both these may be resolved into one; and it may be said in one word, that moral inability consists in the opposition or want of inclination. (YE1: 159)

The distinction amounts to this: *a person S is naturally able to do x provided there is no internal or external impediment to this act.* By contrast, *S is morally able to do x provided S has the strength of inclination to do x. S has a moral inability to do x when there is a want of inclination to do x.* Edwards gives as examples of what he has in mind a moral woman being unable to prostitute herself to her slave, and a child who loves her parents being unable to commit patricide. In both cases there is no natural impediment to the action in question; but there is a moral impediment so strong that it is impossible for all practical purposes for the person in question to carry out the immoral action in view.

In *Freedom of the Will*, Edwards has eighteenth-century freethinkers and "Arminians" in view in deploying this distinction between moral and natural (in)ability. Yet it has application to *Original Sin* as well. If fallen human beings have no natural impediment to living lives according to the moral law, but have a moral inability to do so (because of the crippling effects of original sin), then Edwards seems to have an interesting reason for thinking that fallen creatures may be naturally able not to sin, but morally incapable of refraining from sin. This in turn is consistent with his theological compatibilism, set forth in *Freedom of the Will*, and with what he says about human moral responsibility there.[3] The argument is something like this: God ordains all that comes to pass, including my actions. God ordains that there is no natural impediment to me turning to him to be reconciled. Nevertheless, because of Adam's primal sin, I am morally incapable of doing so; this moral impediment makes it practically impossible for me to turn to God to be reconciled. So God has to take the initiative in reconciling me to himself.

This raises several important questions. The first has to do with moral

---

3. To recap: compatibilism is the notion that determinism is consistent with human free will. *Theological* compatibilism is the idea that the divine determination of all things is consistent with human free will. Incompatibilists claim that determinism is inconsistent with human free will. These come in two varieties: libertarians, who claim that humans have free will, so determinism must be false; and hard determinists, who claim that determinism is true so humans cannot have free will. Each of these views has historic and contemporary defenders.

responsibility and Edwards's theological compatibilism. Given this account of moral and natural (in)ability, how is someone that is naturally capable but morally incapable of a given action morally responsible for their incapacity to act? Edwards appears to adopt a version of what is sometimes called the ledger view of moral responsibility, according to which there is a moral ledger (whether real or metaphorical) against which one's action is measured. One is morally responsible to the extent that one is praise- or blameworthy for the act in question. This touches upon a number of important and related issues in the contemporary literature on free will and action theory, the full treatment of which would take us far from our present concern. Suffice it to say that for Edwards, moral responsibility is about measuring up to God's moral law, and our shortcomings are due to the vitiated nature we have passed onto us via Adam by means of a moral inability to act as we ought to. We can be held accountable for failing in our duty to love and serve God by failing to uphold the moral law because there is no natural impediment to our doing so. Granted, we are morally incapable of serving and loving God absent divine intervention, so we are morally incapable of upholding the moral law, and this incapacity is as certain as any natural inability. However, we are in a state of moral incapacity because (a) we possess original sin, and (b) we perform actual sin on the basis of this inherent disposition to sin, which yields a double guilt. This raises the question of why it is that I am held culpable for possession of original sin, which yields both my moral inability to love and serve God and his moral law, and actual sin that generates a double guilt.

This brings us to our second question, which has to do with the transmission of sin, and is the focus of the rest of the chapter. Suppose Edwards's reasoning is sound and I am morally responsible for Adam's sin. On what basis can I be held responsible for Adam's sin?

Edwards on the Transmission of Original Sin

It seems to me that Edwards's most important contribution to the Christian doctrine of original sin was not his defense of these aspects of the traditional doctrine, but his reworking of the doctrine of the transmission of original sin from Adam to the rest of the human race. This is also a hoary old theological conundrum, not one that was new in the eighteenth century. Nevertheless, the doctrine of original sin was being impugned in the early modern period on the basis of problems associated with its transmission (amongst other things) by freethinkers like John Toland, whose work in this area was the occasion of Edwards's treatise. There are several aspects to this objection raised against the transmission of original sin. The first is that it seems monumentally unjust for one human being to be blamed for the action of another. How can I be culpable for the sin of someone that lived many years before I was born? How can I be included in the guilt accruing to his sin if I did not participate in that sin and did not approve it? Normally, we would think that it is inappropriate to consider punishing the descendent of a notorious criminal for the sins of her ancestor. Yet this is just what is proposed to us in the traditional, Augustinian account of the transmission of original sin. Call this *the injustice problem*. Closely related to this matter of the injustice of this arrangement is a question of its morality. How can God ascribe moral responsibility for the sin and guilt of Adam and Eve to me? What is the warrant for this judgment? What grounds it? What motivates it? Call this *the morality problem*. As with the question of injustice, so with the question of morality: it is difficult to see how one would motivate this claim or in what manner it is warranted. As before, when we consider non-theological cases of sin and guilt we do not commonly think it is morally appropriate to ascribe these qualities to a person unless they are culpable for some crime. If the descendent of a murderer were treated as if she were guilty of the crime of her forebear, we would think this a travesty of moral judgment, not a paradigm. The reason, like the reason motivating the injustice objection, is obvious: my sin and guilt do not normally transfer to someone else. Another individual cannot be punished for my sin because that person is not culpable for having committed the sin I have committed.

This is a commonplace intuition that has been made famous in literature. For instance, in Charles Dickens's *A Tale of Two Cities*, the English barrister Sydney Carton substitutes himself for the French aristocrat Charles Darnay at the guillotine during the French Revolution, dying in his stead. The author sets up the narrative so that the reader has great sympathy with Carton as he is about to die, playing on the fact that he is an innocent performing an act of great heroism and self-sacrifice. "It is a far, far better thing that I do, than I have ever done; it is a far, far better rest that I go to than I have ever known," he famously remarks as he is led to his death. If we did not have the intuition that one cannot justly punish an innocent in place of the guilty, this plot device upon which the novel turns, would be redundant.

I take it that these two issues, that is, the injustice and morality problems for original sin, are aspects of one whole objection to the transmission of original sin. (They also have application to the doctrine of atonement, and a complete theological account of these concerns ought to be at least cognizant of its connection to union with Christ and the transmission of his righteousness to the elect, but that is a topic for another day.[4]) Edwards's response to these twin concerns is to develop an account of transmission that circumvents them by making of Adam and his progeny one metaphysical whole. If Adam's sin *really is* my sin because we are somehow parts of one whole entity that exists across time, then God is not obviously unjust or immoral in ascribing original sin and guilt to Adam's descendants. He writes, "For Adam's posterity are from him, and as it were in him, and belonging to him, according to an established course of nature, as much as the branches of a tree are, according to a course of nature, from the tree, in the tree, and belonging to the tree" (YE3: 385). This "established course of nature" is nothing more than the "established method and order of events, settled and limited by divine wisdom" (YE3: 386). In the following chapter he goes on to say:

> both guilt, or exposedness to punishment, and also depravity of heart, came upon Adam's posterity just as they came upon him, as much as if he and they had all coexisted, like a tree with many branches; allowing only for the difference necessarily resulting from the place Adam stood in, as head or root of the whole, and being first and most immediately dealt with, and most immediately acting and suffering. (YE3: 389)

So, it seems that all of Adam's progeny are united with him in a way similar to the union of different parts of a tree. Just as the branches are joined to the trunk, forming one whole object, so Adam and his progeny are one whole organism, according to a settled course of nature established by divine wisdom. This use of an organic analogy is not new to Ed-

---

4. Recently S. Mark Hamilton has offered an argument for the view that Edwards's doctrine of atonement utilizes the same metaphysical apparatus as his doctrine of the transmission of sin, in order to articulate what might be called a "realist" account of the transference of Christ's righteousness to the elect. See his "Jonathan Edwards on the Atonement," *International Journal of Systematic Theology* 15.4 (2013): 394-415. See also Crisp, "The Imputation of Christ's Righteousness," appendix to *Jonathan Edwards and the Metaphysics of Sin;* and a constructive theological use of this Edwardsian line of thinking in Crisp, "Original Sin and Atonement," in *The Oxford Handbook of Philosophical Theology,* ed. Thomas P. Flint and Michael C. Rea (Oxford: Oxford University Press, 2009), chap. 19.

wards. Other theologians have used it as well. Nor is it clear exactly how this organic analogy is supposed to provide a metaphysical story by means of which we can apprehend how it is that you and I are all united to Adam so that his sin is yours and mine. Later in his treatise, Edwards goes on to add another complication to his account:

> Thus it appears, if we consider matters strictly, there is no such thing as any identity or oneness in created objects, existing at different times, but what depends on God's sovereign constitution . . . for it appears, that a divine constitution is the thing which makes truth, in affairs of this nature.

Moreover,

> It appears, particularly, from what has been said, that all oneness by virtue whereof pollution and guilt from past wickedness are derived, depends entirely on a divine establishment. . . . And I am persuaded, no solid reason can be given, why God, who constitutes all other created union or oneness, according to his pleasure, and for what purposes, communications, and effects he pleases, may not establish a constitution whereby the natural posterity of Adam, proceeding from him, much as the buds and branches from the stock or root of a tree, should be treated as one with him, for the derivation, either of righteousness and communion in rewards, or of the loss of righteousness and consequent corruption and guilt. (YE3: 404-5)

He even goes as far as to say,

> From what has been observed it may appear, there is no sure ground to conclude, that it must be an absurd and impossible thing, for the race of mankind truly to partake of the sin of the first apostasy, so that this, in reality and propriety, shall become their sin; by virtue of a real union between the root and branches of the world of mankind. . . . And therefore the sin of the apostasy is not theirs, merely because God imputes it to them; but it is truly and properly theirs, and on that ground, God imputes it to them. (YE3: 407-8)

Elsewhere, in his sermon "Justification by Faith," Edwards makes the point that the real is the foundation of the legal in the question of justification.⁵ That is, God imputes Christ's righteousness to the elect *because they really are united to him by his work*. Something similar obtains, *mutatis mutandis*, in what he has to say about the union between Adam and his progeny and the transmission of original sin.⁶ There is a real union between Adam and the rest of humanity, a "oneness" established by divine "constitution." On this basis, God may "impute" to fallen human beings the original sin of Adam.

Why only Adam and why only his first sin? Because Adam acts in his primal sin as representative of the rest of humanity as the first human being, according to Edwards. His first sin is the act that disorders his human nature. Thereafter, he is without original righteousness and unable not to sin. Though Adam acts "publicly," as Edwards puts it, in our stead and as our head and representative, we are really united to him so that the metaphysical realism of Edwards's position is doing a lot of work in explaining the transmission of sin. This, coupled with some very positive comments about the scholastic theologian Johannes Stapfer's work, has led some interpreters to the conclusion that Edwards endorses mediate imputation, rather than immediate imputation. Mediate imputation is the view that the moral vitiation of original sin is passed on from Adam to me via the intervening generations, from parents to children, mediately. On this way of thinking, the transmission of sin is akin to the transmission of genetic material, though in the case of sin it does not necessarily have a biological basis. Just as genes are passed down the generations biologically, so sin is passed down the generations morally and spiritually. Imparted, not imputed we might say. By

---

5. "What is real in the union between Christ and his people, is the foundation of what is legal; that is, it is something really in them, and between them, uniting them, that is the ground of the suitableness of their being accounted as one by the Judge" (YE19: 158). The same idea is found elsewhere in Edwards's works, e.g.: "What is real in the union between Christ and his people, is the foundation of what is legal; that is, it is something that is really in them and between them, uniting [them], that is the ground of the suitableness of their being accounted as one by the Judge" ("Miscellany" 568, YE18: 105). See also "Sermon Series II, 1737, n. 419; John 13:23" in WJE Online Volume 52, at http://edwards.yale.edu/. (I owe the latter two references to Mark Hamilton.)

6. This was noticed more than half a century ago by Thomas Schafer. In his groundbreaking essay on Edwards's doctrine of justification he writes, "The same tendency to ground imputed relations in real ones is observable in Edwards' treatment of original sin. He espouses the mediate rather than immediate imputation of Adam's sin and interposes to account for it a theory of identity or 'real union' between each man and Adam which almost replaces imputation altogether." "Jonathan Edwards and Justification by Faith," *Church History* 20 (1951): 55-67; here, n. 37, pp. 65-66.

contrast, immediate imputation is the view that God ascribes original sin to every individual after Adam (barring Christ) by divine fiat and consequent to his primal sin. It is not passed on via natural generation from parents to offspring, but transmitted immediately by divine fiat — as if God simply deals with humanity as a class, attributing Adam's sin to all of them upon his committing the primal sin.[7] Edwards, it is argued, opts for the mediate, not immediate view on the transmission of sin.[8]

But that is not quite right. Only when we factor in Edwards's views about the persistence of human beings through time do we have the full picture concerning his account of sin's transmission. Given the constraints of space, I will offer a synthetic version of Edwards's position in *Original Sin* using a contemporary idiom, and then offer some comments about two possible interpretations of his remarks, and the superiority of one over the other.

His considered view is something like this:

> God treats Adam and his posterity as one entity for the purposes of transmitting original sin. Adam does have a public and representative role as the first human whose primal sin alone causes the deformity of soul that is passed on to all subsequent generations of humans. It is appropriate that he have this role because he was without sin, and was therefore more likely to persevere than any of his progeny. Thus the arrangement is not injurious to human beings. Nor is it unjust, contrary to first appearances. As an oak tree grows from a sapling and a middle-aged man from an infant, so God treats Adam and his progeny as one whole entity extended across space and time that grows and develops across time. John Locke supposes identity through time has to do with sameness of conscious subject. However, this is not a sufficient condition for such sameness at different times. Instead, the persistence of an object is due to divine constitution; to what God wills to be the case. For sameness of consciousness depends on God, who ensures the persistence of an entity across time according to the natural laws he has put

---

7. This is discussed in greater detail in Crisp, "Jonathan Edwards and the Imputation of Sin."

8. We have already noted above that this is Thomas Schafer's view. Charles Hodge in the nineteenth century concurred, with some important qualifications. He regards Edwards's positive remarks about Stapfer's views as an "excrescence" that does not fit with the rest of his treatment of sin. His settled judgment is that "it is, therefore, after all, realism, rather than mediate imputation, that Edwards adopted." See his *Systematic Theology* (Grand Rapids: Eerdmans, 1940 [1871]), vol. 2, pp. 207-8.

in place. Now, created things do not persist across time causing things to happen from one moment to the next. What is past (even a moment ago) no longer exists. So it cannot be the case that what is past causes what is present or future. Rather created things pass out of existence immediately upon being created, like the light reflected from the moon is forever being renewed moment-by-moment, so that the moonlight we see at one moment is numerically distinct from the moonlight of the next. God creates things continuously, moment-by-moment. His preservation of creation is equivalent to his continuously creating the world. If created things cannot persist through time and immediately cease to exist upon being created, then God must be immediately producing all things out of nothing at each moment of creation. Now, suppose this is the case. What "binds" things together across time if it isn't God's constituting different things at different moments into one entity, according to his purposes? He treats these numerically distinct momentary things as one, communicating to them like properties, relations, and circumstances, so that we come to regard them as one. Apply this to the question of the transmission of original sin. When we do, we see that God treats Adam and his progeny as one for this purpose, because divine convention is what constitutes truth in this matter. So any union between Adam and his progeny is grounded in divine fiat, and a kind of real union between the parts thereof, as God constitutes things. Indeed, this real union between Adam and his seed is the foundation of what is imputed in original sin. That is, his sin is truly and properly the sin of his offspring, and on that ground God imputes it to them. Scripture makes it plain that this union between Adam and his progeny in Adam's original sin is unique. It doesn't apply to any other relation between humans (such as a son inheriting guilt for a father's sin), only to this union between Adam and his progeny. (See Ezek. 18:1-20 in this regard.) God's constitution makes it the case that we participate in, and consent to, the apostasy of Adam; we are one with him in his sin; therefore we are rightly treated as sinners and the bearers of original sin and guilt, which is our sin and guilt. (See YE3: 389-409)

Thus Edwards. What are we to make of it? There seem to be several distinct strands to his reasoning, a matter to which we shall return in a moment. Also, he appears to place a lot of store by a rather unusual understanding of continual creation, which appears to conflict with a doctrine of divine conservation (part of a traditional doctrine of providence). However, the most interesting matter for our purposes is how he envisages Adam and his progeny being a whole such that I participate in, and consent to, Adam's sin.

In my earlier work I took the view that Edwards adopts some version of temporal parts doctrine here. On this view spacetime is made up of temporal as well as spatial parts. Things exist across time in virtue of having temporal parts that are aggregated into wholes across time. Jones has a temporal part that existed at noon yesterday, another that existed at noon today, and a third that exists at noon tomorrow. Each part is numerically distinct, but qualitatively near-identical (God "communicates like properties, relations, and circumstances" to these parts, as Edwards puts it). Hence, this is a version of a four-dimensionalist ontology (the fourth dimension being time). The idea is that any object that persists through time does so by having temporal parts that can be "strung together" to form one four-dimensional whole (sometimes called a temporal worm). So Jones is a four-dimensional whole that has numerous temporal parts in somewhat the same sense that he is one physical composite made up of many physical parts, such as his head, limbs, torso, and so forth. Just as the physical parts of Jones are not identical to Jones or even to Jones's body, so on this view the temporal parts of Jones are not identical to Jones either; they must be aggregated together (like his physical parts) in order to compose one whole thing across time.

This seems consistent with what Edwards says in *Original Sin*. However, Michael Rea has suggested a slightly different view, which I now think makes better sense of the whole.[9] To begin with, let us assume the same four-dimensionalist ontology as before. However, instead of a persisting object being composed of numerous temporal parts that are aggregated over time, this view, called stage theory, says that the basic building block is the part, not the whole. The temporal parts are stages of a person. One stage is created and ceases to exist. It is replaced by a numerically distinct stage; this in turn is replaced by another stage when it ceases to exist; and so on. Note that on this way of thinking, the same basic ontology (four-dimensionalism) is "carved" differently, so that temporal stages of a thing are taken to be more fundamental or primitive than the persisting four-dimensional composite, as with the temporal parts doctrine. If the fundamental building blocks of per-

---

9. See Rea, "The Metaphysics of Original Sin." My earlier remarks were made in *Jonathan Edwards and the Metaphysics of Sin*. Paul Helm, in *Faith and Understanding;* Mark Heller, in *Four-Dimensional Hunks of Matter;* and Roderick Chisholm, in *Person and Object* all take a view similar to my earlier view in this regard.

sisting objects are stages, then it looks like each successive stage is a closest continuer from the one immediately prior to it. It is its "successor," so to speak, which is numerically distinct from the previous stage, and is connected to the previous stage by immanent causal relations of some kind. These causal relations obtain between stages so that as one stage is annihilated, it gives rise to or causes the existence of a subsequent stage. On this way of thinking myriad temporal stages are segued together to form what appears to be a whole object across time. To return to our earlier example, whereas Jones is the aggregate four-dimensional entity that has temporal parts that exist at numerous different times on the temporal parts doctrine, on this view "Jones" is a name we may give to an entity that appears to persist through time. In reality, however, there are numerically distinct stages that succeed one another in time (and in sequence) that are phases of one life. The Jones-stage at one time is entirely distinct from the Jones-stage of another time. But the later stage bears a certain causal relationship to the earlier stage close enough for us to treat these two stages as parts of a single life. Importantly, however, on this way of thinking, God could bring it about that there is no single closest continuer to the previous stage. It could be that one stage is immediately succeeded by two or more stages that each have communicated to them what Edwards calls "like properties, relations, and circumstances."

Consider a child building a tower out of toy blocks. The whole tower is composed of the individual blocks, one on top of the other, that represent stages of the upward trajectory of the whole. However, at a certain point in the building of this tower the child might have placed two or more blocks on top of a single block below it in the stack (in order to make a slightly larger stage of the overall block). Upon seeing this tower we might suppose that neither one of these blocks would be the closest successor to the previous block below them; but that both are.

Suppose God does this with Adam just after he has committed the primal sin. The stage of his life immediately after this catastrophic event is the closest continuer to the stage that commits the primal sin. Call this stage of Adam's life *AS* for "Adam the Sinner," and the immediately preceding stage at which the primal sin is committed, *AP* for "Adam committing Primal Sin." However, and importantly, on this view AS is not a single stage that is the closest continuer to AP. Rather, AS shares the property of being the closest continuer to AP along with a myriad of other stages, each of which makes up the first stage of another human life in the total human family scattered across space and time — your life and mine included. There are, we might think, a cloud of AS stages: $AS_1, AS_2, AS_3, AS_4 \ldots$ etc. that are all fissioned stages that are closest continuers with AP, and each of these stages, $AS_1, AS_2, AS_3, AS_4 \ldots$ and so on, is indexed to the life of a particular human individual other than Adam. In other words, we literally share a stage of our lives (presumably, the earliest stage) with Adam, a stage that, through fission, means our lives are united with Adam's life at this particular stage, the stage at which he acquires original sin. For this reason, Rea speaks of this as a fission theory of original sin, which is in many ways a contemporary metaphysical updating of the sort of realist account that we find in Edwards.

On this way of understanding Edwards, his remarks about "the natural corruption of mankind in general and of their consent to, and participation of, the primitive and common apostacy" (YE3: 409) make sense. There is a "real" union between Adam and his progeny, for we all share a stage of Adam's life. This union is brought about by divine agency. Moreover, there is reason why it only obtains in this particular instance, and cannot be generalized over other human relationships: only Adam is far enough back in time for a stage of his life to be a stage in the life of all subsequent humans. Stages in the life of all subsequent humans would not also be stages in his life, and would not necessarily be stages that are shared with all other humans either. This also fits with Edwards's remarks about the representative dimension to Adam's role. His action in primal sin distributes to the rest of humanity via this fission theory.

There is a certain metaphysical elegance to this solution to the problems raised earlier about the transmission of original sin, that is, the injustice and moral problems respectively. For on this view the arrangement is neither unjust nor immoral, because Adam and his progeny really are one entity existing across time, sharing a stage of one life together. Nevertheless, it is counterintuitive. Perhaps one might adopt it as a means of rebutting the injustice and immorality objections, offering it as a sort of metaphysical "just-so" story that may be true for all we know, rather than endorsing it as the fact of the matter. That may provide some help to those struggling with the transmission problem. For if it is regarded merely as a just-so story (i.e., as possibly true, for all we know) this at least shows that the transmission problem does not necessarily provide a defeater that undercuts the doctrine of original sin, because God could have brought about something like the fission-theory account and thereby ensured that Adam's sin *really was* your sin and my sin.

Edwards on Original Sin: Another Look

Problems with Edwards on the Transmission of Original Sin

However, there are other problems in the neighborhood of this one that also need to be dealt with. On the one hand, Edwards appears to want to use an organic analogy between Adam and his progeny in order to provide some motivation for thinking that there is a real union between the two. "The real is the foundation of the legal," so that God is able to "impute" Adam's sin to you and me because we really are united to him as branches to a tree. On the other hand, he wants to suggest that all this is directly and immediately dependent on divine ordination. We are told, "divine constitution is the thing which makes truth, in affairs of this nature." The problem is this: if the reason why I am guilty of Adam's sin is just that God gerrymanders things so that my life is united with Adam's life such that we are one metaphysically scattered object that shares certain properties and parts, then it is not clear why he needs the real to be the foundation of the legal. Divine fiat is doing all the explanatory work.

I suggest that there are, in fact, at least two different theories about the transmission of original sin in Edwards's treatment of the matter — perhaps three, depending on what one makes of his warm remarks about Stapfer's mediate imputation view. These three are not commensurate with each other.

We might think of these as intertwined strands in Edwards's argument that may be teased out. The first strand is the organic analogy, which stands in need of some metaphysical story to motivate it, for it is consistent with more than one metaphysics of transmission. This brings us to the first metaphysical strand of his argument; the four-dimensionalism we have just elaborated. The second strand is the remarks he makes about God "making truth" in affairs of this nature, reducing the whole matter of the mechanism of transmission to divine fiat. In effect, he says that God ordains which temporal stages follow which, whether they are segued together one way or another, or even if there is some sequence at all. This undercuts the four-dimensionalism of the first strand, since if God makes truth in this, and simply orders things as he sees fit by divine fiat, there is no need for a four-dimensionalist ontology to explain how Adam's sin is my sin. God simply arranges things so that this is the fact of the matter because he "makes truth" in ontology. The worry, of course, is that this reduces transmission to a question of divine megrim. No one wants to say that there is no good reason for the arrangement between Adam and his progeny apart from divine fiat. For that does not so much solve the injustice and morality problems as recalibrate them as problems concerning the authorship of sin. If God "makes truth" in this affair, as Edwards says at certain points, then God may be held directly responsible for how things turn out, and we are no further towards an answer to the apparent injustice and immorality of the transmission of original sin. All we can say is "God arranged things thus," which is hardly satisfactory.

The third strand of Edwards's argument concerns his positive remarks about Stapfer (YE3: 391-92), in which he cites the Zurich divine approvingly to this effect:

> The whole of the controversy they have with us about this matter, evidently arises from this, that they suppose the *mediate* and the *immediate* imputation are distinguished one from the other, not only in the manner of conception, but in reality. And so indeed they consider imputation only as *immediate*, and abstractly from the *mediate*; when yet our divines suppose, that neither ought to be considered *separately* from the other. Therefore I chose not to use any such distinction, or to suppose any such thing, in what I've said on the subject; but only have endeavored to explain the thing itself, and to reconcile it with the divine attributes. And therefore I have everywhere conjoined both these conceptions concerning the imputation of the first sin, as inseparable; and judged, that one ought never to be considered without the other. (YE3: 393 n. 1)

Let us be clear: these words are *Stapfer's*, transcribed in English by Edwards from his *Institutiones Theologicae, polemicae universae* of 1756. They are not Edwards's own words. He includes them in a lengthy and approving footnote in the midst of his discussion about the mechanism of transmission for original sin. If we take them at face value, it would appear that Edwards is endorsing the claim that there is no principled distinction between mediate and immediate imputation, given a realist ontology about the transmission of original sin. In one respect this fits with his claim that "the real is the foundation of the legal." For then God could create a four-dimensionalist world where Adam and his progeny share certain stages of their lives and this could be the real foundation upon which sin is "transmitted" from one to the other. Nevertheless, it could be said that God "imputes" Adam's sin to us on the basis of this real union with Adam. It would be like discovering a friend is the son of an enemy and deciding that this real relation he bears to his father means you will treat him with the same enmity you treat his parent. Here too the "real" relation is the foundation of the "legal" imputation — in this case, of the enmity from one person to another. It now seems to me that this endorsement of Stapfer, which has embarrassed some Edwardsians, should be taken seriously as part of his realist metaphysical story about the transmission of original sin. However, even if these two strands are part of a larger consistent whole (viz., our first and third strands respectively), it still appears that Edwards vacillates between this basically realist account and his remarks about God "making truth" in this affair. He would have been better off excising the latter remarks in order to save the realist account.

Edwards's Contribution to Hamartiology

Given the foregoing, what if anything is Edwards's contribution to hamartiology? I suggest that one of the most important aspects of his doctrine of original sin, perhaps the most important aspect, is contained in his response to the transmission problems we discussed earlier, namely, the problems of injustice and morality. The four-dimensionalism he deploys at this juncture of his argument has a certain appeal for those willing to accede to its rather counterintuitive assumptions. However, we need not adopt some version of four-dimensionalism to find this aspect of his argument of interest. One could adopt some version of metaphysical realism without committing to a particular metaphysics of persistence through time as a theological framework for thinking about the transmission problems. In taking up such a model and fusing it with certain metaphysical notions, Edwards was able to offer a powerful defense of Augustinianism against its detractors. Realism of this Augustinian sort has fallen on hard times in recent systematic-theological treatments of original sin.[10] Perhaps it is time to rehabilitate it, taking a leaf out of Edwards's book in order to do so.

---

10. To give just one example, see Henri Blocher's remarks in his *Original Sin: Illuminating the Riddle* (Grand Rapids: Eerdmans, 1999 [1997]). There, in the context of comments on the realism of another Reformed theologian, the nineteenth-century American Presbyterian William Shedd, he remarks, "The realist explanation [of the transmission of original sin and our union with Adam] is fraught with a number of difficulties. Realizing the idea of nature so strongly that it becomes numerically one as a substance, with a history of its own, demands a rather extreme form of Platonism or . . . the acceptance of modern philosophical opinions which we have reason to suspect" (p. 115). Undoubtedly, Edwards would be guilty on both counts: as a Neoplatonist theologian of sorts, and as someone enamored of "modern philosophical opinions which we have reason to suspect."

CHAPTER 7

Bellamy and Edwards on the Atonement

What is the relationship between the doctrine of atonement propounded by Jonathan Edwards and that developed by his disciples in the New Divinity? This question is not as straightforward as it might first appear. Edwards never completed a sustained account of the atonement, and the scattered remarks he did write on the subject appear to pull in rather different directions. For instance, he wrote an enthusiastic preface to *True Religion Delineated*, the work of his protégé, Joseph Bellamy, which offered the first complete account of the New England version of the governmental model of atonement, one of the hallmarks of the New England Theology. Yet it appears that Edwards's most reflective work on this subject in his notebooks stays within the bounds of satisfaction and penal substitution versions of the doctrine.

Behind this puzzle lies a question of doctrinal development. Was the New Divinity governmental theory of the atonement a legitimate extrapolation of basically Edwardsian themes, a kind of Calvinized version of the doctrine in keeping with the New England attempt to re-envision Reformed theology for an American context? Or was it an important departure from the thinking of Edwards, a sign that his theological progeny were not content to pass on his theology but were at least as concerned to put their own imprimatur on the burgeoning movement?

The evidence suggests that the seeds of the New England governmental view of the atonement were sown by Edwards himself. But he did not have the opportunity or, perhaps, the inclination to develop this in his own work.[1] So, the views expressed by Bellamy, Samuel Hopkins, and Jonathan

---

1. Dorus Paul Rudisill makes much the same point when he says "the Atonement was

Edwards Jr., to name the three most important exponents of the doctrine amongst the theologians of the New Divinity, represented, one might think, a doctrinal innovation in one respect. But they were building upon some ideas latent in the work of the elder Edwards, and did, it appears, have his sanction for doing so.[2] Here, then, is an instance of theological development that, though far from straightforward, does not bespeak some sort of declension or departure from the teaching of the master — the "decline and fall" narrative often associated with historiography of the New England Theology.[3] I suggest that this indicates one important way

---

not a theological issue in New England during Edwards's ministerial career. Opportunity for the articulation of his polemic predilection was afforded by other issues." *The Doctrine of Atonement in Jonathan Edwards and His Successors* (New York: Poseidon Books, 1971), pp. 20-21.

2. The most important historic discussion of this matter is Edwards Amasa Park's introduction to *The Atonement: Discourses and Treatises by Edwards, Smalley, Maxcy, Emmons, Griffin, Burge and Weeks* (Boston: Congregational Board of Publication, 1859), which also contains the treatment of the topic by a number of key New England theologians, including Jonathan Edwards Jr. and John Smalley. What emerges from this work is the fact that there was some difference of views about how to understand the atonement within the New England Theology. Rudisill's *The Doctrine of Atonement* is the most accessible published treatment in the modern secondary literature.

3. The *locus classicus* of this "decline and fall" reading of the development of the New England Theology, away from the piety and genius of Edwards to a moribund moralism, is Joseph Haroutunian, *Piety versus Moralism: The Passing of New England Theology from Edwards to Taylor* (Eugene, OR: Wipf and Stock, 2006 [1932]). This monograph set the tone for much subsequent twentieth-century commentary on the movement, but it has been superseded by more nuanced treatments of the New England Theology. A helpful account of the vicissitudes attending the historiography of the New England Theology can be found in Douglas A. Sweeney, "Edwards and His Mantle: The Historiography of the New England Theology," *The New England Quarterly* 74.1 (1998): 97-119. My own reading of the New Divinity is closer to that of scholars like William Breitenbach, who argues (*contra* Haroutunian) that "the leading tendencies of Edwards's system can be discovered by tracing the trajectory of his ideas in the theology of his New Divinity successors." Moreover, "this Edwardsean theology, for all its originality, should be seen as maintaining the fundamental commitment of New England Puritanism to the reconciliation of grace and law." Breitenbach, "Piety and Moralism: Edwards and the New Divinity," in *Jonathan Edwards and the American Experience*, ed. Nathan O. Hatch and Harry S. Stout (New York: Oxford University Press, 1988), p. 178. Also useful in this regard are Joseph A. Conforti, *Jonathan Edwards, Religious Tradition, and American Culture* (Chapel Hill: University of North Carolina Press, 1995), pp. 123-26; and Mark Valeri, *Law and Providence in Joseph Bellamy's New England: The Origins of the New Divinity in Revolutionary America* (New York: Oxford University Press, 1994), especially pp. 14-15 on his debt to Edwards and pp. 123-25 on the atonement.

in which the relationship between the work of Edwards and his theological progeny (at least, in the first phase of the New England Theology, that is, the New Divinity) is more complex than might be thought at first sight, and merits further research.

This chapter is divided into five sections. The first section offers some theological context on the doctrine of the atonement relevant to this historical discussion. The second section focuses on some key ideas in Edwards's soteriology. These are then, in a third section, compared with notions set forth by Joseph Bellamy, Edwards's principal disciple, whose work on the subject became the benchmark for later variations on the New England doctrine of the atonement. A fourth section rounds out the whole by offering reflections on the relationship between the soteriological doctrines of Edwards and Bellamy. I close with some remarks about implications for the broader canvas of the New England Theology.

The aim throughout is to show that the New Divinity men, here represented by Bellamy, were Reformed theologians developing basically Edwardsian insights in a changing intellectual context, which required them to think creatively about the way in which the atonement should be understood.[4] Using ideas that Jonathan Edwards had developed elsewhere in his metaphysics, these divines sought to remedy a lacuna in Edwards's theology, by formulating a version of the doctrine of atonement that made sense of central Reformed convictions whilst also reflecting some of the emerging themes of the New Divinity — themes that were essentially Edwardsian in character. The result was a creative and important contribution to the Reformed tradition, which has been overlooked or sidelined in subsequent systematic theology.

Diversity within the Reformed Tradition on the Atonement

In their recent reader in the New England Theology, Douglas Sweeney and Allen Guelzo introduce the New Divinity doctrine of the work of Christ by pointing out that it departed from the standard Reformed doctrine of a definite, limited atonement. "The judicial model of justification had immediate connections to the nature of the atonement, since a justifica-

---

4. Something of this changing social context is described by Mark Noll in *America's God: From Jonathan Edwards to Abraham Lincoln* (New York: Oxford University Press, 2005), especially chap. 7.

tion accomplished by the merits of Christ could be applied only to those whom Christ consciously intended them for; the elect." This "structured the atonement as a transaction in which the believer had no real role." For this reason, "many of the evangelical movements of the eighteenth century either softened or abandoned the limited atonement model."[5] But this is not quite right. Although many in the Reformed tradition did subscribe to the doctrine of a definite, limited atonement understood in terms of a penal substitutionary model, this was not universally the case. There were a number of Reformed theologians who were much less enamored of the idea that the atonement was limited in sufficiency to the elect alone. Before the Synod of Dort, several different accounts of the scope of the atonement were tolerated within the bounds of Reformed theology. Subsequent to this great conclave of Calvinist divines, there remained divergence within certain confessional boundaries.

To take just one example, Bishop John Davenant, who led the British delegation to the Synod, held to a species of hypothetical universalism.[6] This doctrine distinguishes between the divine intention to provide an atonement sufficient to deal with the sin of all humanity, and God's intention in making it effectual for those to whom faith is given, that is, the elect. Although the distinction may seem like a nice one, it has important theological implications, relevant to discussion of the Reformed credentials of the New Divinity. For if God's antecedent intention was to

---

5. *The New England Theology: From Jonathan Edwards to Edwards Amasa Park*, ed. Douglas A. Sweeney and Allen C. Guelzo (Grand Rapids: Baker Academic, 2006), pp. 133-34. See also Guelzo's *Edwards on the Will: A Century of American Theological Debate* (Eugene, OR: Wipf and Stock, 2008 [1989]), where he seizes upon the New Divinity view as an instance of doctrinal development that was decidedly non-Calvinist, especially in the matter of the scope of the atonement, commenting that "The most startling departure from received Calvinist doctrine which the New Divinity undertook concerned the central doctrine of Christian theology, the atonement" (p. 129). Note, however, that Sweeney is sympathetic to the view expressed in this chapter elsewhere in his work. See, e.g., his *Nathaniel Taylor, New England Theology, and the Legacy of Jonathan Edwards* (New York: Oxford University Press, 2002), chap. 5.

6. Hypothetical universalism is the dogmatic genus of which English hypothetical universalism and the Amyraldism of the School of Saumur (following the Scot John Cameron and his French disciple, Moise Amyraut) are different species — a point that has not always been entirely clear in the literature. An excellent discussion of this can be found in Jonathan D. Moore, *English Hypothetical Universalism: John Preston and the Softening of Reformed Theology* (Grand Rapids: Eerdmans, 2007). I have discussed Davenant's doctrine at greater length in *Deviant Calvinism: Broadening Reformed Theology* (Minneapolis: Fortress, 2014).

bring about a state of affairs whereby all humans could be saved via the atonement of Christ, then the scope of the atonement is not necessarily such that, as Sweeney and Guelzo put it, "justification accomplished by the merits of Christ could be applied only to those whom Christ consciously intended them for; the elect." Nor is it true of such hypothetical universalist theology that it "structured the atonement as a transaction in which the believer had no real role." The consequent decree to bring about the salvation of the elect only obtains precisely because God's initial or antecedent decree is ineffective, on this way of thinking; God foresees that fallen human beings will not choose the salvation his initial decree proffers. The response of faith is a key constituent of this consequent, effective decree.

But matters are more complicated than even this divergence suggests. Recent work on Grotius's doctrine of atonement suggests that Grotius is not necessarily a Grotian. That is, Grotius's doctrine is not obviously the governmental view of the atonement often touted in the literature, though there may be the seeds of such a doctrine in his work.[7]

This is important because it means that the New England "softening" of a limited atonement doctrine into its distinctive version of the governmental theory need not have been quite the deviation from a Reformed consensus it is often thought to be. There are, I suggest, a range of possible options on the divine intention in the atonement, its nature and scope, consistent with the confessionalism of Reformed theology.[8] Sometimes commentators like to distinguish between what is called the "traditional five-point Calvinist" position, which includes commitment to a doctrine of limited atonement. "Four-point Calvinism," that is, Reformed theology that adopts an unlimited scope to the atonement, such as the hypothetical universal-

---

7. See Garry Williams, "A Critical Exposition of Hugo Grotius' Doctrine of the Atonement, in *De Satisfactione Christi*" (D. Phil. thesis, Oxford University, 1999). I discuss this in "Penal Non-Substitution," *Journal of Theological Studies*, NS, 59.1 (2008): 140-68.

8. As G. Michael Thomas has recently pointed out, it cannot be claimed "on the basis of the Reformation and classical period [of the development of Reformed confessionalism subsequently] that there was ever such a thing as a coherent and agreed 'Reformed position' on the extent of the atonement." *The Extent of the Atonement: A Dilemma for Reformed Theology from Calvin to the Consensus (1536-1675)* (Milton Keynes: Paternoster, 1997), pp. 249-50. There were a number of different, related views on a spectrum that were permissible in early Reformed theology, including doctrines that allowed a universal scope to the atonement, favored by the Amyraldians, Anglican hypothetical universalists, and such continental divines as Matthias Martinius, who was a member of the Bremen delegation to the Synod of Dort, where he distinguished himself by vociferously defending this doctrine. (See Thomas, *The Extent of the Atonement*, chap. 7, especially pp. 137-38.)

ists do, is, on this view, something doctrinally inferior, a compromise for those unable to stomach the full five points. This is an unfortunate way of characterizing matters. Whilst there may be good theological reasons for embracing five-point Calvinism and its commitment to a limited or definite atonement, there is nothing *un-Reformed* in the four-point Calvinism of someone like Davenant, or, indeed, Moise Amyraut or John Cameron.

By parity of reasoning, the adoption by the New Divinity theologians of the idea that the atonement is unlimited in scope does not in-and-of-itself tell against the Reformed credentials of its exponents. Consistent Calvinism (as the New England Theology was sometimes called) is not necessarily *in*consistent with the wider Reformed community on this matter. To claim otherwise at the outset is to beg the question at issue by assuming that the only position on the scope of atonement permissible in the Reformed tradition is that of a definite, limited atonement. But this is simply mistaken.

There is a polemical history behind this claim that is not inconsequential. In the mid-nineteenth century, when Princetonian Calvinists were fighting the representatives of the New England Theology for theological supremacy, Charles Hodge (and later, Benjamin Warfield) sought to out-maneuver their opponents by claiming the high Calvinistic ground.[9] Theirs was the formulation of Westminster Calvinism that was truly representative of the tradition; the New England doctrine was a genetic spur that needed to be excised. Today, their version of events is remembered because Princetonian theology outlived that of New England, and had intellectual heirs to receive and transmit it. But when history is written by the victors there is no guarantee the whole story will be told. And there may

---

9. This was a strategy Hodge adopted in other controversies, too, e.g., when dealing with the sacramental Calvinism of John Williamson Nevin — but that is another story. Sweeney discusses the "paper war" between Charles Hodge and Edwards Amasa Park in the mid-nineteenth century about who was the rightful theological heir of Jonathan Edwards in "'Falling Away from the General Faith of the Reformation?': The Contest over Calvinism in Nineteenth-Century America," in *John Calvin's American Legacy*, ed. Thomas J. Davis (New York: Oxford University Press, 2010), pp. 111-46. Hodge makes oblique reference to this dispute in *Systematic Theology* (Grand Rapids: Eerdmans, 1940 [1871]), vol. 2, pp. 578-79. Benjamin Warfield adopts essentially the same position in "Edwards and the New England Theology," reprinted in *The Works of Benjamin B. Warfield* (New York: Oxford University Press, 1932 [1912]), pp. 515-38. There he speaks of the New England theologians' "substitution of the Governmental (Grotian) for the Satisfaction doctrine of the Atonement" (p. 535). This is inaccurate. The New England governmental theory of the atonement was not identical to the Grotian version, as I have argued in "Penal Non-Substitution."

actually be reason to think that the New England doctrine of the atonement is not necessarily beyond the bounds of Reformed theology on the scope of the atonement. The historiography of this work is fraught because this was a doctrine that caused considerable consternation amongst so-called "Old Light" Calvinists (i.e., those, like the Princetonians, committed to a traditional, Westminster Calvinism).

However, even if this is right, there is still the matter of the nature of the atonement, and the divine intention in bringing about the atonement. Is the Consistent Calvinist position in this matter also consistently Reformed? A related concern, which overlaps with this one to some extent, is whether the New England doctrine of the atonement is a development of properly Edwardsian themes. If the answer to this latter query is in the affirmative, then the answer to the former question becomes even more important. For Edwards is claimed by both theological progressives, that is, the "New Lights" of the New England Theology, such as Park, as well as the "Old Lights" of traditional Calvinism, such as the Princetonians. The connection between Edwards and his erstwhile disciples in this central theological matter of the atonement thus has important implications for the theological "orthodoxy" of Edwards himself. These are not incidental concerns; resolving them takes us to the heart of the New England Theology, and, by implication, to the taproot of that tradition — Edwards himself.

But we begin to get ahead of ourselves. Let us turn first to a consideration of the shape of Edwards's doctrine of the atonement. We will then be in a position to ascertain whether his immediate theological heirs departed from, or developed, basically Edwardsian themes on the work of Christ.

Jonathan Edwards on the Atonement[10]

Robert Jenson reports that Edwards's doctrine of the atonement has a different tenor from many defenders of penal substitution. For Edwards, God's rejection of sin is his own problem because he is "antecedently determined to be merciful." Indeed, "Christ's atoning suffering is God's own

10. Since I wrote this chapter, Mark Hamilton has published two excellent essays, "Jonathan Edwards on the Atonement," *International Journal of Systematic Theology* 15.4 (2013): 394-415, and "Jonathan Edwards, Anselmic Satisfaction and God's Moral Government," *International Journal of Systematic Theology* 17.1 (2014): 46-67. Hamilton's essays don't undermine the argument of this chapter, but he does offer a very interesting discussion of the shape of Edwards's doctrine that goes significantly beyond previous work in the literature.

anguish suffered in the historically actual achieving of mercy."[11] The emphasis is upon God's bringing about union with humanity via the work of Christ as an expression of divine love.

Of the many references to the work of Christ that can be found in the works of Jonathan Edwards (and especially in his notebooks[12]), one of the most sustained and carefully drawn is that found in "Miscellany" 774. There, Edwards speaks in language that seems to straddle aspects of traditional satisfaction doctrines of the atonement as well as rectoral notions of God's moral governance of the world:

> Seeing therefore 'tis requisite that sin should be punished, as punishment is deserved and just, therefore the justice of God obliges him to punish sin: for it belongs to God as the supreme Rector of the universality of things, to maintain order and decorum in his kingdom, and to see to it that decency and right takes place at all times, and in all cases. That perfection of his nature whereby he is disposed to this is his justice; and therefore, his justice naturally disposes him to punish sin, as it deserves.[13]

Elsewhere, he makes plain his adherence to a traditional doctrine of penal substitution. Thus, for example, his discussion in his "Controversies" Notebook:

> What I think we may rationally and truly suppose concerning this matter, is this: that as of old God was long preparing his church to receive the doctrine of an atonement for sin by the sufferings of Jesus Christ, the second Adam, and imputing his sufferings to the sinner as one that in that matter stood for the sinner and was his representative, by representing himself as appeased and pardoning the sinner on the account of the sacrifices and vicarious sufferings and death of brute animals, and so long using his church and accustoming the world of mankind to the notion of an atonement by vicarious sufferings.[14]

---

11. Robert W. Jenson, *America's Theologian: A Recommendation of Jonathan Edwards* (New York: Oxford University Press, 1988), p. 124.

12. See, e.g., "Miscellany" entries t, oo, 21, 25, 32, 306, 319, 321b, 357, 366, 388, 398, 424, 449, 451, 506, 516, 589, 594, 622, 698, 728, 764a, 772, 779, 781, 798, 898, 915, 1035, 1076, 1083, 1145, 1211-14, 1217, 1295, 1352.

13. Edwards, "Miscellany" 774, in YE18: 437.

14. Jonathan Edwards, "Controversies" Notebook, WJE Online Volume 27, located at http://edwards.yale.edu/. Compare "Sermon Fourteen" in *A History of the Work of Re-*

Both aspects of Edwards's work were picked up by Edwards Amasa Park in his introductory essay on the New England doctrine prefacing his work, *The Atonement*. Somewhat reluctantly, he acknowledged that Edwards "adopted, in general, both the views and the phrases of the older Calvinists, with regard to the atonement. But like those Calvinists, he made various remarks that have suggested the more modern theory."[15]

A summary of these issues in Edwards's work can be given as follows. God is the moral governor of the cosmos against whom humans have sinned. His honor cannot be besmirched by human wickedness. Indeed, sin against such a being is sin against a being of infinite worth. The status of the person against whom one sins plays an important role in determining the seriousness of the crime and the suitability of punishment required. To sin against a being of infinite worth is to commit an act of heinousness corresponding to the status of the person concerned, in this case the Triune God. Since God is infinitely worthy, the demerit generated by sinning against him must be infinite, because (according to Edwards) the merit or demerit of an action corresponds to the worth of the person at whom the action concerned is aimed. Assume that humans normally commit at least one such sin.[16] Then, all such humans possess an infinite demerit, which they are incapable of remitting. In order to discharge his duty as moral governor of the cosmos, God must ensure that sin is punished; he cannot waive it, or forgive it.[17] Were he to do so, sin would go

---

demption, where Edwards says that Christ's purchase of redemption includes two things: his satisfaction and merit. His work "pays our debt and so it satisfies by its intrinsic value an agreement between the Father and the Son; it procures a title for us to happiness and so it merits. The satisfaction of Christ is to free us from misery, and the merit of Christ is to purchase happiness for us" (YE9: 304).

15. Park, *The Atonement*, introduction, pp. xi-xii.

16. Edwards seems to think all sin is sin against God, irrespective of who the sin is aimed at, because all sin is a failure of benevolence to being in general, and being in general is identified with God (in his dissertation on *True Virtue*). This seems implausible. Exploring it would take us too far afield from our present concern. So, in order to avoid this inconvenience, I offer this weaker premise, that humans normally commit at least one such sin. This leaves open the question of limit cases such as humans that die in childbirth, or in the womb, or are morally incapable, such as the severely mentally handicapped. The claim that all sin is directed against God is discussed by Jonathan L. Kvanvig in "Jonathan Edwards on Hell," in *Jonathan Edwards: Philosophical Theologian*, ed. Paul Helm and Oliver D. Crisp (Aldershot: Ashgate, 2003), pp. 1-12; and William J. Wainwright, "Jonathan Edwards on the Doctrine of Hell," in Helm and Crisp, eds., *Jonathan Edwards*, pp. 13-26.

17. This is the preponderating view one finds in Edwards's remarks on this subject. However, John Gerstner thinks "Miscellany" 306 may be an exception, because Edwards

unpunished and his moral governance (and nature) would be called into question. (Behind this lies the assumption that justice is inexorable and must be served.) Moreover, for any theater of creation, the full panoply of divine attributes must be displayed so that both his justice and his mercy are manifest, thereby vindicating God's nature before his creatures. Thus, sin must be punished in one of two possible ways: in the person of the sinner in hell, in an infinite punishment, or in the person of a suitable vicarious substitute to whom the infinite penal consequences of the demerit can be transferred. God ensures that Christ is the vicar for the elect; he alone is able to take on this task because he alone is both fully human, and therefore able to act on behalf of other humans, and also fully divine, and therefore able to offer up a merit of infinite value that may offset any infinite disvalue generated by human sin.

The act of atonement is a vicarious substitution. It is a provision which, though infinite in value and therefore in principle sufficient to remit the sin of all humanity, is in fact applied only to the sins of the elect. Nevertheless, all human beings are without excuse before God because all human beings are naturally able to turn to Christ and be saved. The reason all humans do not act upon this natural ability is that they are morally incapable of doing so, because of the deformity of sin (a matter that we have already had cause to note in Edwards's work). It is like a man in prison whose jailer comes and unlocks the prison door, but who refuses to leave the prison because of his moral indignation at being incarcerated in the first place. Though there is no natural impediment to his leaving the cell, he is morally incapable of doing so because of his

---

says there that if God had not punished sin, no one could accuse him of wrongdoing. "How could an Anselmian like Edwards say that?" asks Gerstner. But the aim of the "Miscellany" is to establish on what basis it is true to say God must punish sin; Edwards reasons that it cannot be merely on the basis of a bare justice. Rather, it must be that he is obliged "in holiness and wisdom" to punish sin because it would not be a "prudent, decent or beautiful" thing for God to fail so to act. But God is essentially prudent, decent, and beautiful, as well as holy and wise. So he must punish sin. The claim that God could fail to punish sin without being accused of wrongdoing is puzzling, to be sure. But in context, it is clear that whatever he may mean by that, Edwards is not abandoning the Anselmian notion that God must punish sin. His worry seems to be that justice alone, without this richer moral understanding of the divine nature, is not a sufficient reason for thinking that God must punish sin. But taken together with this rich account of the divine nature it is necessary and sufficient to the task. See "Miscellany" 306 in YE13: 391, and Gerstner, *The Rational Biblical Theology of Jonathan Edwards* (Powhatan, VA: Berea Publications, 1992), vol. 2, pp. 435-36.

indignation.[18] In a similar manner, humans are able to come to faith in Christ but refuse to do so (although, for Edwards, this moral inability is as certain as any natural or metaphysical necessity — there is no sense in which the sinner will relent, given time or inducement).

From this synthetic account of Edwards's doctrine, we can see the following things relevant to the question of his relationship to the New Divinity conception of the atonement. First, God is understood as a moral governor, which plays an important role in how Edwards conceives the issues at stake. Second, justice demands that sin be punished; God is essentially just; so sin must be punished. Edwards upholds a strong, Anselmian account of the moral imperative for the punishment of sin. Third (echoing Anselm once again), Edwards provides a reason for thinking that human sin generates an infinite demerit for which only the God-man can atone. Fourth, although the scope of the atonement is limited in intention to the salvation of some fraction of fallen humanity, in keeping with western Catholicism, Edwards affirms that it is sufficient in principle to save all humanity. Nevertheless, fifth, it is effectual only for the elect, who are made morally capable of receiving faith through the suasions of the Holy Spirit. Finally, sixth, Edwards deploys his distinction between human moral and natural ability to argue that even the reprobate have no reason for thinking this action unjust because they are naturally (though not morally) able to come to faith if they so wish. It is just that they are morally incapable of so wishing because of their sinful condition.

This brings us to two important points of contention between Edwards and the New Divinity theologians. The first is that Edwards conceives of the atonement as, in one sense, effectual only for the elect; it is not effectual for the reprobate. The reprobate does not have his sin atoned for by Christ only to then suffer an infinite punishment for that sin in hell. That (so defenders of the definite atonement doctrine maintain) would be an unjust double payment for sin. Edwards can avoid this objection by saying that Christ's work is limited to the elect only, though it has the power in principle to atone for all human sin, just as a vaccine stockpile may be sufficient in principle for an entire population, though it is not administered to the whole population.[19] The sinner in hell does not have

---

18. Jonathan Edwards, YE1: 362-63. We encountered this argument previously in chapter 5.

19. I dealt with the double payment objection in more detail in *Deviant Calvinism*, chap. 8.

the "vaccine" of Christ's atonement applied to him or her; hence, he or she suffers the penal consequences of his or her sin. Second, and following on from this, Edwards clearly endorses the doctrine of penal substitution as the mechanism by which atonement is brought about. It is this core idea that is abandoned by the representatives of the New Divinity.

Joseph Bellamy on the Atonement

We are now in a position to turn to the work of Joseph Bellamy, Edwards's closest disciple. His *True Religion Delineated and Distinguished from All Counterfeits*, published in 1750, became one of the most influential works by any New Divinity author. This is evident in Harriet Beecher Stowe's novel *Oldtown Folks* (1869), where she says of *True Religion*, "Its dissemination was deemed an act of religious ministry, and there is not the slightest doubt that it was heedfully and earnestly read in every good family of New England; and its propositions were discussed everywhere and by everybody."[20] This is important anecdotal evidence of the reception of Bellamy's work, which contains the first treatment of the New Divinity version of the governmental theory of atonement — what I have characterized elsewhere as the doctrine of penal non-substitution.[21] On this view, Christ's work is a penal example that vindicates God's moral governance by showing that the consequences of sin must be dealt with, in order that he may pardon (some) human beings.

Edwards's preface to Bellamy's *True Religion Delineated* states unequivocally that from his own perusal of the discourse he had found that it contained "the proper essence and distinguishing nature of saving religion" which is "deduced from the first principles of the oracles of God, in a manner tending to a great increase of light in this infinitely important subject; discovering truth, and at the same time shewing the grounds of it."[22] He

---

20. Harriet Beecher Stowe, *Oldtown Folks* (Boston: Fields, Osgood and Co., 1869), p. 374. Chapter 29, entitled "My Grandmother's Blue Book" (her copy of *True Religion Delineated*, wrapped in a blue dust cover), is concerned with the influence of the New Divinity through Edwards and Bellamy, and based on recollections of the period in which the New Divinity flourished.

21. See Crisp, "Penal Non-Substitution." That article was a prequel to the present chapter.

22. Jonathan Edwards, preface to Joseph Bellamy, *True Religion Delineated* (Boston: S. Kneeland, 1750), pp. vi-vii.

had read and commented on a manuscript version of the book, and was fulsome in praise of it in private correspondence with his Scottish friend, John Erskine.[23] This has caused not a little puzzlement among scholars. For, plainly, Edwards's doctrine of the atonement is quite different from the governmental view Bellamy's work sets forth. How could he endorse it? An answer to this question can be had if we pay attention to the logical form of Bellamy's doctrine, and compare it to what Edwards himself says. As in the previous section, we shall provide a synthesis of Bellamy's views. We will then be in a position to compare these views with those of Edwards, and to advance a plausible solution to our conundrum.

Bellamy's doctrine is as follows. Like his mentor, Bellamy thinks sin is infinitely heinous and worthy of an infinite punishment in hell. Fallen human beings have the natural ability to avail themselves of faith in order to be saved. But they are morally incapable of doing so, because of the effects of sin. Nevertheless, because there is no natural impediment to reconciliation with Christ, fallen humans who fail to ask for faith are culpable, and punishable in hell for their sin. Unlike Edwards, Bellamy thinks the atonement is, in one respect, unlimited in scope: Christ's work purchases all of humanity. He says, "All [of mankind] were purchased by him, none of these things could have been granted to mankind but for him."[24] Nevertheless, the net result is particular: God gives the elect faith, and it is his intention that the elect are those for whom the work of Christ is effectual through faith.

Hence, there are important parallels between Edwards's doctrine and that of Bellamy, centered around the intention of God in the atonement and in the means by which this is applied to the believer (by faith), as well as the explanation as to why this is a just arrangement despite the fact that the reprobate are not given faith (via the moral vs. natural ability distinction). But there is a difference, having to do with the scope of the atonement. This is tied to Bellamy's understanding of the nature of the atonement.

Unlike Edwards, Bellamy believed that Christ's work is merely a penal

---

23. See Letter 117, to the Rev. John Erskine, in YE16: 347-56. Edwards remarks, "I have had opportunity to read the manuscript and, in my humble opinion, it has a tendency to give as much light in this matter as anything that ever I saw" (YE16: 348). He goes on to say that he is "persuaded his book might serve to give the church of God considerable light as to the nature of true religion, and many important doctrines of Christianity" (YE16: 349). See also Letter 106 to Joseph Bellamy, in the same volume.

24. *True Religion Delineated* (Morris-Town: Henry P. Russell, 1804 [1750]), p. 352. All subsequent references are to this edition.

example, not a penal substitution. In a later summary statement of his views on the atonement, he says,

> The design of the incarnation, life and death of the Son of God, was to give a practical declaration, in the most public manner, even in the sight of the whole intellectual system, that God was worthy of all that love, honor, and obedience, which his law required, and that sin was as great an evil as the punishment threatened supposed; and so to declare God's righteousness, and condemn the sins of an apostate world, to the end God might be just, and yet a justifier of the believer. And this he did by dying in our room and stead.[25]

Being moral governor of the creation, God cannot wink at sin. Were he to do so, his moral governance would unravel because it would be manifestly unjust for God to fail to treat sin with the moral seriousness it deserves. It is impossible for God to fail in such a duty because he is essentially just. Nevertheless, how he goes about discharging this duty is not quite as Edwards conceives it. Christ's work serves to vindicate God's moral governance by showing by example what the moral law demands of those who transgress it, namely, an infinite punishment. Christ's suffering is not infinite in duration, but his is a suitably equivalent suffering, because as the God-man his suffering has an infinite value, generating an infinite merit which he does not need, because he is impeccable and therefore does not require salvation.

On the basis of this work, God is able to forgive human sinners. It is penal in nature, because it demonstrates what the consequences attending sin are, being a suitably equivalent punishment to that which would be meted out to sinners in hell. But it is not a vicarious substitution whereby Christ stands in the place of the sinner, taking upon himself the penal consequences of the sinner's wrongdoing, and suffering in place of the sinner.

---

25. Bellamy, *An Essay on the Nature and Glory of the Gospel of Jesus Christ*, §IV, in *The Works of Joseph Bellamy, D.D.* (Boston: Doctrinal Tract and Book Society, 1853), vol. 2, p. 313. Later he says, "Thus the whole mediatorial scheme is designed, and in its own nature adapted, to do honor to the divine law" (p. 315). Similar sentiments are expressed in *True Religion Delineated*, where he says, "The death of Christ was not designed, at all, to take away the evil nature of sin, or its ill deserts.... But the death of Christ was rather, on the contrary, to acknowledge and manifest the evil nature and ill desert of sin, to the end that pardoning mercy might not make it seem to be less evil than it really is: So that God may freely pardon all our sins, and entitle us to eternal life for Christ's sake" (p. 339; cf. pp. 333, 343).

Although there is a sense in which he stands "in our room and stead," he does so by virtue of offering a suitably equivalent act of atonement that demonstrates the heinousness of sin by his becoming an example of what would happen to human sinners if they were punished for their sins.[26] Because Christ does this, God is able to forgive sinners. His moral governance is vindicated, and Christ's work generates a merit sufficient in principle for the salvation of all humanity. More than that, as we have already seen, according to Bellamy, Christ's work actually purchases all humanity. It is on the basis of this purchase that God may forgive sinners. All humans are naturally able to turn to God for salvation. But they are morally unable to do so without the secret work of the Holy Spirit. It is to the elect alone that God gives the gift of faith that enables them to appropriate the benefits of Christ's atonement.

However, this does seem to generate a problem of double payment for sin. If Christ's work purchases all humanity, yet the reprobate still suffer in hell for their sin, this seems unjust. To this Bellamy replies, "Christ did not die with a design to release them from their deserved punishment, but only upon condition of faith; and so they have no right to release, but upon that condition: it is just, therefore, [that] they should be punished as if Christ had never died, since they continue obstinate to the last."[27]

In other words, without faith, the benefits of Christ's work cannot be applied to a sinner. Bellamy thinks that by appropriating Edwards's distinction between moral and natural ability he can have his cake and eat it. For then, Christ can be said to purchase all humanity acting as penal exemplar. But the effectual application of the benefits of this purchase is, in some sense, conditional upon the exercise of faith. In a similar way, it might be that the government purchases sufficient stores of vaccine for the whole populace, but only distributes it to those citizens who ask to be inoculated.[28] In this way, Bellamy thinks he can do justice to those biblical

---

26. "The truth is, that when Christ laid down his life a ransom for all, he only accomplished what he undertook at the beginning. Christ actually interposed as Mediator immediately upon the fall of man, and undertook to secure the divine honor, by obeying and suffering in the room of a guilty world; and therefore, through him, God did offer mercy to Cain as well as to Abel, and show common favor to the world in general, as well as grant special grace to the elect." *True Religion Delineated*, p. 355.

27. Bellamy, *True Religion Delineated*, p. 354.

28. If the purchase of sinful humanity by the atonement were unconditional, then Bellamy would have a problem with double payment. As it is, by making the effectiveness of the atonement conditional upon its appropriation by faith, he elides this objection. Christ's

passages where Christ's work is said to be for the whole world. But he can also make sense of those passages where Christ's work is said to apply only to an elect, by invoking the moral vs. natural ability distinction: though all sinners have been purchased by Christ's work, not all sinners will avail themselves of this work because not all have been chosen by God to do so. They are still culpable because they are naturally able to avail themselves of Christ's work. But they will never desire to do so because they are morally incapable of doing so as a consequence of their morally vitiated condition. As Bellamy puts it, "God never *designed* to bring the non-elect to glory, when he gave his Son to die for the world. He designed to declare himself *reconcilable* to them through Christ."[29]

Why Edwards Endorsed Bellamy

We are now in a position to offer some explanation as to why it was that Edwards felt able to endorse Bellamy's doctrine, despite the fact that they disagreed about the nature of the atonement. My contention is this: although Edwards could not have failed to see that Bellamy's doctrine provided a different mechanism for atonement than his own, it yielded equivalent outcomes, using several key distinctions he favored in doing so. Although he does not say so, it seems plausible that Edwards was willing to allow latitude on the means by which atonement is brought about provided the result did not violate his own Reformed sensibilities about the restriction of the application of Christ's work to the elect alone. He certainly would have been aware of the leeway within his own tradition on this matter, through reading standard works of divinity, such as Turretin's *Institutes* (in which Turretin discusses the Amyraldian alternative to his own doctrine of satisfaction in detail). I suggest that, allowing for difference over the mechanism of atonement, Edwards was satisfied that Bellamy captured what was non-negotiable in his battle against theological "Arminianism," that is, that the atonement is designed to be effectual only for the elect.[30]

---

work makes human salvation possible; it is only made effectual through the gift of faith, which all humans can ask for (natural ability), though only the elect will avail themselves of (moral inability). Part of the problem in understanding exactly what Bellamy commits himself to is that his language in *True Religion Delineated* is popular, somewhat repetitious, and less rigorous than that of, say, Edwards's *Freedom of the Will*.

29. *True Religion Delineated*, p. 361, emphasis added.

30. "Arminianism" included a wider group than theological Arminianism. For Ed-

Imagine two jazz saxophonists playing Charles Mingus's classic, *Moanin'*. Both interpretations of the music contain similar leitmotifs, riffs, and the same recurring melody. But they are different in important respects, because each musician freely adapts the basic structure of Mingus's work to the set they are playing. Nevertheless, both are playing what are recognizably versions of the same piece of music.[31]

I am suggesting that something analogous applies to the differences between Edwards and Bellamy. They differ concerning their understandings of the mechanism by means of which Christ's work is said to atone for sin. According to Edwards, this is penal substitution; for Bellamy, it is penal non-substitution (his governmental theory). They differ as to the scope of the atonement. According to Edwards, God intends the salvation of the elect and brings about an atonement that is effectual only for the elect.[32] For Bellamy, the atonement is unlimited in scope because Christ purchases all humanity. But his work is made effectual via faith, and God provides such faith only for the elect. So somehow God intends the atonement to be universal in scope, though he also intends it to be limited in effectiveness.[33] As Guelzo observes, "for all its un-limitedness," Bellamy's doctrine in *True Religion Delineated* is "as particular and definite as the more classical constructions of the doctrine, since God in the end always has the final say in who shall be forgiven."[34] Edwards and Bellamy agree

---

wards it was a term that encapsulated a range of theologically liberalizing tendencies in the New England churches, of which theological libertarianism was one particular instance. For discussion of this, see Paul Ramsey's introduction to *Freedom of the Will*, in YE1: 3.

31. Two examples can be found in Charles Mingus's Blue Note album *Moanin'* (1958), which contains two "takes" on the piece, and in the Mingus Big Band version of *Moanin'* in the album *The Essential Mingus Big Band* (2001).

32. "Miscellany" t says this: "Now Arminians, when [they] say that Christ died for all, cannot mean, with any sense, that he died for all any otherwise than to give all an opportunity to be saved; and that, Calvinists themselves never denied. He did die for all in this sense; 'tis past all contradiction" (YE13: 175).

33. In this respect Bellamy's view is similar to Amyraldism, the adherents of which typically adopt a "multiple intentions" account of the atonement: God first intends to save all, but his decree is ineffectual because of human sin; so, in a consequent decree, he intends to save the elect only, via the faith they are given. For discussion of this in the case of John Davenant, see Moore, *English Hypothetical Universalism*, pp. 205-8.

34. Guelzo, *Edwards on the Will*, p. 135. He goes on, "It would not have been difficult at all for Edwards or anyone else to have embraced such an idea of the atonement — indefinite in theoretical scope, limited in actual application — and still insist that he was within the ambit of Westminster Calvinism" (p. 135). That is precisely my point: Edwards

upon the fact that God is a moral governor of the cosmos and that the punishment of sin is intimately connected to that role. They agree upon the heinousness of sin and the necessity for the God-man in order to atone for it. And they agree upon the vital role played by the distinction between moral and natural ability in the appropriation of Christ's work, and in explaining why those who are reprobate remain culpable for their lack of faith.

It would appear that Edwards thought that there was sufficient similarity or family resemblance between his doctrine and that of Bellamy for him to endorse Bellamy's work. It may even have been that Edwards thought Bellamy's conception of the atonement had certain virtues worth stating. At the very least, it appears that what separated them was less important to Edwards than what united them. Both were concerned to articulate Reformed doctrines of the atonement that would provide a theological bulwark against the encroaching tide of "Arminianism" and freethinking, which favored Socinian critiques of traditional atonement theories.

This, I submit, offers a plausible explanation of the fact that Edwards read and understood Bellamy's work and was willing to endorse it despite the differences between them. He was willing to do so because he saw Bellamy's work as a Reformed cousin to his own, with the same aims and equivalent outcomes, but different accounts of the mechanism by which atonement obtains.

Coda

This particular point about the relationship between the doctrines of Edwards and Bellamy leads me to make a wider (and bolder) claim — one for which I cannot offer an argument here, but which might be usefully followed up in another context. In formulating their account of the work of Christ, the theologians of the New Divinity may well have departed from the atonement theory expressed by Edwards, which seems to have been a species of penal substitution. But, from one perspective, in developing their own position they did not deviate from Edwardsian theology as such. Rather, they fused certain elements within a basically Edwardsian scheme,

---

would not have thought Bellamy's doctrine beyond the bounds of what was doctrinally permissible for a Reformed theologian.

particularly an emphasis on the moral government of God in creation, to forge a novel and robust account of the work of Christ.[35] In other words, they innovated *within* an emerging theological tradition, developing a distinctively American strand of Reformed theology. The resulting account of the work of Christ is worthy of much more serious consideration in the academic literature than it has hitherto enjoyed.

---

35. Compare Guelzo, who maintains that "a little reflection will show that the New Divinity doctrine of the atonement represented hardly more than an elaboration of what Edwards himself had laid the foundations for" (*Edwards on the Will*, p. 134).

CHAPTER 8

Edwards on Preaching

One of the most enduring popular images of Edwards is as hellfire preacher, wrapped in the black folds of a Geneva gown, terrorizing the inhabitants of his Northampton parish with lurid sermons about the damnation that is their rightful due. Thus, for example, his infamous sermon, "Sinners in the Hands of an Angry God," where Edwards says that "God holds you over the pit of hell, much as one holds a spider, or some loathsome insect, over the fire, abhors you, and is dreadfully provoked; his wrath towards you burns like fire; he looks upon you as worthy of nothing else, but to be cast into the fire."[1]

Happily, the caricature of Edwards as a hellfire preacher is slowly being displaced by the increasingly sophisticated work being done on his homiletics — although the rehabilitation of the Northampton Sage as preacher is perhaps the least-known aspect of the resurgence of interest in his theology more generally. As the editors of the recent *The Sermons of Jonathan Edwards: A Reader* observe, "Although it may seem obvious to general readers that sermons lie at the heart of a preacher's vocation,

---

1. "Sinners in the Hands of an Angry God," in *A Jonathan Edwards Reader*, ed. John E. Smith, Harry S. Stout, and Kenneth P. Minkema (New Haven: Yale University Press, 1995), p. 97. The definitive classroom text of the sermon is Wilson H. Kimnach, Caleb J. D. Maskell, and Kenneth P. Minkema, eds., *Jonathan Edwards' "Sinners in the Hands of an Angry God": A Casebook* (New Haven: Yale University Press, 2010). It can be also be found in, e.g., *The Norton Anthology of American Literature, Shorter Seventh Edition*, ed. Nina Baym, Wayne Franklin, Philip F. Gura, Arnold Krupat, and Robert S. Levine (New York: W. W. Norton, 2007), a widely used textbook in American Literature courses that reproduces it alongside another Edwards sermon, "A Divine and Supernatural Light."

most scholars have somehow failed to notice this fact as it applies to Jonathan Edwards."[2] Much more attention has been paid to Edwards's major treatises than has been given to his sermon corpus, despite the fact that well over a thousand of his sermons or sermon skeletons (i.e., sermon outlines) are extant. Part of the reason for the neglect of his sermons is because they have been harder to access than his treatises. Sermons by Edwards are still being published for the first time in various collections such as the *Reader* just mentioned and the online Yale edition of Edwards's works. Until recently, only those with access to the sermon manuscripts in specialist libraries could consult this material. But other considerations are also important. For one thing, it is clear that Edwards's treatises are the major documents by which he expected to be remembered. By their very nature sermons are occasional, short pieces that cannot bear the sustained development of ideas that major intellectual works can. (Although, as we shall see, there is an important relationship between Edwards's sermons and some of the major treatises that grew out of them; Edwards pushed the definition of sermon to its rhetorical limit in order to wring from it as much as he could for his written treatises.) What is more, although Edwards was employed as a minister for the majority of his working life, he clearly felt very deeply that his calling involved diligent study and the preparation of major publications. Were this not the case it would be very difficult to explain his working habits: thirteen hours a day in the study and the meticulous use of various notebooks and catalogues as repositories of his ideas, upon which he drew when it came to compiling his major works in the last decade of his life.

As the Yale edition of Jonathan Edwards's works has published more of his homiletical writings,[3] a number of helpful studies have been made of his sermons.[4] One important focus of this work has been on the Puritan

---

2. See Wilson H. Kimnach, Kenneth P. Minkema, and Douglas A. Sweeney, eds., *The Sermons of Jonathan Edwards: A Reader* (New Haven: Yale University Press, 1999), p. xxxviii.

3. The online edition of Edwards's works at Yale University includes a wealth of sermon skeletons and fragments not published in the print edition. After 1742 Edwards began to reduce his sermons from full scripts to small outlines, or "skeletons," to give greater scope for (apparent) extemporizing. For discussion, see Harry S. Stout, "Edwards and Revival," in *Understanding Jonathan Edwards: An Introduction to America's Theologian*, ed. Gerald R. McDermott (New York: Oxford University Press, 2009), pp. 37-52.

4. These include the editorial introductions to the relevant volumes of the Yale Edition of Edwards's Works, especially vols. 9, 10, 14, 17, 19, 22, and 25. Wilson H. Kimnach has been the most important recent interpreter of Edwards's homiletics (and editor of the

emphasis on jeremiad, that is, the mournful complaint of the preacher against the evils of a fallen society. Another has been on the "art of prophesying" — the Puritan understanding of the sermon as a means by which God speaks to the Church by the transposition of Scripture to a contemporary context through careful exposition and application. The relation between published sermons and homiletical oration is something of an intellectual tangle that some recent scholarship has sought to unravel. The published editions of Edwards's sermons are often far more polished in style and language than his extant sermon skeletons or handwritten outlines. Was the sermon form as Edwards inherited and used it primarily an oral or a written means of communication — or (somehow) both? Given the centrality of the sermon as a literary and theological staple of New England Puritan culture, these are important considerations that have only recently begun to receive the attention they deserve.

In the remainder of this chapter, I shall focus on a slightly different, though related question, having to do with the doctrinal content in Edwards's sermons. Although he followed the Puritan model of elucidating text, doctrine, and application, Edwards's understanding of the role of the sermon in conversion, his religious psychology, and his insistence upon laying bare the idea (in the Lockean sense of that term[5]) before the minds of his hearers, meant that getting clear the doctrinal content of his sermons was of particular importance to him. Intellectual understanding and experiential apprehension of the content were intertwined in his

---

key tenth volume in the Yale Works, which gives a general introduction to Edwards's sermon corpus). Another important resource is Kimnach et al., eds., *The Sermons of Jonathan Edwards: A Reader*, which has a helpful editorial introduction to Edwards's homiletics, with a greater focus on the shape of Edwards's sermons than I provide in this chapter. Cf. also Kimnach's "The Sermons: Concept and Execution," in *The Princeton Companion to Jonathan Edwards*, ed. Sang Hyun Lee (Princeton: Princeton University Press, 2005), pp. 243-57.

5. John Locke defines an idea as "Whatsoever the Mind perceives in itself, or is the immediate object of Perception, Thought or Understanding." *An Essay concerning Human Understanding*, ed. Peter Nidditch (Oxford: Oxford University Press, 1979 [1690]), 2.8.8. In commenting on this, E. J. Lowe writes that "Locke's empiricism is at once *atomistic* and *constructivist* in character. In calling it 'atomistic', I mean that Locke regards ideas as falling into two classes, *simple* and *complex*, with complex ideas being analysable into simple components." Locke's work is constructivist because he thinks we can construct complex ideas of which we have no experience from simple ideas of which we have experience. So the complex idea 'unicorn' is constructed from things we have experienced, such as horses and animals with horns. See E. J. Lowe, *Locke* (London: Routledge, 2005), p. 34.

conception of the role homiletics should play in the life of the Church. By focusing on one of his sermons on the person of Christ as a case study I hope to show how these different concerns were combined in his sermons with a view to reaching the affections of those listening, in order to transform them through understanding the "excellency" of the person and work of Christ. Thus, as I shall argue, in the hands of Edwards, the doctrinal sermon becomes a catalyst for moral and spiritual change, not merely the vehicle for expressing propositions that ought to be believed. In this respect, Edwards's homiletics is of a piece with his wider theological concern for doctrine that is not merely understood but experienced. In short, Edwards's sermons were exercises in what, echoing the subject of his treatise on *Religious Affections*, might be called "affective doctrine."

Edwardsian Rhetoric

By all accounts, Edwards was not the most scintillating orator of his age. His voice was somewhat weak, he did not make use of bodily gesture, and for much of his ministry it seems he preferred to stand and read his sermons from the high pulpit of Northampton. His disciple and biographer, Samuel Hopkins, writing of his preaching style, observes that

> His appearance in the desk [i.e., in the pulpit] was with a good grace and his delivery easy, natural and very solemn. He had not a strong, loud voice; but appeared with such gravity and solemnity, and spake with such distinctness, clearness and precision; his words were full of ideas, set in such a plain and striking light, that few speakers have been able to command the attention of an audience as he. His words often discovered a great deal of inward fervour, without much noise or external emotion, and fell with great weight upon the minds of his hearers. He made but little motion of his head or hands in the desk; but spake so as to discover the motion of his own heart, which tended in the most natural and effectual manner to move and affect others.[6]

6. Samuel Hopkins, *The Life and Character of the Late Learned Mr. Jonathan Edwards, President of the College of New Jersey, Together with Extracts from His Private Writings and Diary, and also Seventeen Select Sermons on Various Important Subjects* (Northampton, MA: Andrew Wright, 1804), p. 52. What is more, Hopkins tells us that he wrote out his works mostly in full, and carried the scripts with him into the pulpit from which he mostly *read*, adding in extemporary flourishes as they occurred to him. But, says Hopkins, Edwards

Edwards on Preaching

Yet he was an effective communicator whose sermons had an enormous impact in the Great Awakening,[7] and upon subsequent generations in printed form. And he had a very exalted view of the role of the preacher as the human agent by means of which the Word of God is communicated. In his early notebook musings, Edwards had recorded that "so far forth as the people are obliged to hear what I teach them, so great is my pastoral, or ministerial, or teaching power." It is, he thinks, the degree of *power* attendant upon the Word preached that distinguishes different ministers of Christ. As he puts it, "this is all the difference of power there is amongst ministers, whether apostles or whatever. Thus if I in a right manner am become the teacher of a people, so far as they ought to hear what I teach them, so much power I have."[8]

But all of this raises the question: how is this tension between Edwards the preacher of rather modest oratorical gifts and Edwards the stalwart of the Great Awakening revivals to be explained? The Yale historian of Puritan New England, Harry Stout, offers a distinction between *dramaturgy* and *rhetoric*, which we can appropriate as a means to resolving this problem.[9] Edwards did not possess the physical gifts of someone like George Whitefield, the itinerating Anglican evangelist whose mellifluous, powerful voice and dramatic delivery could command the attention of crowds of thousands in open air meetings without any artificial amplification. But Edwards was a master of rhetoric. This was the source of the power of Edwards's preaching.

Whitefield's ministry transformed New England preaching wherever he went, and deeply influenced Edwards.[10] Whereas Whitefield was an

---

maintained that his method was not the best one, thinking a more completely extemporary style preferable to his own (p. 53).

7. The Great Awakening refers to the religious revivals that swept Great Britain, parts of continental Europe, and the American colonies in the mid-eighteenth century, under the leadership of John and Charles Wesley, George Whitefield, and Edwards, amongst others. It is usually thought to be the movement that gave birth to modern evangelical Christianity.

8. "Miscellany" 40, in YE13: 223. Cf. Kimnach, who remarks that "Like his father and grandfather, Edwards understood the sermon to be primarily a vehicle of power rather than reason or beauty." From "Edwards as Preacher," in *The Cambridge Companion to Jonathan Edwards*, ed. Stephen J. Stein (Cambridge: Cambridge University Press, 2007), p. 105.

9. See Stout, "Edwards and Revival," p. 47.

10. The two best critical studies of Whitefield to date are Harry S. Stout, *The Divine Dramatist: George Whitefield and the Rise of Modern Evangelicalism* (Grand Rapids: Eerdmans, 1991); and Frank Lambert, *"Peddler in Divinity": George Whitefield and the Transatlantic Revivals, 1737-1770* (Princeton: Princeton University Press, 2002).

orator of the first order, whose abilities made even David Garrick, the celebrated eighteenth-century actor, envious,[11] Edwards was principally a thinker. The primary vehicle for his genius was the written, not the spoken, word. Yet Edwards turned this to his advantage. Unable to match Whitefield's dramaturgy, that is, his powerful and sometimes histrionic delivery, Edwards turned to rhetoric — the art of persuasion by words alone, written or preached. As Stout puts it, "Edwards was a genius with words, and he set himself to compose the 'perfect idea' of an awakening sermon."[12] In order to do this, says Stout, Edwards modified "not only his delivery and gestures, but the balance of ideas and the very structure of the composition."[13] Evidence for this Edwardsian emphasis on rhetoric can be found in the use of small duodecimo notes (the pages of which are 7-8 inches in length) that could be "palmed" in the pulpit, for a more apparently extempory delivery, and which often included cues to aid Edwards in extemporizing. It can also be found in the subject matter of his sermons: more "stick," as it were (i.e., references to hell and the need for penitence), and less "carrot" (references to heaven and future rewards).[14]

But any claim of an "extemporizing turn" in Edwards's sermons of the early 1740s, from which time Whitefield's influence upon Edwards and the Great Awakening began to be felt, should not be exaggerated. Although he evidently did bow to pressure in the direction of more informality, even seemingly improvising parts of his sermon delivery (especially during and after the throes of the revivals), it seems that Edwards was not entirely at home in this mode. It is interesting that his "farewell sermon" to his congregation at Northampton, from which he was expelled as minister, was written out in full — the form in which it was subsequently published. (This was not an isolated case: on special occasions Edwards typically wrote out his sermon in full.[15]) And, in the last years

---

11. David Garrick is reported to have expressed a willingness to pay one hundred pounds to be able to say "Oh!" like Whitefield.

12. Stout, "Edwards and Revival," p. 47. Cf. John E. Smith: "It is not surprising to find that by all accounts Edwards's talents were far more literary than oratorical. His weak points appear to have been in voice, gesture and rhythm; his great power was in his masterful use of language." *Jonathan Edwards: Puritan, Preacher, Philosopher* (London: Geoffrey Chapman, 1992), p. 139.

13. Stout, "Edwards and Revival," p. 47.

14. Stout, "Edwards and Revival," p. 47.

15. In his *Life* of Edwards, Samuel Hopkins remarks that Edwards "wrote most of his sermons out in full for near twenty years after he first began to preach; though he did

of his life, whilst a missionary to the Native Americans at Stockbridge, Edwards seems to have spent more time rehashing existing sermons than generating new ones. His attention was by then taken up with composing the major theological and philosophical treatises by which his name is remembered.[16]

But whether attempting to extemporize or reading from a script, Edwards could be a very effective — indeed powerful — preacher. Although his preferred medium was the written, not spoken word, he adapted himself to the oral presentation of his ideas. And, given the written accounts of the effects Edwards's sermons had on some of his hearers, it appears that the practical consequences of his efforts to develop a sophisticated rhetorical style of preaching were successful, even if we allow for some measure of partisanship on the part of those wishing to extol his pulpit endeavors. Take, for instance, the diary entry by the Reverend Stephen Williams who went to hear Edwards deliver his most celebrated sermon, "Sinners in the Hands of an Angry God," at Enfield, Connecticut:

> Went over to Enfield, where we met Dear Mr. Edwards of New Haven who preached a most awakening Sermon from those words Deut. 32:35 — and before ye Sermon was done there was a great moaning and crying out throughout ye whole House. What shall I do to be saved — oh I am going to Hell — oh what shall I do for a Christ, etc. — so that ye minister was obliged to desist. [The] shrieks and cries were piercing and Amazing.[17]

Similarly, Reverend Dr. Trumbell, reporting on the same occasion, writes:

---

not wholly confine himself to his notes in his delivering of them." Hopkins, *The Life and Character of the Late Learned Mr. Jonathan Edwards*, p. 50.

16. Kimnach divides Edwards's preaching into three chronological segments corresponding to the different phases of his career. The first runs up to 1729, when Edwards took sole control of the Northampton pastorate. In that time he was busy mastering the sermon form. The second phase is concurrent with the Great Awakening, running from 1729 to 1742, during which time Edwards viewed the sermon as a means by which to "awaken" and "affect" his congregation. The final phase runs from 1743 to 1758, when Edwards left the pastorate for the presidency of Princeton. During this period he was less concerned with the sermon form than with using the sermon for his other literary projects. See Kimnach, "Edwards as Preacher," p. 106.

17. Cited from a handwritten typescript of Rev. Williams's diary by Stout in "Edwards and Revival," p. 49.

When we went into the meeting house, the appearance of the assembly was thoughtless and vain. The people hardly conducted themselves with common decency. The Rev. Mr. Edwards of Northampton preached; and before the sermon was ended, the assembly appeared deeply impressed, and bowed down with an awful conviction of their sin and danger. There was such a breathing of distress and weeping, that the preacher was obliged to speak to the people and desire silence, that he might be heard.[18]

Several of Edwards's major works began as sermons. His rhetorical approach lent itself to the kind of careful, reasoned discourse that could then be reworked into the chapters of treatises. His *History of the Work of Redemption* was originally a series of sermons preached to his congregation in Northampton; Edwards seems to have intended it as the basis for a significant new body of divinity, but did not live to complete it.[19] His work of moral theology, *Charity and Its Fruits*, published as a series of written sermons, had likewise been preached before his Northampton parishioners.[20] *Religious Affections*, published in 1746, twelve years before his sudden demise in Princeton, was perhaps the most theologically significant work that began life as a sermon series. According to his nineteenth-century biographer, Sereno Dwight, "In its style it is the least correct of any of the works of Mr. Edwards, published in his lifetime." But as a work

---

18. Sereno E. Dwight, *Life of President Edwards* (New York: G. C. & H. Carvill, 1830), p. 605. This is not an isolated case. Compare the reminiscence of one Dr. West of Stockbridge, whom Dwight quotes to the following effect: "On one occasion, when the sermon exceeded two hours in length, he told me that, from the time that Mr. Edwards had fairly unfolded his subject, the attention of the audience was fixed and motionless, until its close; when they seemed disappointed that it should terminate so soon. *There was such a bearing down of truth upon the mind, he observed, that there was no denying it*" (p. 604, emphasis added). The rhetorical tone reported here is unmistakable. The fact that Edwards was a regular itinerant during the height of the Great Awakening does suggest that his services as a preacher were in demand.

19. Edwards in a letter to the Trustees of the College of New Jersey (later Princeton) refers to this work as follows: "I have had on my mind and heart (which I long ago began, not with any view to publication) a great work, which I call *A History of the Work of Redemption*, a body of divinity in an entire new method, being thrown into the form of an history." It was one of several major works left unfinished at the time of Edwards's death. See YE16: 727.

20. Edwards's great-great-grandson, Tryon Edwards, produced an "amended" (i.e., corrupted) version of *Charity and Its Fruits* (New York: Robert Carter and Brothers, 1852). Happily, the text has been restored in the Yale edition, which can be found in YE8.

breathing the "living religion of Christianity," it possesses a "singular excellence" second only to Holy Writ.[21]

Rhetoric, Ideas, and Affections

During his time at Yale College, Edwards had read a number of other early Enlightenment authors, including John Locke, whose work shaped his theological development in important respects.[22] One can trace Locke's influence from Edwards's early notebooks into his mature works, where the same intellectual virtues are privileged. Thus, in his Cover-Leaf Memoranda to his notebook "Natural Philosophy," Edwards writes to remind himself to try "not to silence but to gain readers" (YE6: 192). He speaks of the need for "modesty" to "be seen in the style" of his work. He reminds himself to "be very moderate in the use of terms of art. Let it not look as if I was much read, or conversant with books or the learned world" (YE6: 193). But most importantly for his career as a minister, Edwards, echoing Locke, says this:

> When I would prove anything, to take special care that the matter be so stated that it shall be seen most clearly and distinctly by everyone just how much I would prove; and so to extricate all questions from the least confusion or ambiguity of words, *so that the ideas shall be left naked*. (YE6: 193, emphasis added)

Commitment to simplicity and clarity of expression, and to speech and writing unadorned by reference to the latest fashionable writers and their works, are just as much hallmarks of Edwards the preacher and theologian as they are of Edwards the natural philosopher. His expressed desire to "lay bare the idea" before those to whom he communicated was a Locke-

---

21. Dwight, *Memoir*, in *The Works of Jonathan Edwards*, ed. Edward Hickman (Edinburgh: Banner of Truth Trust, 1974 [1834]), vol. 1, p. lxxxiii. There Dwight observes that as *Religious Affections* was first prepared, "it was a series of sermons, which he preached from his own pulpit, from the text still prefixed to it, 1 Peter i.8," probably in the years 1742-1743, "and afterwards thrown into the form of a treatise by its author."

22. As we have already had cause to note, other early influences include continental Reformed orthodox theologians such as Francis Turretin and Petrus van Mastricht, and the philosophical ideas of Nicholas Malebranche and the Cambridge Platonists, particularly Henry More.

inspired notion from which he never departed. It is a linchpin of what the twentieth-century Harvard historian Perry Miller called Edwards's "rhetoric of sensation." In this connection, Miller writes,

> Edwards' great discovery, his dramatic refashioning of the theory of sensational rhetoric, was his assertion that an idea in the mind is not only a form of perception but is also a determination of love and hate. To apprehend things only by their signs or by words is not to apprehend them at all; but to apprehend them by their ideas is to comprehend them not only intellectually but passionately. For Edwards, in short, an idea became not merely a concept but an emotion.[23]

But *passions* must be distinguished from *affections*, on an Edwardsian way of thinking. Whereas passions overpower a person, making of the person a slave (in David Hume's famous phrase[24]), affections, as Edwards understood the term, had to do with the apprehension of a thing. They were, as John E. Smith puts it, "the response of the self to an *idea*."[25] It is tempting to equate passions and affections with emotional responses to a given stimulus. But this was emphatically not the way Edwards conceived of the matter. In his *Religious Affections*, he made it clear that an affective response to a thing has an intimate connection to the understanding of that thing. It is a reasoned response, not an impulsive or visceral reaction.[26] What is more, for Edwards, true knowledge of a thing is affective knowledge. Or, to put it in more contemporary terms, for Edwards as for Locke, there is a distinction to be made between knowledge by *description*

---

23. Perry Miller, *Errand into the Wilderness* (Cambridge, MA: Harvard University Press, 1956), p. 179. But Miller overstates matters when he goes on to say, "For Edwards it [i.e., his 'refashioning of the rhetoric of sensation'] was the most important achievement of his life and the key to his doctrine and practice." See also Wilson H. Kimnach, "Jonathan Edwards's Pursuit of Reality," in *Jonathan Edwards and the American Experience*, ed. Nathan Hatch and Harry S. Stout (New York: Oxford University Press, 1988), pp. 102-17, which is, in many ways, superior to Miller's work on this topic.

24. "Reason is, and ought only to be the slave of the passions." David Hume, *A Treatise of Human Nature*, 2nd ed., ed. Peter Nidditch (Oxford: Oxford University Press, 1978 [1739-1740]), 2.3.3.4.

25. Smith, *Jonathan Edwards*, p. 33.

26. Compare Smith: "There is a temptation to use the term 'emotions' as a synonym for affections, but this is apt to be misleading unless emotion is taken to mean a felt response to an object, event or situation which is called forth by an *understanding* of the nature of the object." Smith, *Jonathan Edwards*, p. 33, author's emphasis.

and knowledge by *acquaintance*.²⁷ I can know a thing in theory, as a man born blind can know of something called color, though he knows not what it is. Without acquaintance, such knowledge is always notional; it is never affective. And without acquaintance, something vital is missing from our notional descriptive account of a thing. In writing about how it is that the saint has a new sense of things on being regenerated, a "new simple" idea brought about by an act of supernatural grace whereby she now sees the world in an entirely different light, Edwards says this:

> something is perceived by a true saint, in the exercise of this new sense of mind, in spiritual and divine things, as entirely diverse from anything that is perceived in them, by natural men, as the sweet taste of honey is diverse from the ideas men get of honey by only looking on it, and feeling of it. (YE2: 206)²⁸

Tasting honey is knowledge by acquaintance just as an affective understanding of a thing, or the new simple idea the saint has formed in her by faith, is a form of knowledge by acquaintance. Only experience, understood as an event that is lived through and of which one is conscious, can deliver this sort of "lively," affective understanding of a thing. It is not difficult to see how this philosophical distinction between what I am calling description and acquaintance, which he culled from his study of Locke, has important implications for Edwards's desire to "lay bare the idea" in his sermons. His concern was to bring about in his parishioners an affective response — the stimulation needed to generate a true acquaintance with the things of divine grace that could only come with a new simple idea of the world, given in regeneration.

But Edwards was no slavish follower of Locke in the way of ideas. Wallace Anderson makes this clear when he says that "The very notion of an idea, as applied to the immediate objects of sensation, is in Locke's account primarily an epistemological one; simple ideas are, for him, the fundamental building blocks of knowledge." Not so, for Edwards. In his

---

27. Bertrand Russell is often thought to have introduced this distinction into the philosophical literature. But it can be found in Locke and Edwards. For discussion, see Richard Fumerton's article, "Knowledge by Acquaintance vs. Description," in the *Stanford Encyclopedia of Philosophy*, located at http://plato.stanford.edu/entries/knowledge-acquaindescrip/.

28. See also Edwards's sermon, "A Divine and Supernatural Light," in which this analogy with honey is spelled out (YE19: 405-26).

discussions "the term 'idea' as applied to given experience has primarily an ontological import; it serves to establish that the objects we perceive cannot exist except in minds."[29] An important connection is to be made here between the Edwardsian "rhetoric of sensation" and his immaterialist philosophy. Ideas were important to Edwards because, as we saw in the second chapter, he thought the whole world a collection of ideas and minds — matter being a sort of fiction. Thus, in his *Miscellanies* notebook, he writes: "Supposing a room in which none is, none sees in that room, no created intelligence; the things in the room have no being any other way than only as God is conscious [of them], for there is no color, nor any sound, nor any shape, etc." (YE13: 188).[30] And in another place in his early notebooks, "The substance of bodies at last becomes either nothing, or nothing but the Deity acting in that particular manner in those parts of space where he thinks fit. So that, speaking most strictly, there is no proper substance but God himself (we speak at present with respect to bodies only)" (YE6: 215). He even goes as far as to say in *The Mind* that "the brain exists only mentally" so that he speaks "improperly" when he says, "the soul is in the soul only as to its operations" (YE6: 355).[31] Not only was it true that ideas were of fundamental importance in Edwardsian rhetoric. They were the very building blocks of his ontology. For Edwards, ideas were not simply things to be communicated effectively through language. Ideas were also the things of which the world was composed.

For this reason, I want to distinguish between Miller's notion of the "rhetoric of sensation" and what I am calling "affective doctrine." The latter might be thought of as an aspect of the former, or at least, as coming under the aegis of the rhetoric of sensation. Edwards's desire to affect his congregation with homiletical power meant that he made a concerted effort to craft sermons that would be affecting. And since, by his own lights, affections were roused when a person apprehended an idea, it was only natural for Edwards to think that he ought to spend his sermons laying bare those ideas, making them as clear as possible, so as to be as suitable

---

29. Wallace Anderson, introduction to YE6: 102.

30. Referred to by Sang Lee in *The Philosophical Theology of Jonathan Edwards* (Princeton: Princeton University Press, 1988), p. 58.

31. Edwards explicitly denies material substance in "Notes on Knowledge and Existence," where he states in response to Hobbesianism that "What we call body is nothing but a particular mode of perception; and what we call spirit is nothing but a composition and series of perceptions, or an universe of coexisting and successive perceptions connected by such wonderful methods and laws" (YE6: 398).

a vehicle for the suasions of the Holy Ghost as he could make them. As he says in *Some Thoughts concerning the Present Revival of Religion,*

> I think an exceedingly affectionate way of preaching about the great things of religion, has itself no tendency to beget false apprehensions of them; but on the contrary a much greater tendency to beget true apprehensions of them, than a moderate, dull, indifferent way of speaking of 'em.... I should think myself in the way of my duty to raise the affections of my hearers as high as possibly I can, provided that they are affected with nothing but truth, and with affections that are not disagreeable to the nature of what they are affected with.... Our people don't so much need to have their heads stored, as to have their hearts touched; and they stand in the greatest need of that sort of preaching that has the greatest tendency to do this.[32]

To see a concrete example of this, let us turn in the final section of this chapter to consider a particular sermon as a case study of just this sort of homiletical arrangement.

Case Study: "The Excellency of Jesus Christ"

Context

During the winter of 1734-1735, Edwards experienced the first significant "awakening" in his congregation in Northampton. It presaged the later Great Awakening that swept the eastern seaboard of New England in the 1740s and catapulted Edwards to international fame as its principal intellectual apologist. Not only is this early awakening an interesting phenomenon in itself. (It was, at that stage, by far the most significant spiritual transformation Northampton had seen, eclipsing that of the pastorate of Edwards's predecessor and maternal grandfather, Solomon Stoddard.) It was also significant enough to be memorialized by the congregation of Northampton. They financed the publication of the only collection of sermons Edwards published during his lifetime, all of which came from this period of his ministry. The collection was entitled, with typical eighteenth-century prolixity, *Five Discourses on Important Subjects, Nearly Concerning*

---

32. Edwards, *Some Thoughts concerning the Present Revival of Religion* (YE4: 386-88).

the *Great Affair of the Soul's Eternal Salvation* (Boston, 1738) — hereinafter *Five Discourses*.[33] In the estimation of Wilson Kimnach, "The publication of Edwards's five discourses in 1738 marked the high point of his pastoral preaching." He goes on to say that "taken as a whole," the sermons Edwards preached during this period in the 1730s "have a technical mastery and consistency of finish unmatched elsewhere in his career."[34]

For these reasons, it is worth studying the *Five Discourses* as case studies of Edwards's most carefully crafted sermon style, and as repositories of his concern to communicate affective doctrine to his listeners and readers. The preface to the sermons is the only place in which he offers anything like an argument for his particular approach to homiletics. In it, Edwards explains that all the discourses except "The Excellency of Jesus Christ" were originally preached during the "late wonderful work of God's power and grace" (YE19: 794), that is, the Northampton revival in 1734-1735. But of the sermons printed, only "The Excellency of Christ" appeared at Edwards's specific behest, added, as he says, "on my own motion" rather than that of his congregation. It was included because he thought that "a discourse on such an evangelical subject would properly follow others that were chiefly awakening," showing something of the excellency of Christ, as he put it, after having enunciated the necessity of salvation in the four preceding sermons. It is also noteworthy that Edwards was "earnestly importuned" for a published version of this sermon "by some other town in whose hearing it was occasionally preached" (YE19: 797). So "The Excellency of Christ" is an important example of a finished sermon, delivered on more than one occasion to different congregations, which had brought about just the sort of affecting result that would encourage a writer like Edwards to think it worth seeing through to publication.

In his preface to *Five Discourses*, Edwards offers a defense of the rather provincial style of his preaching, reflected in the printed versions of the five sermons. His words here echo his earlier notebook entry on the need for an unadorned, modest style of writing in order to lay bare his ideas before his listeners and readers. To this end, he observes that the four sermons (including "The Excellency of Jesus Christ") that follow the ex-

---

33. The *Five Discourses* appear in YE19, in which the preface is included as an appendix. This is quite unsatisfactory, given that these discourses were seen through the press by Edwards himself in a particular form that the editor has chosen to ignore. Thankfully, a complete text of the whole symposium, including the preface, can be found in *The Works of Jonathan Edwards*, vol. 1, pp. 620-89.

34. Kimnach, "Edwards as Preacher," p. 115.

tensively reworked "Justification by Faith Alone" "have but little added to them" for publication "and now appear in that very plain and unpolished dress in which they were first prepared and delivered" (YE19: 797).[35] They do not exhibit "such ornaments as politeness and modishness of style and method." Yet, if he is not able "to preach or write politely," nevertheless God has blessed "a very plain and unfashionable way of preaching" (YE19: 797). Such conventional self-deprecation, a typical feature of much eighteenth-century literature, should not be taken at face value. Edwards is not offering an apology for a plain, Puritanical style of sermon so much as he is rebuking the cultivated "modishness" that was at that time increasingly prevalent in the pulpits of New England.

Finally, by way of introducing "The Excellency of Christ," it is interesting that part of the argument of the preface to *Five Discourses* involves a defense of the careful, logically rigorous, and sophisticated doctrinal style of Edwards's discourse on "Justification by Faith," the first sermon in the series. Edwards acknowledges that "Justification" is the one sermon that has been significantly revised since its original declamation. Nonetheless, what he says of it is pertinent to the other sermons, including "The Excellency of Christ," the homily Edwards had personally elected to include. Here too, he takes a combative stance, this time against those who found in older theology too much by way of "speculative niceties" and "subtile distinctions" (YE19: 795).[36] Against the supposedly "plain and easy" style of much "modern" divinity, Edwards writes with ironic haughtiness that

> prejudice against distinctions in divinity, I humbly conceive, is carried to a great extreme. So great, and general, and loud a cry has been raised by modern philosophers and divines, against the subtile distinctions of the Schoolmen, for their learned impertinence, that many are ready to start at anything that looks like nice distinction, and to condemn it for nonsense without examination. Upon the same account, we might expect to have St. Paul's epistles, that are full of very nice distinctions, called nonsense, and unintelligible jargon, had not they the good luck,

---

35. However, as M. X. Lesser points out in introducing the sermon in YE19, it is clear that this work had much more added to it for publication than the other sermons printed in the book. It is a fifth longer than its manuscript counterpart. See Lesser's introduction in YE19: 562.

36. Of course Locke was also an opponent of scholastic distinctions. Edwards is no Lockean in this respect!

to be universally received by all Christians, as part of the holy Scriptures. (YE19: 795)

Careful, logical, even "nice" distinctions, so characteristic of Edwards's treatises, are also hallmarks of his sermons. In this respect, "The Excellency of Christ" is no different from "Justification by Faith." Although, as we have just noted, something of his self-deprecation in the preface to *Five Discourses* is simply a matter of eighteenth-century social and literary custom, it is surely true that Edwards's stand against "fashionable" divinity and "modish" sermons signals something important about his own approach to sermon construction and delivery. He is interested in aligning himself with an older, plain Puritan style, rather than with the fad for more cosmopolitan disquisitions that had been imported from across the Atlantic. His desire to lay bare the idea before his congregation in Lockean style, and the importance he placed upon affections in matters touching religion, are part-and-parcel of this attempt to hold the high moral ground on the sermonic form he inherited from the Puritans. In his preface, he stresses his commitment to both a "very plain unfashionable way of preaching" and the "clear and rational" enquiry modeled by the scholastic theology in which he had been educated, and which was so much part of his own *modus operandi*. With this in mind, we turn to consider the text of "The Excellency of Christ."

Text

The biblical text for the sermon is taken from Revelation 5:5-6, where in the heavenly throne room John of Patmos encounters the "Lion of the Tribe of Judah, the Root of David," who is paradoxically also "a Lamb as it had been slain" — a representation of Christ. This entity to whom is given a multitude of apparently contradictory titles is the only one able to open the Book of the Seven Seals, the record of God's decrees. The concatenation of these different titles given to Christ is the focus of Edwards's discourse, and yields the thesis of the sermon, namely, that "there is an admirable conjunction of diverse excellencies in Jesus Christ" (YE19: 565). The discourse is then divided into a section dealing with how these diverse excellencies meet in the person of Christ, and another on how they are manifest in his actions.

Edwards makes clear that the apparently contradictory nature of the titles given to Christ owes to our limited epistemic vantage. The difference between these titles "is chiefly relative, and in our manner of conceiving them." He gives two examples to make the point. First, Christ is infinitely high, or great, and yet infinitely condescends to take on human nature and suffer an ignominious death on behalf of fallen human beings (YE19: 565-66). Second, Christ is both infinitely just and infinitely gracious. His justice is "strict with respect to all sin." But his grace is "sufficient to bestow all good" and "all things" upon fallen human beings (YE19: 567). These are not necessarily contradictory attributes, though they may initially appear to be so. One entity could be both transcendent and yet immanent. Likewise, an entity could be both just and gracious in his or her dealings with others. But Edwards also addresses apparently contradictory predicates found conjoined in Christ which would be thought contradictory in any other person. Among these he includes the following seven pairs: Christ's infinite glory and lowest humility; his infinite majesty and transcendent meekness; his deepest reverence to God as well as equality with God; his infinite worthiness of good and yet patient suffering of evil; his spirit of obedience and yet dominion over the whole creation; his absolute sovereignty and perfect resignation; and his self-sufficiency and entire trust and reliance on God (YE19: 567-72).

Edwards cannot claim in all seriousness that these attribute-pairs are formally inconsistent or even yield a contradiction; they do not. Rather, the claim seems to be that such a concatenation of "diverse excellencies" in one person is peculiar to Christ. As Edwards puts it, only in Christ do all these different things "meet together." Only Christ is able to be both obedient and yet the master of creation, an absolute sovereign perfectly resigned to his ignoble death at the hands of his creatures, entirely self-sufficient and yet absolutely reliant upon God, and so forth. But Edwards goes on to isolate three of these diverse excellencies in particular as being "impossible to be exercised towards the same object" — except in the case of Christ. These are his justice, mercy, and truth (YE19: 572). Christ has an "infinite regard" to divine justice and to the truth of God, and yet he is also the savior of the world. Although Edwards does not spell out exactly why Christ alone can exhibit these different attributes at once, the idea seems to be that no other being could be both the perfect upholder and executive of divine justice and yet also be the harbinger of divine mercy to those condemned under the moral law of God. In this respect, Christ is unique among all those who possess a human nature, because he is also a divine person.

The second part of the sermon switches from discussion of the admirable conjunction of diverse excellencies in Christ to an elaboration of how this is manifested. It is found, first, in the very act of Incarnation through which the infinite Second Person of the Trinity condescends to assume human nature (YE19: 573-74). But it also appears in the particular acts he performed as God Incarnate from his infancy onwards (YE19: 574-75). And it is most clearly demonstrated in his atonement (YE19: 576-81). For in this act, his "infinite regard" for divine justice meets his infinite mercy towards fallen humanity. Finally, Edwards refers to Christ's diverse excellencies to his current state of exaltation in heaven, which is the specific subject of Revelation 5, and in the prospect of his return to judge the quick and the dead (in which context, Edwards turns to Revelation 20:11, which pictures the Last Judgment).

Application

This is strong theological meat. Edwards does not skimp on the doctrinal content of his sermon; and he certainly makes every effort to lay bare the idea that forms the thesis of the discourse. It is in the application section of the sermon that he seeks to make this content *affective*. After impressing on his hearers/readers the importance of this doctrine for understanding the multitude of different attributes of Christ revealed in Scripture, Edwards employs the Puritan convention of castigating and imploring his audience "to accept of him, and close with him as your Savior" (YE19: 583). He contrasts the "despicable" state of fallen human beings with the diverse excellencies of Christ in his capacity as Savior, and impresses upon his audience that Christ, though "awful" in his majesty, is also a "creature as well as the Creator" and has stooped to save fallen human beings (YE19: 584). He wonders what his audience is afraid of, that he or she does not accept Christ; or what he or she could desire in a Savior other than the diverse excellencies found in Christ alone (YE19: 585). His language is replete with the sort of heartfelt appeals one would expect in such an evangelical discourse: "O thou poor, distressed soul! Whoever thou art that art afraid that you never shall be saved, consider this that Christ mentions is your very case, when he calls to them that labor and are heavy laden!" And "How does Christ here graciously set before you his own winning, attractive excellency!" (YE19: 587). Moreover, he takes every occasion to press home the central doctrinal message in his petitions: "As there is such an admirable meeting of diverse excellencies in Christ, so there is everything in him to render him worthy of your love and choice, and to win and engage it" (YE19: 588).

But it is not just that Edwards refers his audience back to the thesis of his sermon in his application of it to their circumstances. He also develops his doctrinal theme further through his affective appeals. He deliberately conflates heartfelt and doctrinal language so as to *affect* his audience (in the Edwardsian sense of "affect" outlined earlier) in characteristically effusive emotional language.

So, he speaks of Christ closing the infinite distance between God and human beings in order that he may "engross our regard in every way" and that "he may be the center" of our regard for God, that we may "love and delight" in him who is "the greatest instance of these sweet virtues, that ever was, or will be," and so on (YE19: 589-90). This culminates at the end of the discourse in two important doctrinal "improvements," or applications, which drive home the affective aspect of the sermon. The first is his claim that the excellencies of Christ's human nature do not add to the excellency of his person, but rather "are additional manifestations of his glory and excellency to us" (YE19: 590). The second is that in virtue of being united to Christ through regeneration, the sinner is united to God — a union that will eventually include becoming "partakers of the Son's enjoyment of God, and having his joy fulfilled in ourselves" (YE19: 593). Admission to the church, which is the body of Christ (Edwards takes the organic language of union with Christ very seriously indeed), means being part of one society or family, "that the church should be as it were admitted into the society of the blessed Trinity" (YE19: 594).[37]

Christ's human excellencies cannot add to the overall excellency of his person because he is already a perfect being in virtue of being a member of the holy Trinity. Clearly, a perfect being cannot be made *more perfect* by the addition of further attributes: he already has an infinite conjunction of excellencies. But the addition of his human excellencies in the Incarnation do make Christ *appear* more excellent to fallen human beings by manifesting his glory and excellency to us. So the Incarnation has this important function for Edwards: it makes God visible to us, and gives us additional reasons for esteeming and loving him. This is a clear instance

---

37. This is a theme Edwards develops in greater detail in his dissertation, *God's End in Creation*, where he endorses a doctrine of theosis: "If the happiness of the creature be considered as it will be, in the whole of the creature's eternal duration, with all the infinity of its progress, and infinite increase of nearness and union to God; in this view, the creature must be looked upon as united to God in an infinite strictness" (YE8: 534).

of affective doctrine and an extension of the thesis with which Edwards opened the sermon.

The sermon culminates with Edwards impressing upon his readers/hearers that union with Christ includes union with God. This is an important and recurrent theme in Edwards's theology, in which human salvation is much more than merely the saving of one's soul from damnation. He also reiterates that the union between God and the believer brought about through the work of Christ could not obtain without the Incarnation. We have a "more free and full enjoyment of him" than "we could have had if he had remained only in the divine nature" (YE19: 593). So it is only by God becoming incarnate, and (as it were) closing the infinite gap between God and fallen humanity, that union with God is possible. By setting forth the trajectory of salvation in this manner, Edwards indicates how doctrine and religious affection ought to go hand-in-hand. We might put it like this: only by tasting and seeing the admirable conjunction of diverse excellencies laid bare in Christ, can fallen human beings know and enjoy communion and union with God.

Conclusion

The connection between Edwards's understanding of the role of religious affections and the truth of doctrine has been explored before. As we have seen, as far back as Perry Miller, the Edwardsian "rhetoric of sensation" has been the subject of scholarly comment.[38] This chapter takes the discussion forward by focusing on one of Edwards's discourses at a time in his career when he was producing the most polished of his sermons. We have seen that Edwards was at pains to set forth careful, logically rigorous arguments for substantive doctrinal points in his sermons. But he was not content to leave it there. Doctrine had to be instilled in his hearers, so that it had a demonstrable, practical effect upon their lives. This is the affective dimension to Edwards's homiletics. And it is clear that, through his mastery of rhetoric, Edwards was able to impress upon those who heard him the affective nature of doctrine through sheer force of words and the

---

38. See, for example, the critical reaction of Vincent Tomas, in "The Modernity of Jonathan Edwards," *The New England Quarterly* 25.1 (1952): 60-84; and (more recently) the measured response by Michael J. McClymond in "Spiritual Perception in Jonathan Edwards," *Journal of Religion* 77.2 (1997): 195-216.

relentless logic of his delivery. Edwards may not have had the hortatory presence of Whitefield in his open-air rallies. But what he lacked in natural gifts of oratory, he made up for in the studied power of words. "Sticks and stones may break my bones, but words will never harm me" — so children are often taught. Edwards is remarkable as a thinker and preacher because he demonstrates how mistaken such sentiment is. In his hands, words became tools to unlock the hearts and souls of his hearers and readers. Edwards's power lay in the *text* of his sermons. His words really did change the way his congregation saw this world, and how they viewed the next.

CHAPTER 9

On the Orthodoxy of Jonathan Edwards

Suppose you came across the work of a long dead theologian that included the following summary statement of what he believed regarding the divine nature and God's relationship to the created order:

> God is a simple pure act, by which I mean God is essentially without composition and is such that there is no real distinction between his being (that he is) and his act (what he does). Indeed, God is the only entirely realized entity. In this respect, and in keeping with much Protestant and medieval thought, we can affirm that God is entirely distinct from his creation. He exists *a se*, which is to say he exists independently of that which he has created. And he is supremely free in all his acts, constrained only by his own nature, in bringing about what he does. He is infinitely beautiful, infinitely glorious and perfect in his nature and in all his ways. He is excellent. But excellency is an attribute that pertains only to those things which are beautiful, and beauty is something which implies an internal structure or set of relations within an entity. To be beautiful is to have "parts" or "relations" that, taken together, make the thing in question more complete, and therefore more excellent, than it would be without these relations. Although a simple, internally undifferentiated entity might have a certain austere beauty in virtue of its mereological simplicity, it is less wondrous and less excellent than something that includes symmetry, proportion, and parts or relations that consent with one another in a regularity. Such an excellent entity is greater than one without such relations because such an entity is beautiful in a much more complex manner than the mereological simple,

in virtue of the aesthetic relations it bears and the internal structure of its being.

God is a maximally excellent being. He is triune in his very nature. The three divine persons of the Godhead share a common divine essence. Yet there are real distinctions in God pertaining to the individuation of the divine persons. The Father is uncreated being; the Son or Logos is the divine idea of wisdom; the Holy Spirit is the bond of love, the agape of God, God in act. These distinctions are predicated on the so-called relations of origin, that is, those relations that distinguish one person from another. These comprise: "being the source of the Trinity," which is an attribute of the Father alone; "being eternally begotten of the Father before all ages," which belongs to the Son; and "being eternally spirated by the Father and the Son," the distinguishing attribute of the Holy Ghost.

Thus, God is a simple pure act; a being of superlative excellence; and essentially triune. He is eternal, existing outside of time and space. Yet he brings time and space into existence *ex nihilo*. Indeed, God's creation is not merely the product of his free eternal decision, but the necessary output, even overflow or emanation, of his nature. For God has an essential disposition to create. What is more, since he is a being perfect in every respect, it would be inconceivable for him to create a world that was an inferior product. For the ultimate end of all God's works is to bring himself glory. In creatures such an attribute would be a vice rather than a virtue, for placing the glorification of a limited being at the head of all one's works rather than the exaltation of a perfect being is vanity and pride. But placing the glorification of the most perfect being as the conclusion of all one's ways is a virtue, since there is nothing greater, and nothing better at which one may aim. It would be unfitting and inappropriate for God to direct himself to the glorification of anything other than himself in all his ways. Hence, God's ultimate end in creation is the glorification of himself. God's essential disposition to create is an eternal disposition that can only find its realization in the creation of a world *ad extra*. Hence, God eternally creates a world with time, and this is an essential product of the creativity of God. Indeed, God's perfect nature dictates that he creates the best possible world, since it would be a dereliction of his perfection for him to create a world less than perfect and there is an axiologically structured hierarchy of possible worlds including a best of all possible worlds. This world is just such a product of the divine agency.

The world comprises all created minds and their ideas, which exist "in" God. "Matter" is a fiction; there are no material objects strictly speaking, though there are objects that have properties such as "being hard," "being extended in space," etc. But these are no more than sensations, percepts, ideas — there is nothing over and above such ideal entities that must be taken account of in metaphysics. The world exists in God as a set of stable ideas. But the world is not an entity that persists through time upon being created by God. Rather, God creates a four-dimensional set of numerically distinct world-stages that exist across time, and that he segues together seriatim, according to his good pleasure and will. This means that the world is created whereupon it immediately ceases to exist, to be replaced by a second momentary facsimile world created *ex nihilo*. This too immediately ceases to exist and is replaced by another facsimile . . . and so on, each world-stage being succeeded by another seriatim, in the divine mind. Thus the "world" (i.e., the created order as it exists across space and time) is in reality a collection of world-stages. What is more, God causes these world-stages to obtain in the sequence they do, giving them the appearance of continuity through apparently stable laws and principles of operation. But God is the sole cause of the obtaining of these world-stages as well as being the causal agent responsible for all that obtains in these world-stages. Creatures are merely the occasions of God's action.

Such a picture of God's relation to the creation is undoubtedly striking, combining as it does aspects of classical theism, theological aesthetics, panentheism, and the doctrines of continuous creation and occasionalism (about which, more presently). Far from being the product of some febrile imagination, however, this summary represents the views of the eighteenth-century colonial British, New England Puritan Jonathan Edwards. Those enamored of the more practical and pastoral aspects of Edwards's writings may find this a rather different thinker from the author of the *Religious Affections*, the hagiographical *Life of David Brainerd*, or sermons like "God Glorified in Man's Dependence." But Edwards was a man of many parts, like a number of early modern thinkers.

Several recent treatments of Edwards's philosophical theology have argued that the sort of view given in the summary statement above represents Edwards's considered position on the relationship between God and creation — an important theme in his work.[1] However, this does raise

---

1. See John J. Bombaro, *Jonathan Edwards's Vision of Reality: The Relationship of God to the World, Redemption History, and the Reprobate* (Eugene, OR: Pickwick Publications, 2012);

a concern regarding the orthodoxy of Edwardsian theology that students of the Northampton Sage must face.

Edwards's thought has had a mixed reception in the two hundred and fifty years since his death. Although in recent times he has been hailed as "America's Theologian" and lauded as a thinker of the first rank, he has in the past been the subject of several attempts to impugn his orthodoxy. Edwards himself was a staunch supporter of the theological *status quo* despite the fact that the metaphysics he used to underpin his theology was far from conventional, and led to the development of the New England Theology — a movement not known for its adherence to tradition and creed.

It is this strange Edwardsian combination of high Calvinism and early Enlightenment philosophy that prompts the concern of this chapter. It would seem that, on the basis of the précis of his philosophical theology just given, Edwards is caught on the horns of a dilemma. Call it the Edwardsian Dilemma. It can be phrased like this: *Either Edwards must admit that his Theology Proper implies that God is not metaphysically simple, or he must embrace pantheism.* Neither of these two options would have been particularly palatable for a theologian of his pedigree, since Puritans were nothing if not classical and traditional in the theistic conception of God that they espoused.

However, from the perspective of contemporary constructive theology, the lesser of two evils would be to embrace the idea that God is not metaphysically simple in the classical sense. There are, of course, modern theologians who would be delighted to find in Edwards a precursor to their own predilection for a species of panentheism along with the denial of a classical conception of the divine. However, for those who look to Edwards in support of the classical, orthodox doctrine of God this is cold comfort. Nevertheless, both contemporary panentheists and classical theists will likely unite in their conviction that if Edwards was faced with a dilemma of the sort envisaged here, he ought to prefer a less than absolutely simple God over pantheism. For that way leads beyond the bounds of orthodox Christian doctrine, whereas a less than absolutely simple God means only

---

Crisp, *Jonathan Edwards on God and Creation* (New York: Oxford University Press, 2012); and Douglas Elwood, *The Philosophical Theology of Jonathan Edwards* (New York: Columbia University Press, 1960). Similar views can be found in Kyle C. Strobel, *Jonathan Edwards's Theology: A Reinterpretation* (London: T&T Clark, 2012); and William J. Wainwright, "Jonathan Edwards," in *Stanford Encyclopedia of Philosophy*, http://plato.stanford.edu/entries/edwards/. For a rather different view of Edwards's theology see Lee, *The Philosophical Theology of Jonathan Edwards* (Princeton: Princeton University Press, 1988).

that, all things considered, Edwards was not strictly a theologian in the classical theistic mold, which is a much less controversial outcome, though an important one nonetheless.[2]

My argument proceeds in three parts. In the first, I show that on one plausible interpretation of his work, Edwards cannot consistently hold that God is absolutely metaphysically simple in a traditional sense. Then, in a second part, I argue that given a slightly different construal of Edwardsianism, pantheism obtains. In a third part I offer an analysis of which alternative is less damaging for the integrity (and orthodoxy) of Edwards's thought.

I presume throughout the not uncontroversial assumption that if Edwards's work does contain the sort of structural tensions, even inconsistencies, maintained here, he must embrace one or other of the horns of this dilemma to avoid incoherence. Given Edwards's habits of mind and theological temperament, this line of approach is, I think, a charitable rather than a critical one. Edwards was, after all, a theologian deeply concerned to ensure his work was coherent and aimed at truth. It might be argued that the dilemma outlined here fails to capture other options that were open to Edwards — that is, that it is not a *forced* dilemma, strictly speaking. In which case, Edwards is not necessarily faced with a choice between two equally unpleasant alternatives; a third option may be available to him. However, for reasons that will become clear in what follows, I do not think this is plausible. The deep structures of Edwards's metaphysics appear to present him with a real difficulty which he cannot escape without embracing significant theological revision to his doctrine of God in a manner incompatible with the classical theism of his heritage and schooling. Thus, I shall argue, Edwards *is* faced with a forced dilemma. Although he does not appear to have been aware of this particular implication of his work, it is an implication. A hard decision must therefore be made in order to stave off incoherence or unorthodoxy. Happily, however, much of Edwardsian doctrine can be preserved by opting for a more modest account

---

2. Of course, some may conclude that any doctrine of God that prescinds from the doctrine of divine simplicity as it has been traditionally understood is outside the bounds of orthodoxy. This would certainly be true for Roman Catholics, for whom the doctrine is an established dogma (affirmed at Lateran IV and Vatican I). However, I think that in the current theological climate there is much less sympathy for this claim than there is for the claim that pantheism is unorthodox. For, presumably, one could believe that God is less than simple and still hold to the Catholic creeds. But one cannot really do that if one is a pantheist.

of the unity of the divine nature. This does constitute a departure from Edwards's stated views. But such revision is needed in order to "repair" or "amend" Edwards's thought so as to avoid the problem raised by the dilemma.

Divine Simplicity, Occasionalism, and Panentheism

Let us begin by briefly outlining what divine simplicity, occasionalism, and panentheism are. I take it that the doctrine of divine simplicity is, minimally, the view according to which God is essentially non-composite. There may be different strains of this doctrine in the history of Christian theology.[3] But even if it is regarded as primarily an apophatic doctrine, designed to anchor Christian Trinitarianism within monotheism (thereby preventing it from drifting towards tritheism) but offering much less by way of positive content when it comes to predication, it is usually thought to include certain cataphatic elements. One of these is that each of the divine attributes implies all the others. Another is that each divine attribute implies the divine essence. This is certainly how it has been understood in the recent literature, and even amongst the majority of those who have sought to defend it against contemporary revisionists.

Edwards clearly endorses this doctrine. He does not elaborate upon it, or offer a detailed account of it. But he accepts it as part of the theological heritage bequeathed to him by his forebears. His references to it are just what one would expect of someone for whom it is a given, something uncontroversial, part of the warp and weave of his doctrine of God. In *Freedom of the Will*, he speaks of God's "perfect and absolute simplicity,"[4] whilst in *Religious Affections* he says, "A love to God for the beauty of his moral attributes, leads to, and necessarily causes a delight in God for all his attributes; for his moral attributes cannot be without his natural attributes: for infinite holiness supposes infinite wisdom, and an infinite capacity and greatness; and *all the attributes of God do as it were imply each other*."[5] This idea that the attributes of God imply one another is a constituent of the traditional doctrine of divine simplicity. In his unpublished work

---

3. Richard Muller has argued to this effect in his magisterial *Post-Reformation Reformed Dogmatics: The Rise and Development of Reformed Orthodoxy, ca. 1520 to ca. 1725* (Grand Rapids: Baker Academic, 2003), vol. 3, pp. 32-33, 276.
4. YE1: 377.
5. YE3: 256-57, emphasis added.

on the Trinity, Edwards says similar things. His *Discourse on the Trinity* begins with Edwards saying that "there are *no* distinctions to be admitted of faculty, habit and act, between will, inclination and love" in God, "but that it is all *one simple act*."[6] Moreover, in speaking of the Second Person of the Trinity as the Divine Idea, Edwards says that the perfect view God has of his own essence is one "in which there is *no distinction of substance and act, but it is wholly substance and wholly act*" such that the "idea God hath of himself is absolutely himself."[7]

The claim that Edwards upheld the doctrine of divine simplicity has been disputed in some recent studies.[8] Whenever he refers to this doctrine in his mature published works, however, he endorses it. Furthermore, in the very text in which some scholars have thought him to be distancing himself from the doctrine, that is, in the unpublished *Discourse on the Trinity*, his opening gambit is to reiterate the doctrine. This presents very strong *prima facie* evidence for the conclusion that he affirmed the doctrine of divine simplicity — something that a number of Edwards scholars now recognize.[9]

Next, we come to occasionalism. This is the doctrine according to which God is the sole causal agent in the world, creatures being merely the occasions of God's action. So, on this way of thinking, when I raise my arm *I* intend to raise my arm, but the cause of the raising of my arm is not *my* bringing about that intention in the actual raising of my arm. Nor is it that I am a necessary but insufficient cause of the bringing about of the raising of my arm, where God is a concurrent cause of my action — as is the case in traditional Thomist accounts of God's causal activity in the world. God

---

6. YE21: 113, emphasis added.
7. YE21: 116, emphasis added.
8. See Amy Plantinga Pauw, "'One Alone Cannot Be Excellent': Jonathan Edwards on Divine Simplicity," in *Jonathan Edwards: Philosophical Theologian*, ed. Paul Helm and Oliver D. Crisp (Aldershot: Ashgate, 2003), pp. 115-25, and her monograph, *"The Supreme Harmony of All": The Trinitarian Theology of Jonathan Edwards* (Grand Rapids: Eerdmans, 2002); as well as Michael McClymond's essay, "Hearing the Symphony: A Critique of Some Critics of Sang Lee's and Amy Plantinga Pauw's Accounts of Jonathan Edwards's View of God," in *Jonathan Edwards as Contemporary: Essays in Honor of Sang Hyun Lee*, ed. Don Schweitzer (New York: Peter Lang, 2010), pp. 67-92.
9. See Bombaro, *Jonathan Edwards's Vision of Reality*; Crisp, *Jonathan Edwards on God and Creation*; Strobel, *Jonathan Edwards's Theology*; and Stephen R. Holmes, "Does Jonathan Edwards Use a Dispositional Ontology? A Response to Sang Hyun Lee," in Helm and Crisp, eds., *Jonathan Edwards: Philosophical Theologian*, pp. 99-114. See also Wainwright's *Stanford Encyclopedia* article, "Jonathan Edwards."

does not work in conjunction with secondary causes like created agents in order to bring actions about, on this view. Instead, God brings the action about directly. I may intend to raise my arm. But, says the occasionalist, that basic action does not cause the non-basic action of the raising of my arm. God does that. As my arm is raised, it appears that I have caused this via my intention to raise my arm. But in fact, my intention was merely the occasion of a divine action that brought about the raising of my arm. Hence, I am not the cause of the raising of my arm.

Were this the whole story, occasionalism would be a thesis about how the actions of creaturely agents are brought about by God, not a thesis about how God brings about what appear to be creaturely actions *simpliciter*. But in fact, it appears that matters are slightly more complicated than this straightforward picture of occasionalism would suggest. For it transpires that occasionalism does entail that God is the sole causal agent of *all* creaturely actions, not merely of non-basic creaturely actions. Intentions are actions of a basic sort, that is, they are actions I perform without using some other means by which to bring the action about. I simply and immediately form the intention to do a particular thing. But, given the central claim of occasionalism that God is the sole causal agent, it looks like my intention to raise my arm is not an action I cause. It is the occasion of God's causing me to form an intention to raise my arm, which results in God causing the raising of my arm. But then it looks like occasionalism is not merely a thesis about how the realization of my intentions in action is directly caused by God, contrary to first appearances. It is a much more radical thesis that implies no mundane action is caused by moral agents other than God. But, of course, this more radical thesis jeopardizes the very idea that there are moral agents other than God.

Evidence that Edwards held a doctrine of occasionalism is not hard to come by: he explicitly endorses it in his treatise *Freedom of the Will*, where he says that the relation that exists between the antecedent and its consequent "is perhaps rather an occasion than a cause, most properly speaking."[10] Similar sentiments are expressed elsewhere. Consider, for example, his comments in "Of Atoms," one of his early philosophical works:

> the substance of bodies at last becomes either nothing, or nothing but the Deity acting in that particular manner in those parts of space where he thinks fit. So that, speaking most strictly, there is no proper sub-

10. YE1: 180-81.

stance but God himself. . . . Since . . . solidity or body is immediately from the exercise of divine power, causing there to be resistance in such a part of space, it follows that motion also, which is the communication of body, solidity, or this resistance, from one part of space to another successively . . . is from the immediate exercise of divine power so communicating that resistance, according to certain conditions which we call the laws of motion. . . . Hence we see what's that we call the laws of nature in bodies, to wit: the stated methods of God's acting with respect to bodies, and the stated conditions of the alteration of the manner of his acting.[11]

Here, as with the doctrine of divine simplicity, it is not insignificant that both in his early unpublished philosophical works and in his mature published works, Edwards can be found endorsing the same view of causation as occasionalism.[12]

Panentheism is not so much a particular view as it is a family of views about the relationship between God and creation.[13] Nevertheless, all pan-

---

11. YE6: 215-16. See also "Miscellany" 267, where Edwards says: "The mere exertion of a new thought is a certain proof of a God. For certainly there is something that immediately produces and upholds that thought; here is a new thing, and there is a necessity of a cause. It is not antecedent thoughts, for they are vanished and gone; they are past, and what is past is not" (YE13: 373). The reasoning underlying this rather cryptic entry seems to be something like this. Past thoughts no longer exist because they are past; things that are past and therefore non-existent cannot generate present things that do exist because *ex nihilo nihil fit*; so some cause other than past thoughts must bring about present thoughts; only a thinking thing can bring about present thoughts; only God is an eternal thinking thing that persists from one moment to the next; so only God can bring about present thoughts; therefore God exists. But clearly, if God is the only agent capable of bringing about present thoughts this also establishes that God causes present thoughts (in creatures). Though this is not sufficient for occasionalism, it is an important step towards the view that God is the only causal agent.

12. See also Philip L. Quinn, "Divine Conservation, Continuous Creation, and Human Action," in *The Existence and Nature of God*, ed. Alfred J. Freddoso (Notre Dame: University of Notre Dame Press, 1983), pp. 55-79, as well as his "Divine Conservation, Secondary Causes, and Occasionalism," in *Divine and Human Action*, ed. Thomas V. Morris (Ithaca: Cornell University Press, 1988), pp. 50-73. For alternative views on Edwardsian occasionalism see Sang Lee, *The Philosophical Theology of Jonathan Edwards*; and Stephen Daniel, "Edwards' Occasionalism," in Schweitzer, ed., *Jonathan Edwards as Contemporary*, pp. 15-32.

13. The most comprehensive recent typology of panentheisms can be found in John Cooper's book, *Panentheism: The Other God of the Philosophers — From Plato to the Present* (Grand Rapids: Baker Academic, 2006).

entheists agree that God and creation are not distinct entities as the classical theist thinks. Instead (so it is often reported) God is to the world as the soul is to the body. The world is contained "within" God, but God is not exhausted by the world; he is greater than the world.

Although (as previously noted) the attribution of a doctrine of divine simplicity and of occasionalism to Edwards is not uncontroversial, ascribing panentheism to him is perhaps the most contested of these three claims. Nevertheless, a number of reputable Edwards scholars maintain that he does hold to some version of this doctrine, and there is evidence of it in his work.[14] Sometimes, in fact, Edwards says rather unguarded things that border on pantheism (roughly, the idea that God and the world are identical). For instance, his comment that "being includes in it all that we call God, who *is*, and there is none else besides him."[15] Or again, "God is the sum of all being and there is no being without his being; all things are in him, and he in all."[16] But his more measured remarks are consistent with panentheism, not pantheism. The clearest indication comes from his dissertation, *God's End in Creation*. There he says things like, "This propensity in God to diffuse himself may be considered as a propensity to himself diffused, or to his own glory existing in its emanation." Or again, "God looks on the communication of himself, and the emanation of the infinite glory and good that are in himself to belong to the fullness and completeness of himself, as though he were not in his most complete and glorious state without it."[17] What is more, *"that a disposition in God, as an original property of his nature, to an emanation of his own infinite fullness, was what excited him to create the world; and so that the emanation itself was aimed at by him as a last end of the creation."*[18] In the last section of this dissertation, Edwards even goes as far as to say this:

---

14. John Cooper says, "All things considered, his affirmation that 'the whole is *of* God, and *in* God, and *to* God' [in YE8: 531] is best construed philosophically as panentheism that borders on Spinozan pantheism" (*Panentheism*, p. 77). Similar sentiments are expressed by Douglas Elwood, in *The Philosophical Theology of Jonathan Edwards*; and, more recently, John Bombaro, *Jonathan Edwards's Vision of Reality*, especially appendix A; and Crisp, *Jonathan Edwards on God and Creation*, chap. 7. But this line of interpretation is resisted by, among others, Sang Lee in *The Philosophical Theology of Jonathan Edwards*, chap. 7, and, more recently, Steven Studebaker and Robert Caldwell III, in *The Trinitarian Theology of Jonathan Edwards: Text, Context, and Application* (Aldershot: Ashgate, 2012), chap. 9.

15. "Miscellany" 27a, in YE13: 213.
16. "Miscellany" 880, in YE20: 123.
17. YE8: 439.
18. YE8: 435, emphasis original.

In the creature's knowing, esteeming, loving, rejoicing in, and praising God, the glory of God is both exhibited and acknowledged; his fullness is received and returned. Here is both an *emanation* and *remanation*. The refulgence shines upon and into the creature, and is reflected back to the luminary. The beams of glory come from God, and are something of God, and are refunded back again to their original. So that the whole is *of* God, and *in* God, and *to* God; and God is the beginning, middle and end in this affair.[19]

This Neoplatonism (for that is what it amounts to) is something Edwards picked up from his voracious reading, particularly in the writings of Cambridge Platonists like Henry More, an early influence on Edwards.[20] But like Plotinus, Edwards is a kind of idealist, and his Neoplatonism, baptized into the Reformed faith, implies the doctrine that the world exists "in" God and that it is "emanated" by God. The precise shape of Edwards's panentheism need not detain us here.[21] The fact that he is a panentheist should be evident, however.

It would appear, even from this brief sketch, that finding some state of affairs where these three doctrines are compossible is a tall order. Let us set the doctrine of occasionalism to one side for the present, and focus on the conjunction of divine simplicity with panentheism. If God is metaphysically non-composite in the strong sense implied in most classical, orthodox Christian theology, then he is absolutely without parts. But panentheism seems to imply that the creation is a "part" of God, though not identical to God, for that would be pantheism. In which case, creation is a "part" of God that is somehow contained "within" the Godhead. It is not difficult to see the problem this generates: the panentheistic God cannot be non-composite in any strong sense since he appears to have (at least) two "parts": that aspect of his nature which is independent of the creation; and the creation which is the necessary product of his creative nature.

This is worrisome enough. But there are even deeper problems for Edwards. Suppose God is simple in the absolute sense. Then, all his attri-

---

19. YE8: 531.

20. For discussion of early philosophical influences on Edwards, see Wallace Anderson's editorial introduction to YE6 and, on Edwards's reading, YE26.

21. See Bombaro, *Jonathan Edwards's Vision of Reality*, appendix A; Crisp, "Jonathan Edwards' Panentheism," in Schweitzer, ed., *Jonathan Edwards as Contemporary*, pp. 107-26; and Elwood, *The Philosophical Theology of Jonathan Edwards*.

butes imply each other and imply the divine nature. Indeed, there appears to be no distinction between the divine attributes and the divine nature. In keeping with a number of other Reformed and western Catholic theologians, this appears to be the doctrine Edwards adopts. Now, conjoin this strong doctrine of divine simplicity to panentheism. If there are no real distinctions in God and if the creation exists "within" the divine nature, then it appears that creation is identical to the divine nature. But then pantheism obtains.

What if Edwards is only committed to some weaker account of God's relation to the world? Suppose the creation is a set of "stable" divine ideas that are communicated by God, or emanated by him *ad extra*, so that the world is the "overflow" of the divine nature in some shadowy existence outside God. Even if this is right it is still the case that God has a set of ideas about the creation that are identical to each other and to the divine nature. This alone would be a serious concern for the integrity of Edwards's doctrine. Taken together with occasionalism, this would mean that the creation has an attenuated existence as a series of numerically distinct, shadowy world-stages that exist across spacetime. Although such a view is not unorthodox, strictly speaking, it is surely an impoverished doctrine of creation and one that will likely have little appeal to contemporary theologians unsympathetic to Christian appropriations of Neoplatonism.

There is another avenue open to the defender of a broadly Edwardsian account of these things. This is to revise his doctrine of absolute divine simplicity. If God were simple but not absolutely simple, then it would be possible for him to have distinct states, including distinct mental states, and then he could have a set of ideas of the created order that would not imply one another or the divine nature. It would appear, however, from what I have earlier argued in this volume, that Edwards stands firmly within the Reformed and western Catholic tradition and would have almost certainly not have been willing to entertain a softened form of divine simplicity as a viable alternative. The preponderance of his scattered remarks align with a doctrine of absolute simplicity. However, it is worth pausing over Miscellany 135, where Edwards says this:

> Many have wrong conceptions of the difference between the nature of the Deity and created spirits. The difference is no contrariety, but what naturally results from his greatness and nothing else, such as created spirits come nearer to, or more imitate, the greater they are in their powers and faculties. So that if we should suppose the faculties of a

created spirit to be enlarged infinitely, there would be the Deity to all intents and purposes, the same simplicity, immutability, etc.[22]

Taken at face value, this implies something quite different from a traditional doctrine of divine simplicity, since were we able *(mirabile dictu)* to enlarge the powers and capacities of a human soul so as to become a divine soul the net result would not be an absolutely simple being but a metaphysically simple super-soul. It would be non-fissile, since it would not be composed of more fundamental parts; in that sense it would be metaphysically simple. But it would not be *absolutely* simple (i.e., without any parts or composition whatsoever) because it would have distinct mental states and properties. Since this would undermine Edwards's otherwise apparently staunch support for a traditional-sounding doctrine of divine simplicity, and since this is a thought experiment, I think we can charitably assume Edwards did not mean readers of this miscellany to think that God's simplicity is exactly the same as the simplicity of a human soul. Nevertheless, it is noteworthy that in this Miscellany, what he has to say is more metaphysically capacious, that is, allowing for a more modest account of divine simplicity than his other scattered comments on this doctrine might lead one to expect.

If we were to take this modest account of divine simplicity in Miscellany 135 at face value, as one way of rendering Edwards's doctrine coherent, how would this help the advocate of such a refashioned Edwardsianism?

Imagine that God is simple in this modest sense: he is a metaphysically simple substance, like a soul. I take it that souls are non-composite because they are not composed of any more fundamental elements. They are mereological simples or primitives. Bodies, by contrast, are not mereological simples because they are composed of more fundamental elements, e.g., quarks, electrons, and so on. Whereas bodies are in principle fissiparous because they are composed of parts, souls are not. They cannot be divided; they have no location; they are not extended in space. God is like a soul in this regard. He is not fissiparous; indeed, it is a necessary truth that he is not fissiparous. Nor does he have location; and he is not extended in space. So he is simple in a strong sense, but — importantly for present purposes — not a sense that compromises his having distinct mental states, and, therefore, distinct properties. Were Edwards to adopt this modest account of simplicity, then he could claim that God is simple (i.e., a meta-

22. YE13: 295.

physical primitive); that the world exists as a set of divine ideas "in" the divine mind; and that God emanates the created order as a shadowy ideal work that exists *ad extra*. With the exception of this revision to our understanding of divine simplicity and its metaphysical implications we would require no other substantive changes to Edwardsian doctrine.

This represents one way (taken together with a Neoplatonic construal of his panentheism) that Edwards could avoid the Edwardsian Dilemma, with which we began. There is a cost to such revision. But the Edwardsian might think it a cost worth bearing, given the more pressing need for some sort of theological resolution to the Edwardsian Dilemma. This revision to Edwards's doctrine does preserve the internal consistency of his overall metaphysical vision of reality, given a Neoplatonic interpretation of his panentheism. But it does leave intact the moral problems raised by his doctrine of occasionalism. However, there appears to be little that can be done to aid Edwards in that particular theological problem.[23] For the Edwardsian occasionalist appears to be committed to the following inconsistent claims:

1. *God is the only causal agent.* The actions of created "agents" are the occasions of divine action, strictly speaking.
2. *God is the only moral agent.* Created agents do not persist whole and complete from one moment to the next. They are composed of an infinite number of temporal "stages" that are aggregated by divine fiat into one temporally extended individual across time. But this means no created agent exists for long enough to be the cause of moral actions, which means, in turn, that no created agent is capable of being a moral agent.
3. *God is causally but not morally responsible for evil.* God is the agent by means of which wickedness obtains in the creation; since he is the only causal agent, this follows trivially from (1). But God is not morally responsible for the wicked actions of created agents. Created agents are responsible for their wicked actions.

The problem is, there appears to be no moral wiggle room for the Edwardsian here. If God is the only causal agent (because occasionalism obtains)

---

23. This is pointed out in Crisp, *Jonathan Edwards and the Metaphysics of Sin* (Aldershot: Ashgate, 2005). Some similar themes are explored in Joseph Prud'homme and James Schelberg, "Disposition, Potentiality, and Beauty in the Theology of Jonathan Edwards: A Defense of His Great Doctrine of Original Sin," *American Theological Inquiry* 5.1 (2012): 25-53.

and if God is the only moral agent (because occasionalism + continuous creation obtains), then it looks like no created agent causes anything to obtain. Indeed no created agent exists for long enough to be morally responsible for actions that are temporally extended. Since almost all significant moral actions are temporally extended (i.e., they take time to commit), this means that almost all — perhaps *all* — moral actions are not actions that can be ascribed to created agents. If God is the only causal agent, it looks like he is the only moral agent too.

Someone may object to the accuracy of this portrait of Edwards. We have already noted in Chapter 6 that Michael Rea characterizes Edwards (I think rightly) as an early modern thinker who conceives of human beings along the lines of stage theory.[24] This view states that objects that are extended through time, like human beings, are four-dimensional. That is, they exist across time in virtue of possessing different momentary temporal stages (i.e., numerically distinct temporal counterparts) that, when aggregated together, form one temporally extended life. The Rea of noon yesterday and the Rea of noon today are two numerically distinct stages that are aggregated together in one temporally extended life that comprises the sum of such stages. Through immanent causal relations one stage is linked to the next such that a later stage may be the successor or closest continuer of the earlier stage, though they are numerically distinct. Suppose Edwards believes this (and I think Rea mounts a strong argument for the claim that this is indeed the Edwardsian position). Then it looks like the Rea of noon yesterday and the Rea of noon today are stages of one four-dimensional entity and the crime of Rea yesterday may be attributed to the Rea of today. In other words, we can tell some story, based on this ontology, according to which numerically distinct stages may compose a single temporally extended life, such that we may attribute moral properties that obtain at one stage to the later stages of the life of such an entity as it exists across time.

However, setting to one side the strangeness of such an ontology, it will not work in Edwards's favor because there are no immanent causal relations between different stages of a single four-dimensional entity that are not directly and immediately caused by God. Edwards is, after all, an occasionalist. Since almost no moral action obtains in an instant, it would

---

24. See Michael C. Rea, "The Metaphysics of Original Sin," in *Persons: Divine and Human*, ed. Peter van Inwagen and Dean Zimmerman (Oxford: Oxford University Press, 2007), pp. 319-56.

appear that Edwards is faced with at least this very significant moral problem: God is causally and morally responsible for the vast majority of creaturely evil. That is a very serious drawback to his position.

It would seem that in order to avoid the conclusion that God is morally as well as causally responsible for all events that take place in the world, the Edwardsian must distance herself from occasionalism, despite the fact that it is an integral part of the Edwardsian account of the transmission of original sin.[25] So, even if we can provide an account of Edwards's metaphysics that is able to accommodate panentheism and a weak version of divine simplicity, occasionalism provides a significant — indeed, fatal — objection to the consistency of Edwards's position. Or, more precisely, if we factor occasionalism and continuous creation into the equation, then Edwards must embrace the unpleasant and unorthodox consequence that God is the cause of (at least) the overwhelming majority of creaturely evil. Thus, if he grasps the first horn of the dilemma, he will be skewered on it.

God, the World, and Pantheism

But what about the other horn of the dilemma, that is, the worry that if Edwards embraces absolute divine simplicity his view collapses into pantheism? We have already noted this prospect in passing. The concern can be put like this. Suppose God is absolutely simple. Add to this the claim that panentheism is true. Then, God's attributes all imply each other and all imply the divine nature. The divine nature contains the created order, which exists as a set of divine ideas. So (minimally) each fundamental element of the created order implies every other and implies the divine nature. But then there is no metaphysical wiggle room between God and creation: the creation is either numerically or qualitatively identical to God, and pantheism obtains.

This is not a new criticism of Edwards. In the nineteenth century there were grumblings about the implications of Edwardsian metaphysics. Perhaps the best-known critic of the Edwardsian position along these lines was the stanch Princeton Presbyterian, Charles Hodge. In his *Systematic Theology* he writes:

---

25. Edwards, *Original Sin*, IV. III, in YE3. Compare Crisp, *Jonathan Edwards and the Metaphysics of Sin*.

It necessarily follows that if God is the only substance He is the only agent in the universe. All things out of God being every moment called into being out of nothing, are resolved into modes of God's efficiency. If He creates the soul every successive instant, He creates all its states, thoughts, feelings, and volitions. The soul is only a series of divine acts. And therefore there can be no free agency, no sin, no responsibility, no individual existence. The universe is only the self-manifestation of God. This doctrine, therefore, in its consequences, is essentially pantheistic.[26]

As we have already noted, Hodge's objection can only stand if God and the world are identical. But Edwards explicitly denies that this is the case — he is a panentheist, not a pantheist. Nevertheless, Hodge is onto something. Edwards's position could be construed in a way that yields pantheism. For, in addition to the aspects of his metaphysics we have already considered, Edwards is also an idealist who speaks of God "communicating" himself in his act of continuously creating world-stages that he segues together according to his good purpose and will. As William Schweitzer has recently put it, "For Edwards, the content of what God communicates to his intelligent beings is, ultimately, *himself.*"[27] The idealism that Edwards defended meant that "all ideas have their origin and substance in God's idea he has of himself, which is indeed the Second Person of the Trinity. . . . All reality resides in the divine mind, and there can be nothing in creation that did not come from, and forever remains grounded in, the Trinity."[28] Finally, "not only do our ideas necessarily originate from God's idea, they are also 'immediately' communicated to us by God while our bodies 'passively receive' them."[29] Although he does not plumb the depths of Edwardsian idealism, Schweitzer's comments are salutary. God continuously communicates himself to his creatures as he continuously creates world-stages, segued together in the divine mind. Creatures are passive recipients of God's communications, not just in the sense that God communicates the whole of reality from himself at each moment, but also in the sense that all that is created, the creatures included, are mere mo-

---

26. Hodge, *Systematic Theology* (Grand Rapids: Eerdmans, 1940 [1871]), vol. 2, p. 220. For a recent discussion of other pantheistic objections to Edwardsian metaphysics, see Studebaker and Caldwell III, *The Trinitarian Theology of Jonathan Edwards*, chap. 9.

27. Schweitzer, *God Is a Communicative Being: Divine Communicativeness and Harmony in the Theology of Jonathan Edwards* (London: T&T Clark, 2012), p. 20.

28. Schweitzer, *God Is a Communicative Being*, p. 21.

29. Schweitzer, *God Is a Communicative Being*, p. 22.

mentary stages that exist temporarily, flitting, as it were, across the divine mind from whence they originate as divine communications.

When this picture of God's immediate communicativeness in continuous creation of an ideal world is placed alongside Edwards's views about divine simplicity, it is difficult to escape Hodge's conclusion that Edwards is a pantheist in spite of himself. For an ideal world that exists in the divine mind, that is a series of world-stages immediately communicated by God, and that comprises a set of divine ideas that are identical to one another and to the divine nature entails pantheism. For what is pantheism but the thesis that God and the created order are identical? As per traditional versions of divine simplicity, and in keeping with Edwards's published views in *Religious Affections* that "all the attributes of God do as it were imply each other,"[30] it would appear that Edwards is hoist by his own petard. The creation is a set of momentary divine ideas; divine ideas are identical to one another; and divine ideas are identical to God. But this is just pantheism. As Hodge puts it, "the universe is only the self-manifestation of God."

Forcing the Choice

Faced with this dilemma, what is the Edwardsian to do? These are deep waters, and it is always a rather tricky thing to begin suggesting ways in which the metaphysics of a particular thinker might be "amended" or "corrected" in order to avoid certain perceived pitfalls. Nevertheless, given the seriousness of the position the Edwardsian finds himself in, there may be good reason to attempt just this. (It should be noted that there is a long tradition of Edwards's disciples amending his ideas, as a cursory glance at the history of the New England Theology will tell.) The obvious change has already been suggested, namely, embracing a less stringent concept of divine simplicity. This would avoid the second horn of the dilemma. Edwards (or the Edwardsian) would not then be committed to pantheism. For a God that has distinct mental states and distinct properties could presumably have an infinite number of divine ideas that are not identical to one another or to the divine nature. Note that this does nothing to ameliorate the strangeness of Edwardsian metaphysics. But we have been concerned not with the fact that Edwardsian philosophical theology is exotic, but with the fact that it appeared to generate the Edwardsian Dilemma. By

---

30. YE3: 256-57.

adopting a weaker account of divine simplicity, the Edwardsian avoids the second horn of the dilemma.

But the cost is embracing the first horn. As we have seen, this means holding to occasionalism and continuous creation and the moral consequences of the conjunction of these two views. Thus, even if the Edwardsian avoids the second horn of the dilemma by means of a weaker doctrine of divine simplicity, the first horn cannot be avoided without further revision to Edwards's stated views. In other words, the Edwardsian must jettison occasionalism as well as a strong doctrine of divine simplicity in order to avoid both horns of the dilemma.

Bibliography

Works by Jonathan Edwards

a. *The Yale Edition: The Works of Jonathan Edwards*. 26 volumes. New Haven: Yale University Press, 1957-2008.

YE1 — *Freedom of the Will*. Edited by Paul Ramsey. 1957.
YE2 — *Religious Affections*. Edited by John E. Smith. 1959.
YE3 — *Original Sin*. Edited by Clyde A. Holbrook. 1970.
YE4 — *The Great Awakening*. Edited by C. C. Goen. 1972.
YE5 — *Apocalyptic Writings*. Edited by Stephen J. Stein. 1977.
YE6 — *Scientific and Philosophical Writings*. Edited by Wallace E. Anderson. 1980.
YE7 — *The Life of David Brainerd*. Edited by Norman Pettit. 1984.
YE8 — *Ethical Writings*. Edited by Paul Ramsey. 1989.
YE9 — *A History of the Work of Redemption*. Edited by John F. Wilson. 1989.
YE10 — *Sermons and Discourses, 1720-1723*. Edited by Wilson H. Kimnach. 1992.
YE11 — *Typological Writings*. Edited by Wallace E. Anderson and David Watters. 1993.
YE12 — *Ecclesiastical Writings*. Edited by David D. Hall. 1994.
YE13 — *The "Miscellanies": Nos. a-z, aa-zz, 1-500*. Edited by Thomas A. Schafer. 1994.
YE14 — *Sermons and Discourses, 1723-1729*. Edited by Kenneth P. Minkema. 1997.
YE15 — *Notes on Scripture*. Edited by Stephen J. Stein. 1998.
YE16 — *Letters and Personal Writings*. Edited by George S. Claghorn. 1998.
YE17 — *Sermons and Discourses, 1730-1733*. Edited by Mark Valeri. 1999.
YE18 — *The "Miscellanies": Nos. 501-832*. Edited by Ava Chamberlain. 2000.

Bibliography

YE19 — *Sermons and Discourses, 1734-1738*. Edited by M. X. Lesser. 2001.
YE20 — *The "Miscellanies": Nos. 833-1152*. Edited by Amy Plantinga-Pauw. 2002.
YE21 — *Writings on the Trinity, Grace and Faith*. Edited by Sang Hyun Lee. 2002.
YE22 — *Sermons and Discourses, 1739-1742*. Edited by Harry S. Stout and Nathan O. Hatch. 2003.
YE23 — *The "Miscellanies": Nos. 1153-1360*. Edited by Douglas A. Sweeney. 2004.
YE24 — *The Blank Bible*. Edited by Stephen J. Stein. 2006.
YE25 — *Sermons and Discourses, 1743-1758*. Edited by Wilson H. Kimnach. 2006.
YE26 — *Catalogues of Books*. Edited by Peter J. Thuesen. 2008.

b. Other Editions of Jonathan Edwards

Jonathan Edwards. *Charity and Its Fruits*. Edited by Tryon Edwards. New York: Robert Carter and Brothers, 1852.
———. *The Works of Jonathan Edwards*. Volume 1. Edited by Edward Hickman. Edinburgh: Banner of Truth Trust, 1974 [1834].
Jonathan Edwards's "Sinners in the Hands of an Angry God": A Casebook. Edited by Wilson H. Kimnach, Caleb J. D. Maskell, and Kenneth P. Minkema. New Haven: Yale University Press, 2010.
A Jonathan Edwards Reader. Edited by John E. Smith, Harry S. Stout, and Kenneth P. Minkema. New Haven: Yale University Press, 1995.
The Sermons of Jonathan Edwards: A Reader. Edited by Wilson H. Kimnach, Kenneth P. Minkema, and Douglas A. Sweeney. New Haven: Yale University Press, 1999.

Other Sources

Alston, Wallace M., and Michael Welker, eds. *Reformed Theology: Identity and Ecumenicity*. Grand Rapids: Eerdmans, 2003.
Anselm of Canterbury. *S. Anselmi, Cantuariensis Archepiscopi. Opera Omnia, Tomus Primus et Tomus Secundus*. Edited by F. S. Schmitt. Stuttgart: Friedrich Frommann Verlag, 1984 [1968].
———. *Basic Writings*. Edited and translated by Thomas Williams. Indianapolis: Hackett, 2007.
Arminius, Jacob. *The Works of James Arminius*. Edited by James Nichols, William Nichols, and W. R. Bagnall. Volumes 1 and 2: London: Longman, Hurst, Rees, Orme, Browne, & Green, 1825-1828; Volume 3: London: Thomas Baker, 1875; reprinted, Grand Rapids: Baker, 1986.

Bibliography

Bellamy, Joseph. *The Works of Joseph Bellamy, D.D.* 2 volumes. Boston: Doctrinal Tract and Book Society, 1853.

———. *True Religion Delineated.* Morris-Town: Henry P. Russell, 1804 [1750].

Blackburn, George A., ed. *Life Work of John L. Girardeau, D.D., LL.D.* Columbia, SC: The State Company, 1916.

Blocher, Henri. *Original Sin: Illuminating the Riddle.* Grand Rapids: Eerdmans, 1999 [1997].

Bombaro, John J. *Jonathan Edwards's Vision of Reality: The Relationship of God to the World, Redemption History, and the Reprobate.* Eugene, OR: Pickwick Publications, 2012.

Breitenbach, William. "Piety and Moralism: Edwards and the New Divinity." In *Jonathan Edwards and the American Experience.* Edited by Nathan O. Hatch and Harry S. Stout. New York: Oxford University Press, 1988. Pp. 177-204.

Brower, Jeffrey E. "Simplicity and Aseity." In *The Oxford Handbook to Philosophical Theology.* Edited by Thomas P. Flint and Michael C. Rea. Oxford: Oxford University Press, 2009. Pp. 105-28.

Bushnell, Horace. *Christ in Theology.* Hartford, CT: Brown and Parsons, 1851.

Caldwell, Robert W., III. *Communion in the Spirit: The Holy Spirit as the Bond of Union in the Theology of Jonathan Edwards.* Milton Keynes: Paternoster, 2006.

Calvin, John. *Institutes of the Christian Religion.* Edited by John T. McNeill. Translated by Ford Lewis Battles. Philadelphia: Westminster Press, 1960 [1559].

Carse, James. *Jonathan Edwards and the Visibility of God.* New York: Charles Scribner's Sons, 1967.

Chisholm, Roderick. *Person and Object.* London: George Allen and Unwin, 1976.

Choy, Kivin S. K. "Calvin's Defense and Reformulation of Luther's Early Reformation Doctrine of the Bondage of the Will." PhD dissertation, Calvin Theological Seminary, 2010.

Conforti, Joseph A. *Jonathan Edwards, Religious Tradition, and American Culture.* Chapel Hill: University of North Carolina Press, 1995.

Cooper, John W. *Panentheism: The Other God of the Philosophers — From Plato to the Present.* Grand Rapids: Baker Academic, 2006.

Crisp, Oliver D. *Deviant Calvinism: Broadening Reformed Theology.* Minneapolis: Fortress, 2014.

———. "How 'Occasional' Was Edwards' Occasionalism?" In *Jonathan Edwards: Philosophical Theologian.* Edited by Paul Helm and Oliver D. Crisp. Aldershot: Ashgate, 2003. Pp. 61-77.

———. *Jonathan Edwards and the Metaphysics of Sin.* Aldershot: Ashgate, 2005.

———. "Jonathan Edwards on Divine Simplicity." *Religious Studies* 39.1 (2003): 23-41.

———. *Jonathan Edwards on God and Creation*. New York: Oxford University Press, 2012.

———. "Jonathan Edwards' Panentheism." In *Jonathan Edwards as Contemporary: Essays in Honor of Sang Lee*. Edited by Don Schweitzer. New York: Peter Lang, 2010. Pp. 107-26.

———. "Original Sin and Atonement." In *The Oxford Handbook of Philosophical Theology*. Edited by Thomas P. Flint and Michael C. Rea. Oxford: Oxford University Press, 2009. Chap. 19.

———. "Penal Non-Substitution." *Journal of Theological Studies*, NS, 59.1 (2008): 140-68.

———. *Retrieving Doctrine: Essays in Reformed Theology*. Downers Grove, IL: IVP Academic, 2011.

Crisp, Oliver D., and Douglas A. Sweeney, eds. *After Jonathan Edwards: The Courses of the New England Theology*. New York: Oxford University Press, 2012.

Cross, F. L., and E. A. Livingstone, eds. *The Oxford Dictionary of the Christian Church*. Third edition. New York: Oxford University Press, 1997.

Dallimore, Arnold. *George Whitefield*. 2 volumes. Edinburgh: Banner of Truth, 1970; 1980.

Danaher, William J., Jr. *The Trinitarian Ethics of Jonathan Edwards*. Louisville: Westminster John Knox, 2004.

Daniel, Stephen H. "Edwards' Occasionalism." In *Jonathan Edwards as Contemporary: Essays in Honor of Sang Hyun Lee*. Edited by Don Schweitzer. New York: Peter Lang, 2010. Pp. 15-32.

———. *The Philosophy of Jonathan Edwards: A Study in Divine Semiotics*. Bloomington: University of Indiana Press, 1994.

Davies, Brian. "Simplicity." In *The Cambridge Companion to Christian Philosophical Theology*. Edited by Charles Taliaferro and Chad Meister. Cambridge: Cambridge University Press, 2010.

Dekker, Eef. "Jacob Arminius and His Logic: Analysis of a Letter." *Journal of Theological Studies*, NS, 44 (1993): 118-42.

———. "Was Arminius a Molinist?" *Sixteenth Century Journal* 27.2 (1996): 337-52.

Dwight, Sereno E. *Life of President Edwards*. New York: G. C. & H. Carvill, 1830.

Elwood, Douglas. *The Philosophical Theology of Jonathan Edwards*. New York: Columbia University Press, 1960.

Frankfurt, Harry. *The Importance of What We Care About*. Cambridge: Cambridge University Press, 1988.

Fumerton, Richard. "Knowledge by Acquaintance vs. Description." In *Stanford Encyclopedia of Philosophy*. http://plato.stanford.edu/entries/knowledge-acquaindescrip/

Bibliography

Gerstner, John H. *The Rational Biblical Theology of Jonathan Edwards*. Volume 2. Powhatan, VA: Berea Publications, 1992.

Girardeau, John L. *Calvinism and Evangelical Arminianism*. Harrisburg, PA: Sprinkle Publications, 1984 [1890].

———. *Philosophical Questions*. Edited by George A. Blackburn. Richmond, VA: The Presbyterian Committee of Publication, 1900.

———. *The Will in Its Theological Relations*. Columbia, SC: W. J. Duffie, 1891.

Guelzo, Alan C. *Edwards on the Will: A Century of American Theological Debate*. Eugene, OR: Wipf and Stock, 2008 [1989].

Gunter, W. Stephen, trans. *Arminius and His Declaration of Sentiments: An Annotated Translation with Introduction and Theological Commentary*. Waco, TX: Baylor University Press, 2012.

Hamilton, S. Mark. "Jonathan Edwards, Anselmic Satisfaction and God's Moral Government." *International Journal of Systematic Theology* 17.1 (2014): 46-67.

———. "Jonathan Edwards on the Atonement." *International Journal of Systematic Theology* 15.4 (2013): 394-415.

Hansen, Collin. *Young, Restless, Reformed: A Journalist's Journey with the New Calvinists*. Wheaton, IL: Crossway, 2008.

Haroutunian, Joseph. *Piety versus Moralism: The Passing of New England Theology from Edwards to Taylor*. Eugene, OR: Wipf and Stock, 2006 [1932].

Harris, James A. *Of Liberty and Necessity: The Free Will Debate in Eighteenth-Century British Philosophy*. Oxford: Oxford University Press, 2005.

Hatch, Nathan, and Harry S. Stout, eds. *Jonathan Edwards and the American Experience*. New York: Oxford University Press, 1988.

Heller, Mark. *The Ontology of Physical Objects: Four-Dimensional Hunks of Matter*. Cambridge: Cambridge University Press, 1990.

Helm, Paul. "A Forensic Dilemma: John Locke and Jonathan Edwards on Personal Identity." In *Jonathan Edwards: Philosophical Theologian*. Edited by Paul Helm and Oliver D. Crisp. Aldershot: Ashgate, 2003. Pp. 45-60.

———. *Calvin at the Centre*. Oxford: Oxford University Press, 2010.

———. *Faith and Understanding*. Edinburgh: Edinburgh University Press, 1997. Chap. 7: "Jonathan Edwards on Original Sin."

———. *John Calvin's Ideas*. Oxford: Oxford University Press, 2005.

———. "Jonathan Edwards and the Parting of the Ways." *Jonathan Edwards Studies* 4.1 (2014): 42-60.

———. "The Human Self and the Divine Trinity." In *Jonathan Edwards as Contemporary: Essays in Honor of Sang Hyun Lee*. Edited by Don Schweitzer. New York: Peter Lang, 2010. Pp. 93-106.

Helm, Paul, and Oliver D. Crisp, eds. *Jonathan Edwards: Philosophical Theologian.* Aldershot: Ashgate, 2003.

Heppe, Heinrich. *Reformed Dogmatics.* Translated by G. T. Thomson. London: Collins, 1950.

Hight, Marc, and Joshua Bohannon. "The Son More Visible: Immaterialism and the Incarnation." *Modern Theology* 26.1 (2010): 120-48.

Holmes, Stephen R. "Does Jonathan Edwards Use a Dispositional Ontology? A Response to Sang Hyun Lee." In *Jonathan Edwards: Philosophical Theologian.* Edited by Paul Helm and Oliver D. Crisp. Aldershot: Ashgate, 2003. Pp. 99-114.

———. *God of Grace and God of Glory: An Account of the Theology of Jonathan Edwards.* Edinburgh: T&T Clark, 2000.

Hodge, Charles. *Systematic Theology.* Volume 2. Grand Rapids: Eerdmans, 1940 [1871].

Hopkins, Samuel. *The Life and Character of the Late Reverend, Learned, and Pious Mr. Jonathan Edwards, President of the College of New Jersey, Together with a Number of Sermons on Various Important Subjects.* Boston: S. Kneeland, 1765.

———. *The Life and Character of the Late Learned Mr. Jonathan Edwards, President of the College of New Jersey, Together with Extracts from His Private Writings and Diary, and also Seventeen Select Sermons on Various Important Subjects.* Northampton, MA: Andrew Wright, 1804. [This is a different edition of Hopkins's work.]

Hume, David. *A Treatise of Human Nature.* Second edition. Edited by Peter Nidditch. Oxford: Oxford University Press, 1978 [1739-1740].

Immink, F. Gerrit. "The One and Only: The Simplicity of God." In *Understanding the Attributes of God. Contributions to Philosophical Theology.* Volume 1. Edited by Gijsbert van den Brink and Marcel Sarot. Frankfurt am Main: Peter Lang, 1999. Pp. 99-119.

James, William. *The Varieties of Religious Experience: A Study in Human Nature, Being the Gifford Lectures on Natural Religion Delivered at Edinburgh in 1901-1902.* New York: Longmans, Green, and Co., 1902.

Jenson, Robert W. *America's Theologian: A Recommendation of Jonathan Edwards.* New York: Oxford University Press, 1988.

———. "Christology." In *The Princeton Companion to Jonathan Edwards.* Edited by Sang Hyun Lee. Princeton: Princeton University Press, 2005. Chap. 6.

Kimnach, Wilson H. "Edwards as Preacher." In *The Cambridge Companion to Jonathan Edwards.* Edited by Stephen J. Stein. Cambridge: Cambridge University Press, 2007. Pp. 103-24.

———. "Jonathan Edwards's Pursuit of Reality." In *Jonathan Edwards and the*

American Experience. Edited by Nathan Hatch and Harry S. Stout. New York: Oxford University Press, 1988. Pp. 102-17.

———. "The Sermons: Concept and Execution." In *The Princeton Companion to Jonathan Edwards.* Edited by Sang Hyun Lee. Princeton: Princeton University Press, 2005. Pp. 243-57.

Kimnach, Wilson H., Kenneth P. Minkema, and Douglas A. Sweeney, eds. *The Sermons of Jonathan Edwards: A Reader.* New Haven: Yale University Press, 1999.

Kvanvig, Jonathan L. "Jonathan Edwards on Hell." In *Jonathan Edwards: Philosophical Theologian.* Edited by Paul Helm and Oliver D. Crisp. Aldershot: Ashgate, 2003. Pp. 1-12.

Lambert, Frank. *"Peddler in Divinity": George Whitefield and the Transatlantic Revivals, 1737-1770.* Princeton: Princeton University Press, 2002.

Lee, Sang Hyun. *The Philosophical Theology of Jonathan Edwards.* Princeton: Princeton University Press, 1988.

Lee, Sang Hyun, ed. *The Princeton Companion to Jonathan Edwards.* Princeton: Princeton University Press, 2005.

Leftow, Brian. "Why Perfect Being Theology?" *International Journal for Philosophy of Religion* 69 (2011): 103-18.

Locke, John. *An Essay concerning Human Understanding.* Edited by Peter Nidditch. Oxford: Oxford University Press, 1975 [1690].

Lowe, E. J. *Locke.* London: Routledge, 2005.

Lucas, Sean Michael. "'He Cuts Up Edwardsism by the Roots': Robert Lewis Dabney and the Edwardsian Legacy in the Nineteenth-Century South." In *The Legacy of Jonathan Edwards: American Religion and the Evangelical Tradition.* Edited by D. G. Hart, Sean Michael Lucas, and Stephen J. Nichols. Grand Rapids: Baker Academic, 2003. Pp. 200-214.

Luther, Martin. *The Bondage of the Will.* Translated by J. I. Packer and O. R. Johnston. London: James Clarke, 1957.

Mann, William E. "Anselm on the Trinity." In *The Cambridge Companion to Anselm.* Edited by Brian Davies and Brian Leftow. Cambridge: Cambridge University Press, 2004. Chap. 11.

Marsden, George. *Jonathan Edwards: A Life.* New Haven: Yale University Press, 2003.

McClymond, Michael J. "Hearing the Symphony: A Critique of Some Critics of Sang Lee's and Amy Plantinga Pauw's Accounts of Jonathan Edwards's View of God." In *Jonathan Edwards as Contemporary: Essays in Honor of Sang Hyun Lee.* Edited by Don Schweitzer. New York: Peter Lang, 2010. Pp. 67-92.

Bibliography

———. "Spiritual Perception in Jonathan Edwards." *Journal of Religion* 77.2 (1997): 195-216.

McClymond, Michael J., and Gerald R. McDermott. *The Theology of Jonathan Edwards*. New York: Oxford University Press, 2012.

Miller, Perry. *Errand into the Wilderness*. Cambridge, MA: Harvard University Press, 1956.

Moore, Jonathan D. *English Hypothetical Universalism: John Preston and the Softening of Reformed Theology*. Grand Rapids: Eerdmans, 2007.

Muller, Richard A. *God, Creation, and Providence in the Thought of Jacob Arminius*. Grand Rapids: Baker, 1991.

———. "Grace, Election, and Contingent Choice: Arminius's Gambit and the Reformed Response." In *The Grace of God, The Bondage of the Will*. Volume 2. Edited by Thomas R. Schreiner and Bruce A. Ware. Grand Rapids: Baker, 1995. Pp. 251-78.

———. "Jonathan Edwards and the Absence of Free Choice: A Parting of the Ways in the Reformed Tradition." *Jonathan Edwards Studies* 1.1 (2011): 3-22.

———. *Post-Reformation Reformed Dogmatics: The Rise and Development of Reformed Orthodoxy, ca. 1520 to ca. 1725*. Volume 3. Grand Rapids: Baker Academic, 2003.

Murray, Michael J., and Michael C. Rea. *An Introduction to the Philosophy of Religion*. Cambridge: Cambridge University Press, 2008.

Nichols, Stephen R. C. *Jonathan Edwards's Bible: The Relationship of the Old and New Testaments*. Eugene, OR: Pickwick, 2013.

Niebuhr, Richard R. "Being and Consent." In *The Princeton Companion to Jonathan Edwards*. Edited by Sang Hyun Lee. Princeton: Princeton University Press, 2005. Pp. 34-43.

Noll, Mark. *America's God: From Jonathan Edwards to Abraham Lincoln*. New York: Oxford University Press, 2005.

The Norton Anthology of American Literature, Shorter Seventh Edition. Edited by Nina Baym, Wayne Franklin, Philip F. Gura, Arnold Krupat, and Robert S. Levine. New York: W. W. Norton & Co., 2007.

O'Connor, Timothy. *Persons and Causes: The Metaphysics of Free Will*. New York: Oxford University Press, 2000.

Park, Edwards Amasa, ed. *The Atonement: Discourses and Treatises by Edwards, Smalley, Maxcy, Emmons, Griffin, Burge and Weeks*. Boston: Congregational Board of Publication, 1859.

Piper, John. *God's Passion for His Glory: Living the Vision of Jonathan Edwards*. Wheaton, IL: Crossway, 1998.

Bibliography

Plantinga, Alvin. "How to Be an Anti-Realist." *Proceedings and Addresses of the American Philosophical Association* 56.1 (1982): 47-70.

———. *Warranted Christian Belief.* New York: Oxford University Press, 2000.

Plantinga Pauw, Amy. "'One Alone Cannot Be Excellent': Jonathan Edwards on Divine Simplicity." In *Jonathan Edwards: Philosophical Theologian*. Edited by Paul Helm and Oliver D. Crisp. Aldershot: Ashgate, 2003. Pp. 115-25.

———. "The Future of Reformed Theology: Some Lessons from Jonathan Edwards." In *Towards the Future of Reformed Theology: Tasks, Topics, Traditions*. Edited by David Willis and Michael Welker. Grand Rapids: Eerdmans, 1999. Pp. 456-69.

———. *"The Supreme Harmony of All": The Trinitarian Theology of Jonathan Edwards*. Grand Rapids: Eerdmans, 2002.

———. "The Trinity." In *The Princeton Companion to Jonathan Edwards*. Edited by Sang Hyun Lee. Princeton: Princeton University Press, 2005. Chap. 4.

Prud'homme, Joseph, and James Schelberg. "Disposition, Potentiality, and Beauty in the Theology of Jonathan Edwards: A Defense of His Great Doctrine of Original Sin." *American Theological Inquiry* 5.1 (2012): 25-53.

Quinn, Philip L. "Divine Conservation, Continuous Creation, and Human Action." In *The Existence and Nature of God*. Edited by Alfred J. Freddoso. Notre Dame: University of Notre Dame Press, 1983. Pp. 55-79.

———. "Divine Conservation, Secondary Causes, and Occasionalism." In *Divine and Human Action*. Edited by Thomas V. Morris. Ithaca: Cornell University Press, 1988. Pp. 50-73.

Rea, Michael C. "The Metaphysics of Original Sin." In *Persons: Divine and Human*. Edited by Peter van Inwagen and Dean Zimmerman. Oxford: Oxford University Press, 2007. Pp. 319-56.

Reid, Jasper. "The Metaphysics of Jonathan Edwards and David Hume." *Hume Studies* 32.1 (2006): 52-82.

Rogers, Katherin A. *Anselm on Freedom*. Oxford: Oxford University Press, 2008.

———. *The Neoplatonic Metaphysics of Anselm of Canterbury*. Lampeter: Edwin Mellen Press, 1997.

Rowe, William. *Can God Be Free?* Oxford: Oxford University Press, 2004.

Rudisill, Dorus Paul. *The Doctrine of Atonement in Jonathan Edwards and His Successors*. New York: Poseidon Books, 1971.

Schafer, Thomas A. "Jonathan Edwards and Justification by Faith." *Church History* 20 (1951): 55-67.

Schreiner, Thomas R., and Bruce A. Ware, eds. *The Grace of God, The Bondage of the Will*. Volume 2. Grand Rapids: Baker, 1995.

Schweitzer, Don, ed. *Jonathan Edwards as Contemporary: Essays in Honor of Sang Hyun Lee*. New York: Peter Lang, 2010.

Schweitzer, William M. *God Is a Communicative Being: Divine Communicativeness and Harmony in the Theology of Jonathan Edwards*. London: T&T Clark, 2012.

Smith, John E. *Jonathan Edwards: Puritan, Preacher, Philosopher*. London: Geoffrey Chapman, 1992.

Stanglin, Keith D. "Arminius and Arminianism: An Overview of Current Research." In *Arminius, Arminianism, and Europe: Jacobus Arminius (1559/60-1609)*. Edited by Th. Marius van Leeuwen, Keith D. Stanglin, and Marijke Tolsma. Leiden: Brill, 2009. Pp. 3-24.

Stanglin, Keith D., and Thomas A. McCall. *Jacob Arminius: Theologian of Grace*. New York: Oxford University Press, 2012.

Stowe, Harriet Beecher. *Oldtown Folks*. Boston: Fields, Osgood and Co., 1869.

———. *The Minister's Wooing*. New York: Derby and Jackson, 1859.

Stout, Harry S. *The Divine Dramatist: George Whitefield and the Rise of Modern Evangelicalism*. Grand Rapids: Eerdmans, 1991.

———. "Edwards and Revival." In *Understanding Jonathan Edwards: An Introduction to America's Theologian*. Edited by Gerald R. McDermott. New York: Oxford University Press, 2009. Pp. 37-52.

Strobel, Kyle C. "Jonathan Edwards and the Polemics of Theosis." *Harvard Theological Review* 105.3 (2012): 259-79.

———. *Jonathan Edwards's Theology: A Reinterpretation*. London: T&T Clark, 2012.

Studebaker, Steven M. "Jonathan Edwards' Social Augustinian Trinitarianism: An Alternative to a Recent Trend." *Scottish Journal of Theology* 56 (2003): 268-85.

———. *Jonathan Edwards' Social Augustinian Trinitarianism in Historical and Contemporary Perspectives*. Piscataway, NJ: Gorgias Press, 2008.

Studebaker, Steven M., and Robert W. Caldwell III. *The Trinitarian Theology of Jonathan Edwards: Text, Context and Application*. Aldershot: Ashgate, 2012.

Sweeney, Douglas A. "Edwards and His Mantle: The Historiography of the New England Theology." *The New England Quarterly* 74.1 (1998): 97-119.

———. "'Falling Away from the General Faith of the Reformation?': The Contest over Calvinism in Nineteenth-Century America." In *John Calvin's American Legacy*. Edited by Thomas J. Davis. New York: Oxford University Press, 2010. Pp. 111-46.

———. *Nathaniel Taylor, New England Theology, and the Legacy of Jonathan Edwards*. New York: Oxford University Press, 2002.

Sweeney, Douglas A., and Allen C. Guelzo, eds. *The New England Theology: From Jonathan Edwards to Edwards Amasa Park*. Grand Rapids: Baker Academic, 2006.

Bibliography

Swinburne, Richard. *The Coherence of Theism.* Revised edition. Oxford: Oxford University Press, 1993 [1977].

Tanner, Norman P., ed. *Decrees of the Ecumenical Councils.* Volume 1 *(Nicaea I — Lateran V).* Washington, DC: Georgetown University Press, 1990.

Thomas, G. Michael. *The Extent of the Atonement: A Dilemma for Reformed Theology from Calvin to the Consensus (1536-1675).* Milton Keynes: Paternoster, 1997.

Tiessen, Terrance L. *Providence and Prayer: How Does God Work in the World?* Downers Grove, IL: IVP, 2000.

Tomas, Vincent. "The Modernity of Jonathan Edwards." *The New England Quarterly* 25.1 (1952): 60-84.

Turretin, Francis. *Institutes of Elenctic Theology.* Volume 1. Edited by James T. Dennison Jr. Translated by George Musgrave Giger. Phillipsburg: Presbyterian and Reformed, 1992.

Valeri, Mark. *Law and Providence in Joseph Bellamy's New England: The Origins of the New Divinity in Revolutionary America.* New York: Oxford University Press, 1994.

Van Asselt, Willem, J. Martin Bac, and Roelf T. te Velde, eds. *Reformed Thought on Freedom: The Concept of Free Choice in Early Modern Reformed Theology.* Grand Rapids: Baker Academic, 2010.

Visser, Sandra, and Thomas Williams. *Anselm.* New York: Oxford University Press, 2009.

Wainwright, William J. "Jonathan Edwards." In *Stanford Encyclopedia of Philosophy.* http://plato.stanford.edu/entries/edwards/.

———. "Jonathan Edwards and 'Particular Minds.'" *International Journal for Philosophy of Religion* 68 (2010): 201-13.

———. "Jonathan Edwards on the Doctrine of Hell." In *Jonathan Edwards: Philosophical Theologian.* Edited by Paul Helm and Oliver D. Crisp. Aldershot: Ashgate, 2003. Pp. 13-26.

———. "Jonathan Edwards, William Rowe, and the Necessity of Creation." In *Faith, Freedom, and Responsibility.* Edited by Jeff Jordan and Daniel Howard-Snyder. Lanham, MD: Rowman and Littlefield, 1996. Chap. 9.

———. "Original Sin." In *Philosophy and the Christian Faith.* Edited by Thomas V. Morris. Notre Dame: University of Notre Dame Press, 1988. Pp. 31-60.

———. *Reason and the Heart: A Prolegomenon to a Critique of Passional Reason.* Cornell Studies in Philosophy of Religion. Ithaca: Cornell University Press, 2006.

Warfield, Benjamin B. "Edwards and the New England Theology." In *The Works of Benjamin B. Warfield.* New York: Oxford University Press, 1932 [1912]. Pp. 515-38.

Bibliography

Wierenga, Edward. "Augustinian Perfect Being Theology and the God of Abraham, Isaac, and Jacob." *International Journal for Philosophy of Religion* 69 (2011): 139-51.
Williams, Garry. "A Critical Exposition of Hugo Grotius' Doctrine of the Atonement in *De Satisfactione Christi*." D. Phil. thesis, Oxford University, 1999.
Witt, William Gene. "Creation, Redemption, and Grace in the Theology of Jacob Arminius." PhD dissertation, University of Notre Dame, 1993.
Zwingli, Ulrich. *On Providence and Other Essays*. Translated by Samuel Macauley Jackson. Durham, NC: The Labyrinth Press, 1983 [1922].

Index

Aesthetics, 4, 5, 42, 166
Amyraldian theology, 6, 91, 127n6, 128n8, 139
Anselm of Canterbury, xv, 16, 17-25, 134. Works: *Monologion*, 20-25; *Proslogion*, 19-20, 34
Aquinas, Saint Thomas, 17, 19n5, 64; Thomism, 33, 46, 62, 64, 65
Arianism, 11, 31, 36, 39
Arminianism, 7, 60, 62, 79, 89, 110, 139, 141
Arminius, Jacob, xv-xvi, 60, 74, 77; on God and creation, 62-69. Work: *Private Disputations*, 63, 64
Asselt, Willem J. van, 80, 82, 84, 105
Atonement, 124-42; Bellamy on, 135-39; Edwards's doctrine of, 130-35; governmental model, 124, 134, 135, 140; limited atonement, 128; penal substitution, 124, 130-35, 140; satisfaction, 124
Augustinian theology, 11, 16, 22, 27, 33, 46; original sin, 108, 112

Barmen Declaration, 2
Belgic Confession, 2
Bellamy, Joseph, xv-xvi, 13, 124; on atonement, 135-39. Work: *True Religion*, 135
Berkeley, Bp. George, 12
Bodies, 27, 28, 29, 176
Boethius, 36n1, 48
Bushnell, Horace, 36n1

Caldwell, Robert, 37, 39, 46
Calvin, John, 3, 9, 26, 60, 100, 101, 106; Calvinism, 2, 79, 81, 89, 124, 167; old/new light Calvinism, 130; Thomist Calvinism, 78. *See also* Libertarian Calvinism
Cambridge Platonists, 12, 151n22, 174
Cartesianism, 29
Chalmers, Thomas, 7, 83
Christology, 146
Classical theism, 16, 17, 166, 168
Cooper, John, 76
Covenant of works, 100-103
Creation: continuous creation, 12-13, 29, 30, 66, 73, 166, 179-80; Creator/creation distinction, 16, 20, 26, 30-32, 32n35, 164; Edwards's doctrine of, 27-33, 69-77; emanation, 28-29, 29n27, 76, 165, 174; *ex nihilo*, 21, 64, 73, 165
Cunningham, William, 7, 83

Index

Danaher, William, 37, 45
Davenant, Bp. John, 127, 129
Deism, xviii, 4, 41
Divine determinism, xvii, 6, 68, 70, 71, 94, 110n3; hard determinism, 81; soft determinism, 81
Dort, Synod of, 2, 61n1, 102, 125, 127
Double guilt, 8, 109, 111
Duns Scotus, John, 17, 33, 64

Edwards, Jonathan: and beast of Tierra del Fuego, as example of libertarian free choice, 91; doctrine of creation, 27-33, 69-77; doctrine of God, 25-33, 69-77; doctrine of the atonement, 130-35; on free will, 87-94. Works: *Charity and Its Fruits*, 150; *Discourse on the Trinity*, 40, 41, 56, 170; "The Excellency of Jesus Christ," 156; *Five Discourses*, 155-56; *Freedom of the Will*, 6, 34, 40, 83, 87-88, 109-10, 169, 171-72; *God's End in Creation*, 10, 12-13, 55, 70, 75-76, 173; *Justification by Faith*, 114; "Justification by Faith Alone," 157-58; *The Mind*, 27, 42, 154; "Miscellanies," 27, 41, 69, 131, 154, 175-76; *Of Atoms*, 27, 29-30; *On Being*, 27; *Original Sin*, 74, 107, 110, 118; *Religious Affections*, 9, 40, 150, 152, 166, 169, 181; "Sinners in the Hands of an Angry God," 143; *True Virtue*, 10
Edwardsian dilemma, 167-69, 177, 179-82
Enlightenment, 34, 42
Erskine, John, 136
Evangelicalism, xiv, 62
Excellency, doctrine of, 12, 37, 42-44, 51, 58

Filioque, 48
Formula Consensus Helvetica, 102-3
Free will, xvi, 80-106; compatibilism, 81, 87, 89, 93, 102, 104, 110-11; Edwards on, 87-94; incompatibilism, 84, 110n3; libertarianism, 80, 82, 84, 89, 93, 99, 103, 104, 110n3. See also Libertarian Calvinism

Gallic Confession, 102
Girardeau, John, xvi, 83, 94-104. Works: *Calvinism and Evangelical Arminianism*, 98; *The Will in Its Theological Relations*, 94, 98
God: divine aseity, 20, 41, 58, 65, 70, 164; divine attributes, 48, 53-54, 64, 69; divine goodness, 43n15; divine knowledge, 21-22; divine simplicity, 17-20, 19n5, 21, 32, 37, 39-42, 44, 46, 58, 63, 64, 69, 169-70, 174-79; divine sovereignty, xviii, 94; Edwards's doctrine of God, 25-33, 69-77; God as pure act, 40, 47-48, 57, 63, 67, 69, 164; natural knowledge of God, 33-34. See also Divine determinism; Holy Spirit; Son; Trinity; Tritheism
Great Awakening, 147
Grotius, 128

Heidelberg Catechism, 2
Helm, Paul, 91n14, 102, 105
Hobbes, Thomas, 3-4, 27n20; Hobbesian materialism, 3
Hodge, Charles, 2, 15, 78, 83, 116n8, 129, 179-81
Holmes, Oliver Wendell, 36n1
Holmes, Sherlock, 99
Holmes, Stephen, 37, 44-45, 52, 54-57
Holy Spirit, 9, 40, 44, 47, 48, 49, 69, 84, 134, 138, 155
Hopkins, Samuel, 3, 13, 14, 124
Hypothetical universalism, 127, 128

Idealism, 12, 27; theistic idealism, 27, 33
Incarnation, 160-61

Index

James, William, 9
Jenson, Robert W., 130

Laws, physical, 30
Lee, Sang Hyun, 37, 45, 52-53
Leibniz, Gottfried Wilhelm von, 6
Libertarian Calvinism, 83, 84, 85-86, 106
Locke, John, 7, 88, 151, 158
Luther, Martin, 96n31, 106

Machen, J. Gresham, 15
Mastricht, Petrus van, 3
McCall, Thomas, 61, 64, 65, 67, 79
McClymond, Michael, 39
McDermott, Gerald, 39
Middle Knowledge. *See* Molinism
Miller, Perry, 152, 162
Minds, 27; divine mind, 28
Modalism. *See* Sabellianism
Molinism, 60, 67-68, 77-78
Moltmann, Jürgen, 2
Monasticism, 34
Monergism, 109
Muller, Richard, 19n5, 62, 65, 80n1, 81n3, 82, 105

Nevin, John Williamson, 129n9
New Divinity. *See* New England Theology
New England Theology, 7, 13-15, 83, 91, 124-25, 127, 134, 167, 181
New Haven Theology. *See* Yale College/Divinity School

Occasionalism, 73, 170-72, 177, 178-79
Original sin, 8-9, 86, 107-23, 179. *See also* Double guilt

Panentheism, 13, 75-76, 78, 166, 172-74, 174-79
Pantheism, 75n54, 76, 78, 179-81
Park, Edwards Amasa, 129, 132
Perfect being theology, 12, 17

Perichoresis, 37, 41, 45, 49-50, 53, 57, 58
Piper, John, 62
Plantinga, Alvin, 10
Plantinga Pauw, Amy, 37, 39n6, 45
Puritanism, 33, 42, 76, 82, 144-45, 158, 166

Rauschenbusch, Walter, 15
Rea, Michael, 178
Reason, 35, 48
Reformed Orthodoxy, 32, 39, 46, 60, 82
Reformed scholastics. *See* Reformed Orthodoxy
Remonstrants, 60, 61n1
Resistance, 29

Sabellianism, 36
Schleiermacher, Friedrich, 9
Scots Confession, 2, 102
Second Helvetic Confession, 102
Semi-Pelagianism, 60
Socinianism, 41, 141
Sola fide, 1
Sola gratia, 1
Sola scriptura, 1, 60
Soli deo gloria, 1
Solus Christus, 1
Son: as divine idea, 46-47, 48, 59, 165; as divine understanding, 49; eternal generation of, 22-24, 27
Souls, 31, 176
Spinoza, Baruch, 76
Spirits: created, 28, 30, 43, 48, 54, 55; finite, 31-32; infinite, 32; uncreated, 43
Stapfer, Johannes, 115, 121-23
Stoddard, Solomon, 155
Stout, Harry, 147-48
Stowe, Harriet Beecher, 135
Stranglin, Keith, 61, 64, 65, 67, 79
Strobel, Kyle, 38, 49, 53-57
Studebaker, Steven, 37, 39, 46

Index

Swinburne, Richard, 31
Synergism, 60, 109

Taylor, Nathaniel, 13
Theosis, 10, 73
Thirty-Nine Articles, 2
Trinity, 10-11, 16, 36-59, 161, 165; essence and persons, 44-45, 48, 53; models of, 45-46, 58; and monotheism, 41, 51, 169; as mutual love, 44; natural knowledge of, 34-35; relations of origin, 48, 165; social trinitarianism, 41, 53; threeness, 39
Tritheism, 41, 45, 169
Turretin, Francis, 3, 81n2, 91n14, 139

Unitarianism, 41. *See also* Hypothetical universalism

Virtue ethics, 10
Voluntarism, 66

Wainwright, William, 10
Warfield, B. B., 15, 129
Westminster Confession, 2, 82, 103, 129
Whitfield, George, 147-48, 163

Yale College/Divinity School, 13, 151
"Young, restless, and Reformed," 62

Zwingli, Huldrych, 81n4

www.ingramcontent.com/pod-product-compliance
Lightning Source LLC
Chambersburg PA
CBHW031253230426
43670CB00005B/166